The JESUS YOU CAN'T IGNORE

WHAT YOU MUST LEARN FROM *the* BOLD CONFRONTATIONS *of* CHRIST

JOHN MACARTHUR

THOMAS NELSON
Since 1798

NASHVILLE   DALLAS   MEXICO CITY   RIO DE JANEIRO

With thanks to Kent Stainback, a kind
and generous friend with whom I share
a deep love of the Truth.

© 2008 by John MacArthur.

Published in Nashville, Tennessee, by Thomas Nelson. Thomas Nelson is a registered trade-
mark of Thomas Nelson, Inc.

Edited by Phillip R. Johnson.

Thomas Nelson, Inc. titles may be purchased in bulk for educational, business, fund-raising,
or sales promotional use. For information, please e-mail SpecialMarkets@ThomasNelson.com.

All Scripture quotations in this book, except those noted otherwise, are from the New King
James Version, © 1982 by Thomas Nelson, Inc. Used by permission. All rights reserved.

Quotations marked NASB are from the New American Standard Bible® ©, The Lockman
Foundation 1960, 1962, 1963, 1968, 1971, 1972, 1973, 1975, 1977, 1995. Used by permission.

Quotations marked KJV are from the King James Version of the Bible.

ISBN 978-1-4002-0297-3 (trade paper)
ISBN 978-1-4002-8075-9 (IE)

Library of Congress Cataloging-in-Publication Data

MacArthur, John, 1939–
  The Jesus you can't ignore : what you must learn from the bold confrontations of
Christ / John MacArthur.
    p. cm.
  ISBN 978-1-4002-0206-5 (HC)
  1. Jesus Christ—Person and offices. 2. Apologetics. 3. Truth—Religious aspects—
Christianity. 4. Christian life. I. Title.
  BT203.M26 2009
  232.9'5—dc22

                                                                2009003574

Printed in the United States of America
11 12 13 14 RRD 6 5 4 3

Contents

❈

CONTENTS

CONTENTS

Acknowledgments

My deep gratitude, as always, goes to the staff at Grace to You who maintain and distribute the archive of sermons from which I draw all the material for my books. I study and preach and move on to the next passage each week. The Grace to You staff record my sermons, transcribe them, edit them for broadcast, and catalogue everything I ever say from the pulpit. A book like this, which surveys the entire public ministry of Christ, is drawn from hundreds of sermons covering three of the gospels, representing forty years of verse-by-verse preaching. Without the work of so many who remember and record what I say, I would have a difficult time retrieving thoughts and compiling material that I originally developed years ago. The work of writing a book like this—time consuming as it is—would be utterly impossible for me without the help of so many.

Special thanks to Arlene Hampton, who transcribes all my sermons (and has done so for years); Mike Taylor, who oversees editorial, production, and the archiving of everything we publish through Grace to You; Garry Knussman, who edits and proofreads material (usually on very short notice); and the rest of the gifted staff at Grace to You, virtually all of whom at one time or another have had a hand in caring for the recordings, transcripts, and other elements that figure into a book like this. They are a wonderful and loyal group of colaborers—a constant support to me in countless ways.

Special thanks to Phil Johnson, who has compiled, combined, abridged, and edited the material in this book, translating it from those hundreds of sermons to about 250 pages of prose. When trying to capture the passion and the substance of so many sermons in such few pages, it helps to have a like-minded editor, and Phil is definitely that.

Thanks also, as always, to Brian Hampton, Bryan Norman, and the whole team at Thomas Nelson for their help, encouragement, and patience while this book was in the works. Thanks also to Robert Wolgemuth and his team, whose assistance and insights have been an indispensable support to me in my writing ministry for several years now.

—John MacArthur

Prologue

❧

The idea to write this book occurred to me a couple of years ago when I was doing research for *The Truth War* and simultaneously preaching through Luke. The book I was *writing* was a study of Jude v. 3 ("contend earnestly for the faith"), which is a straightforward command to fight for the truth that has been delivered to us. I was dealing with the implications of that text in light of changing evangelical attitudes about truth and certainty. I also wanted to examine the influence of postmodernism, doctrinal minimalism, and various Emergent trends within the contemporary evangelical movement. So before I began writing, I spent some months reading all the literature I could find representing postevangelical points of view.

A common theme stood out in the books I was reading. They all suggested in one way or another that if Christians want to reach unbelieving people in a postmodern culture, we need to be less militant, less aggressive, less preachy, and less sure of our own convictions. According to those authors, Christians should meet other worldviews with *conversation,* not *conflict.* The writers all tended to place an inordinate stress on the supposed importance of always being as agreeable as possible. They more or less assumed that a friendly quest for common ground and mutual goodwill is *always* morally superior to any kind of earnest contention. It sometimes sounded as if they could imagine nothing more useless—or more despicable—than Christians engaging in polemical battles over our articles of faith.

Those books also exhibited a strong bias against any kind of certitude. Their authors all seemed deeply bothered by the fact that in the current intellectual climate, unbelievers usually think Christians sound arrogant and small-minded when we declare that the Bible is infallibly true and Jesus is Lord over all. They were especially uncomfortable with the idea of saying that other religions are *false*. Instead, they said, we should embrace and adapt to the shift in secular attitudes toward truth and certainty. Our dialogue with people of differing faiths and conflicting worldviews now needs to be a give-and-take exchange. That means listening sympathetically, always being flexible with our own point of view, affirming as much as we possibly can, agreeing more than we disagree, carefully avoiding points of truth that are likely to offend, and always seeking common ground.

In other words, because we live in a highly sophisticated but epistemologically challenged culture, certainty about spiritual things automatically comes across as either arrogant or naïve. We should therefore now approach differing faith perspectives as peacemongers rather than as preachers. Some went so far as to suggest that even our corporate worship services should feature open dialogue about various points of view instead of a sermon where one person simply expounds on what the Bible teaches. They also said we need to be prepared at the outset to make concessions and compromises as part of the dialogue process. In the words of one author, "It's important to note that dialogue is not debate; for dialogue to be effective, we need to resist the urge to cut people off and fix what they say. Healthy dialogue involves entering into the reality of the other. . . . In dialogue you are not allowed to stay right where you are; you must move toward the perspective of the other person."[1] More than one book I read suggested that a dance is a better metaphor than warfare to describe how Christians ought to interact with other worldviews.

So much for verse 3 of Jude.

The book I was preaching through, however, revealed practically the opposite pattern. Jesus' interaction with the religious experts of His time was rarely even cordial. From the time Luke first introduces us to the Pharisees in Luke 5:17 until his final mention of the "chief priests and rulers" in Luke 24:20, every time the religious elite of Israel appear as a group in Luke's narrative, there is conflict. Often Jesus Himself deliberately provokes the hostilities. When He speaks to the religious leaders or about them—whether in public or in private—it is usually to condemn them as fools and hypocrites (Luke 11:40; 12:1; 13:15; 18:10–14). When He knows they are watching to accuse Him of breaking their artificial Sabbath restrictions or their manmade systems of ceremonial washing, He deliberately defies their rules (Luke 6:7–11; 11:37–44; 14:1–6). On one occasion, when He was expressly informed that His denunciations of the Pharisees were insulting to the lawyers (the leading Old Testament scholars and chief academicians of that time), Jesus immediately turned to the lawyers and fired off a salvo at them, too (Luke 11:45–54).

AVOID FOOLISH AND IGNORANT DISPUTES

Now, we need to keep this in proper perspective. I'm not suggesting that every disagreement is an occasion for open combat, or even harsh words. Far from it. Many disagreements are so petty that it would be utterly unprofitable to engender strife over them. Merely personal conflicts, debates over arcane or unclear things, and semantic disputes usually fall in that category (2 Timothy 2:14, 23; 1 Corinthians

1:10). Not every issue on which we might hold strong opinions and disagree is of primary importance.

Furthermore, no one who is mentally and spiritually healthy *enjoys* conflict for conflict's sake. No one who thinks biblically would ever relish strife or deliberately indulge in "disputes over doubtful things" (Romans 14:1). Most of us know people who are overtly pugnacious or incurably argumentative about practically everything. That is not at all what Jesus was like. And Scripture gives us no warrant to be like that. Petty or insignificant personal disagreements usually *ought* to be either charitably set aside or settled by friendly dialogue. Anyone who is prepared to pick a fight over every minor difference of opinion is spiritually immature, sinfully belligerent—or worse. Scripture includes this clear command: "If it is possible, as much as depends on you, live peaceably with all men" (Romans 12:18).

But *sometimes*—especially when a vitally important biblical truth is under assault; when the souls of people are at stake; or (above all) when the gospel message is being mangled by false teachers—*sometimes*, it is simply wrong to let a contrary opinion be aired without any challenge or correction. One of the worst things a believer can do is show a kind of feigned academic respect or artificial cordiality to the purveyors of serious, soul-destroying error (Psalm 129:4–8; 1 Corinthians 16:22). The notion that an amiable conversation is *always* superior to open conflict is quite contrary to the example Christ Himself has given us.

FIGHT THE *GOOD* FIGHT

It may not always be easy to determine whether a disagreement is merely petty or truly weighty, but a careful, thoughtful application of biblical wisdom will usually settle whatever questions we may have about the relative importance of any given truth. Scripture makes clear, for example, that we must take a zero-tolerance stance toward anyone who would tamper with or alter the gospel message (Galatians 1:8–9). And anyone who denies the deity of Christ or substantially departs from His teaching is not to be welcomed into our fellowship or given any kind of blessing (2 John 7–11).

The principle is clear: the closer any given doctrine is to the heart of the gospel, the core of sound Christology, or the fundamental teachings of Christ, the more diligently we ought to be on guard against perversions of the truth—and the more aggressively we need to fight the error and defend sound doctrine.

Differentiating between truly essential and merely peripheral spiritual truths does require great care and discernment. The distinction is not always immediately obvious. But it is not nearly as difficult to draw that line as some people today pretend it is. Even if the line does seem a little fuzzy here and there, that's no reason to eliminate the distinction altogether, as some postevangelicals seem determined to do.

Many today are advocating an ultraminimalist approach, paring back the list of essential doctrines to what's covered by the Apostles' Creed (or in some cases, an even shorter list of very broad generalities). That doesn't really promote harmony; it merely muddies all doctrine. After all, many rank heretics, ranging from Unitarians to Socinians to Jehovah's Witnesses, will formally affirm the Apostles' Creed. The problem is that they don't agree on what the creed *means*. Even the largest branches of Christian belief—Catholics, Eastern Orthodox, and Protestants—don't agree among themselves on the meaning of crucial expressions in the creed. It is useless as a standard by which to measure which truths are primary and which ones are secondary.[2]

But Scripture suggests that the gospel, not a third-century creed, is the best gauge for determining the true essentials of Christianity. If you genuinely understand and affirm the gospel, you will automatically have sound views on justification by faith, substitutionary atonement, the deity of Christ, the historicity of the resurrection, the truthfulness and authority of Scripture, and every other doctrine that is "of first importance" (1 Corinthians 15:3 NASB). Conversely, if you go astray—even subtly—on any vital principle of gospel truth, your whole worldview will be adversely affected. Misconstrue the gospel or adapt it to suit a particular subculture's preferences and the inevitable result will be a religion of works and a system that breeds self-righteousness.

That is exactly what Jesus' conflict with the Pharisees was all about. They represented a style of religion and a system of belief that was in direct conflict with the very heart of the gospel He proclaimed. He offered forgiveness and instant justification to believing sinners. Israel's religious leaders manufactured massive systems of works and ceremonies that in effect made justification itself a human work. In the words of the apostle Paul, "they [were] ignorant of God's righteousness, and seeking to establish their own righteousness" (Romans 10:3).

There was simply no way for Christ to avoid conflict with them. So instead, He made the most of it. He used their false religion as a foil for the truth He taught. He let their hypocrisy serve as a backdrop against which the jewel of His holiness shone more brightly. And He set His grace in opposition to their self-righteousness in a way that made the distinction between justification by faith and works-religion impossible to miss.

A TIME TO REFRAIN FROM EMBRACING

That was His *consistent* approach, too. Simply put, Jesus never took the irenic approach with heretics or gross hypocrites. He never made the kind of gentle private appeals contemporary evangelicals typically insist are necessary before warning others about the dangers of a false teacher's error. Even when He dealt with the most respected religious figures in the land, He took on their errors boldly and directly, sometimes even holding them up for ridicule. He was not "nice" to them by any postmodern standard. He extended no pretense of academic courtesy to them. He didn't invite them to dialogue privately with Him about their different points of view. He didn't carefully couch his criticisms in vague and totally impersonal terms so that no one's feelings would be hurt. He did nothing to tone down the reproach of His censures or minimize the Pharisees' public embarrassment. He made his disapproval of their religion as plain and prominent as possible every time He mentioned them. He seemed utterly unmoved by their frustration with His outspokenness. Knowing that they were looking for reasons to be offended by Him, He often did and said the very things He knew would offend them most.

It is surely significant that the approach Jesus took in dealing with religious error is so sharply different from the methods favored by most in the church today. It's pretty hard to imagine Jesus' treatment of the Pharisees getting a positive notice in the pages of *Christianity Today.* And does anyone really think His polemical style would gain the admiration of the average evangelical academician?

The way Jesus dealt with His adversaries is in fact a serious rebuke to the church of our generation. We need to pay more careful attention to how Jesus dealt with false teachers, what He thought of religious error, how He defended the truth, whom He commended and whom He condemned—and how little He actually fit the gentle stereotype that is so often imposed on Him today.

Furthermore, His attitude toward false doctrine should also be ours. We cannot be men-pleasers and servants of Christ at the same time.

That is the thesis of this book. We're going to move chronologically through the gospel accounts of how Jesus handled the religious elite of Israel. We'll look at how He spoke to individuals, how He responded to organized opposition, how He preached to multitudes, and what He taught His own disciples. The practical lesson regarding how we should conduct ourselves in the presence of false religion is consistent throughout: corruptions of vital biblical truth are not to be trifled with, and the purveyors of different gospels are not to be treated benignly by God's people. On the contrary, we must take the same approach to false doctrine that Jesus did, by refuting the error, opposing those who spread the error, and contending earnestly for the faith.

Introduction

❧

ac·a·dem·ic (ak e-DEM ik) *adj.* **1.** abstract, speculative, or conjectural with very little practical significance. **2.** pertaining to scholars and institutions of higher learning rather than to lay people or children. **3.** of interest as an intellectual curiosity, but not particularly useful in real-world applications. **4.** provoking curiosity and analysis rather than passion or devotion. **5.** pedantic, casuistical; good for making a display of erudition but otherwise trivial. **6.** belonging to that realm of scholastic theory and intellectual inquiry where certainty is always inappropriate. **7.** not worth getting agitated about.

Spiritual truth is not "academic" by any of the above definitions. What you believe about God is the most important feature of your whole worldview.

Look at it this way: of all the things you might ever study or reflect on, nothing could possibly be greater than God. So your view of Him automatically has more far-reaching ramifications than anything else in your belief system. What you think of God *will* automatically color how you think about everything else—especially how you prioritize values; how you determine right and wrong; and what you think of your own place in the universe. That in turn will surely determine how you act.

The same principle is as true for the rank atheist as it is for the most faithful believer in Christ. The practical and ideological effects of skepticism are as potent as those of heartfelt devotion—only in the opposite direction. Someone who rejects God has repudiated the only reasonable foundation for morality, accountability, true spirituality, and the necessary distinction between good and evil. So the atheist's private life will inevitably become a living demonstration of the evils of unbelief. To whatever degree some atheists seek to maintain a public veneer of virtue and respectability—as well as when they themselves make moral judgments about others—they are walking contradictions. What possible "virtue" could there be in an accidental universe with no Lawgiver and no Judge?

People who profess faith in the Almighty but refuse to think seriously about Him are also living illustrations of this same principle. The hypocrisy of the superficially religious has a practical and ideological impact that is as profoundly consequential as the faith of the believer or the unbelief of the atheist. In fact, hypocrisy has potentially even more sinister implications than outright atheism because of its deceptiveness.

It is the very height of irrationality and arrogance to call Christ Lord with the lips while utterly defying Him with one's life. Yet that is precisely how multitudes live (Luke 6:46). Such people are even more preposterous examples of self-contradiction than the atheist who imagines he can deny the Source of all that's good and yet somehow be "good" himself. But the hypocrite is not only more *irrational*; he is also more *contemptible* than the out-and-out atheist, because he is actually doing gross violence to the truth while pretending to believe it. Nothing is more completely diabolical. Satan is a master at disguising himself so that he appears good rather than evil. He "transforms himself into an angel of light. Therefore it is no great thing if his ministers also transform themselves into ministers of righteousness, whose end will be according to their works" (2 Corinthians 11:14–15).

It is no accident, then, that Jesus' harshest words were reserved for institutionalized religious hypocrisy. He waged a very aggressive public controversy against the chief hypocrites of His era. That conflict began almost as soon as He entered public ministry and continued relentlessly until the day He was crucified. In fact, it was the main reason they conspired to crucify Him. So Jesus' campaign against hypocrisy is a prominent, if not dominant, emphasis in all four gospels. It is the very theme we'll be surveying in this book.

But our starting point is a truth that should be self-evident: it really *does* matter whether we believe the Bible is true or not; and it likewise matters whether our faith is earnest or not.

WHAT DO HISTORY AND SCRIPTURE SAY ABOUT THE IMPORTANCE OF SOUND BELIEFS?

To any sober-minded person, the importance of thinking rightly and seriously about God is obvious. Certainly, no intelligent mind in past generations would ever have suggested that what we believe about God doesn't ultimately matter much. Study the history of philosophy, and one feature that stands out most prominently is this very theme. Philosophers have always been obsessed with God. Whether they have assumed His existence, questioned it, denied it, or looked for rational arguments to prove or disprove it, they have universally understood that what a person believes about God is basic to everything else.

Of course, one of the central themes of the Bible is the importance of believing the truth about God. This is not something the Bible merely hints at or lightly glosses over. Statement after statement in Scripture emphatically declares that our view of God is the most fundamental spiritual issue of all: "Without faith it is impossible to please Him, for he who comes to God must believe that He is, and that He is a rewarder of those who diligently seek Him" (Hebrews 11:6). "He who does not believe is condemned already, because he has not believed in the name of the only begotten Son of God" (John 3:18). "We are of God. He who knows God hears us; he who is not of God does not hear us. By this we know the spirit of truth and the spirit of error" (1 John 4:6).

In biblical terms, the difference between true faith and false belief (or unbelief) *is* the difference between life and death, heaven and hell. "Brethren, if anyone among you wanders from the truth, and someone turns him back, let him know that he who turns a sinner from the error of his way will save a soul from death and cover a multitude of sins" (James 5:19–20; cf. 2 Timothy 2:15–26). Paul told the Thessalonians he was thankful to God for them, because "God from the beginning chose you for salvation through sanctification by the Spirit and *belief in the truth,* to which He called you by our gospel, for the obtaining of the glory of our Lord Jesus Christ" (2 Thessalonians 2:13–14, emphasis added). And Jesus Himself said, "If you abide in My word, you are My disciples indeed. And you shall know the truth, and the truth shall make you free" (John 8:31–32). The apostle John wrote, "You have an anointing from the Holy One, and you know all things. I have not written to you because you do not know the truth, but because you know it, and that no lie is of the truth" (1 John 2:20–21).

Until the past few years, no Christian who claimed to believe the Bible would have entertained the slightest doubt about the importance of a right view of God. But these days it seems the visible church is dominated by people who simply are not interested in making any careful distinctions between fact and falsehood, sound doctrine and heresy, biblical truth and mere human opinion. Even some of the leading voices among evangelicals seem intent on downplaying the value of objective truth.

That, of course, is precisely the path the greater portion of the Western intellectual world has taken in these postmodern times. Certainty and conviction are badly out of fashion—especially in the realm of *spiritual* things. Dogmatism is the new heresy, and all the old heresies are therefore now welcome back at the evangelical campfire. Academic freedom is extended to all of them (as long as they are not deemed socially unacceptable or politically incorrect by secular society's *fashionistas)*. The word *faith* itself has come to signify a theoretical approach to spiritual things in which every religious belief is placed alongside contrary opinions, admired, analyzed, and appreciated—but not really *believed* with anything like earnest conviction.

In this postmodern climate where *no* truth is held to be self-evident, nothing is more dissonant or strident sounding than the person who genuinely believes that God has spoken, that He managed to make His Word clear, and that He will hold us accountable for whether we believe Him or not. Postmodern epistemology argues instead that *nothing* is ultimately clear or incontrovertible—least of all spiritual, moral, or biblical matters.

WHERE ARE TODAY'S EVANGELICALS HEADED?

The evangelical movement used to be known for two nonnegotiable theological convictions. One was a commitment to the absolute accuracy and authority of Scripture—as the revealed Word of God, not as a product of human imagination, experience, intuition, or ingenuity

(2 Peter 1:21). The other was a strong belief that the gospel sets forth the only possible way of salvation from sin and judgment—by grace through faith in the Lord Jesus Christ.

In recent years, however, evangelicals have been freely imbibing the spirit of the age. Multitudes—including many in positions of spiritual leadership—have quietly jettisoned those two convictions (or simply stopped talking and thinking about them). Evangelicalism has now ceased to be anything like a coherent movement.[1] It has instead become an amorphous monstrosity where practically every idea and every opinion demands to be brought to the table for discussion, received politely by all, and shown equal respect and honor.

As a result, today's evangelicals seem unable to put their finger on anything that makes them truly distinctive. When they try to stake out their own position or explain to nonevangelicals who they are, they sometimes unwittingly confess that conformity to this world and its way of thinking has become the very thing that defines them.[2]

That's not to suggest that contemporary evangelicals have managed to send anything like a clear, coherent, or uniform message. Formal statements of the evangelical position have become so vague and devoid of real conviction that no one seems sure whether they actually mean anything anymore. Chic values such as diversity, tolerance, collegiality, agreeableness, and academic freedom seem to have eclipsed biblical truth in the evangelical hierarchy of virtues. Today's worldly evangelicals are clearly caught in the riptide of popular postmodern opinion.

In May 2008, a new "Evangelical Manifesto" was released to the secular and religious press with considerable fanfare. It was drafted and signed by a disparate group of evangelical and post-evangelical scholars who have distinguished themselves by various means. Some are known mainly as champions for practically every left-wing political cause; others are best-known for writing philosophical apologetics in defense of a more conservative worldview. A couple were "evangelicals" only in the sense that they have tried to marry neoorthodox doctrine with the new evangelical style.

The 2008 Manifesto hit with a resounding thud and was widely panned by critics in the media (and deservedly so) for its lack of clarity throughout—especially its failure to state its own purpose in plain language. But the one word that seemed to be the key to the document was *civility*. That term was used countless times in the press conference where the Manifesto was unveiled. Given the way those who drafted and signed the document were using the term, the underlying assumption plainly was that "civility" always obliges us to disagree "agreeably," and avoid at all costs any hint of combativeness or serious contention. In fact, it seems fair to suggest that one of the main objectives of the document—if not the whole point—was to distance today's evangelical movement from any hint of militancy or "fundamentalism" in the way we interact with ideas that are non-evangelical or anti-Christian.[3]

It seems that zeal for the essential doctrines of biblical Christianity has become virtually as unacceptable among evangelicals and post-evangelicals as it always has been in the world at large. The new rules call for perpetually friendly conversation, ideological largesse, non-judgmental transparency, and ecumenical tranquility.[4] Especially when the discussion turns to doctrine, today's typical evangelical invariably acts as if a docile dialogue is morally preferable to any kind of conflict. After all, we mustn't ever be so passionate about what we believe that we express any serious disdain for alternative ideas.

In such a climate, evangelical dialogue about doctrine seems to have become a mostly aimless conversation for conversation's sake. The goal isn't to arrive at any common understanding or settled conviction about what's true and what's false. Instead, the whole point seems to be to get as many different opinions into the mix as possible, and then perpetuate the lavish, lighthearted friendliness of the discussion indefinitely.

HOW SHOULD WE THEN DEFEND THE FAITH?

To review, then, here are the new rules of post-evangelical engagement: All our differences over biblical and theological matters are supposed to remain blithely congenial and complacently detached from any sort of passion in a purely academic-style exchange of ideas and opinions. *Truth* isn't our primary goal. (How naive that would be!) We don't even need to be seeking *consensus,* much less biblical orthodoxy. After all, diversity is one of the few virtues postmodern culture has achieved, and we must honor that. Likemindedness and formal confessions of faith are seen by secular society as tools of tyranny and repression. Such things breed certitude, moral judgments, and charges of heresy, and these are all out of place in our culture. At the end of the day, then, if we can congratulate ourselves on our own "civility," we should be satisfied with that.

Don't miss the point: it's OK to disagree. (After all, contradiction, dissent, disputes over words, and especially deconstruction are the main instruments of the postmodern dialectic.) It's even acceptable to *voice* your disagreements—as long as you pillow each criticism between positive comments about whatever you are critiquing. But no one is really supposed to take his or her own theological convictions seriously enough to regard anything as *absolute* truth.

Above all, we're not supposed to lodge any *serious* objection to someone else's religious opinions. Talk about a gross breach of etiquette! Only the most lowbrow kind of anti-intellectual philistine would ever dare lift his voice in these post-evangelical times and suggest that something someone else says about God is heresy.

So it seems the sole test of someone's authenticity in the new evangelical climate is whether he can welcome the old unorthodoxies on board and yet maintain an invincibly agreeable tone—without ever marginalizing, discounting, or totally repudiating anyone else's opinion. That approach is deemed the very height of humility by the new postmodern standard; whereas contending seriously for any particular point of view is reflexively dismissed as arrogant, small-minded, and even cruel—especially if the point of view you are fighting *for* involves historic evangelical principles.

Did I say "fighting"? No idea is more politically incorrect among today's new-style evangelicals than the old fundamentalist notion that *truth* is worth fighting for—including the essential propositions of Christian doctrine. In fact, many believe that arguments over religious beliefs are the most pointless and arrogant of all conflicts. That can be true—and *is* true in cases where human opinions are the only thing at stake. But where God's Word speaks clearly, we have a duty to obey, defend, and proclaim the truth He has given us, and we should do that with an authority that reflects our conviction that God has spoken with clarity and finality. This is particularly crucial in contexts where cardinal doctrines of biblical Christianity are under attack.

Incidentally, the core truths of Scripture are *always* under attack. Scripture itself clearly teaches that the main battleground where Satan wages his cosmic struggle against God is *ideological*. In other words, the spiritual warfare every Christian is engaged in is first of all a conflict between truth and error, not merely a competition between good and wicked deeds. The chief aim of Satan's strategy is to confuse, deny, and corrupt the truth with as much fallacy as possible, and that means the battle for truth is *very* serious. Being able to distinguish between sound doctrine and error should be one of the highest priorities for every Christian—as should defending the truth against false teaching.

Take such a stand today, however, and you will be scolded by a cacophony of voices telling you that you are out of line and you need to shut up. The "war" metaphor simply doesn't work in a postmodern culture, they insist. Postmodern epistemologies start and end with the presupposition that any question of what's true or false is merely academic. Our differences are all ultimately trivial. Only the tone of our discussion is *not* trivial. Every hint of militancy is inappropriate in these sophisticated times. After all, we're all fallen creatures and limited in our ability to comprehend the great truths about God, so we're never justified in responding harshly to people who hold different views.

WHAT WOULD JESUS DO?

Even some of the better minds in the evangelical movement seem to have capitulated to the notion that theology is academic, and therefore the only proper way to assess others' theological opinions is with a cool scholastic detachment. They agree—or at least *act* as if they agree—with those who say it's always better to have a friendly conversation than a conflict over doctrinal differences.

One pundit wrote an essay to that effect, and someone anonymously sent me a copy. The sender enclosed an unsigned note saying he was disappointed and completely put off by the title of my book *The Truth War.* He had not actually read the book himself (and did not intend to) because he said he could tell already that I am hopelessly closed-minded. But he wanted to express his outrage and disbelief that a "clergy-person" of my stature in these enlightened times would equate religious beliefs with *truth*—much less treat the quest for truth as a "war." He was certain Jesus would never take such a militant stance.

The essay enclosed with the note was written by someone else, and that author likewise expressed strong misgivings "about the usefulness of the 'war' metaphor in Christianity." *What would Jesus do?* the writer wondered. Wasn't Jesus' own ministry characterized by kindness and pacifism instead of combat and contention? Didn't He call His true followers to seek love and unity, not conduct crusades? Didn't He say, "Blessed are the peacemakers"? Doesn't the whole spirit of militancy (especially ideological aggression against others' *beliefs*) seem completely out of place in this postmodern era? Don't common sense and cultural sensitivity both suggest that we ought to shelve the vocabulary of combat altogether and focus principally on the theme of reconciliation?

The writer of that essay tried hard to play down the significance of the militant language employed in numerous places throughout the New Testament. He seemed to imagine that if today's evangelicals were encouraged to think of the struggle between truth and error as anything more serious than a sack race on the lawn at summer camp, the church would soon be overrun with Christian jihadists wearing bandoliers, waving real weapons, and waging a literal flesh-and-blood incursion against teachers of false religions.

Of course, no credible Christian who is committed to Scripture as our supreme authority has ever proposed a literal, earthly holy war. That's not what *spiritual* warfare is about, and Scripture is unequivocal on that: "We do not wrestle against flesh and blood" (Ephesians 6:12). And "the weapons of our warfare are not carnal" (2 Corinthians 10:4).

Nevertheless, the postmodern mind sometimes seems unable to make any meaningful distinction between armed physical combat with weapons intended to kill people and spiritual combat with truth intended to save them from spiritual death.

CNN, for example, aired a special series in 2007 titled "God's Warriors," with a major segment subtitled "God's *Christian* Warriors." The program was far from objective, and the segment that focused on Christianity seemed to have little point other than attempting to suggest that there is a kind of moral parity between Muslim jihadists who blow innocent people up and Christians who believe Jesus Christ is the world's only true Savior. "Their battle to save the world has caused anger, division and fear," CNN reporter Christiane Amanpour solemnly intoned in her introduction to the segment about evangelicals.[5] The series threw Christian fundamentalists into the same category with Islamic jihadists. Naturally, that generated a lively discussion in various online forums. Some Christians who commented about the CNN special sounded disturbingly ambivalent on the question of whether or not Christians *deserve* to be lumped with terrorists and suicide bombers. Have Christians actually earned this reputation by being too contentious about their beliefs? Is it now time for us to repudiate every hint of fighting and conflict, purge the language of warfare from our lexicon, stop clashing with worldly opinions and unbiblical religious ideas, and pursue peace and harmony rather than controversy with other worldviews? Several of them also toyed with the question, "What would Jesus do?" One person wrote:

We have over-used and over-emphasized the "war" metaphor in Christianity. It is a tired metaphor that brings up too many "modern" world images when we live in a post-modern, post-Christian world. I'm not sure the "Prince of Peace" would have been a fan of or even sung along with Onward Christian Soldiers.[6]

In another Internet forum a few weeks later, someone wrote,

I don't think Jesus ever fought a truth war. He didn't go around proactively defending his theology and opposing everyone else's. I am not saying that he didn't see the other religions as false. But I don't think he would have ever started a Truth War on earth. Jesus actively lived out his truth (since he Himself was truth) and had intense conversations about truth on a need-only basis. And even those were not letters sent all over the countryside— they were one-on-one conversations with the men themselves. People were drawn to the truth that Jesus lived out, not because they were defeated in a doctrine battle.[7]

All those sentiments are wrong, and dangerously so. But before we analyze the error, let's acknowledge that the right response is not to run to the opposite extreme. Christians are not to be pugnacious. Love of conflict is no less sinful than craven cowardice.

Spiritual warfare is necessary because of sin and the curse—not because there's anything inherently glorious or virtuous about fighting. Zeal without knowledge is spiritually deadly (Romans 10:2), and even the most sincere passion for the truth needs to be always tempered with gentleness and grace (Ephesians 4:29; Colossians 4:6). Eager enthusiasm for calling down fire from heaven against blasphemers and heretics is far from the spirit of Christ (Luke 9:54–55).

To acknowledge that the church often needs to fight for truth is not to suggest that the gospel—our one message to a lost world—is somehow a declaration of war. It most certainly is not; it's a manifesto of peace and a plea for reconciliation with God (2 Corinthians 5:18–20). Conversely, those who are *not* reconciled to God are at war with Him all the time, and the gospel is a message about the only way to end that war. So ironically, the war to uphold the truth is the only hope of peace for the enemies of God.

I do agree that *usually* it is far better to be gentle than to be harsh. Peacefulness is a blessed quality (Matthew 5:9); pugnaciousness is a disqualifying character flaw (Titus 1:7). Patience is indeed a sweet virtue, even in the face of unbelief and persecution (Luke 21:19). We always ought to listen sufficiently before we react (Proverbs 18:13). A kind word can usually do far more good than a curt reaction, because "a soft answer turns away wrath, but a harsh word stirs up anger" (Proverbs 15:1)—and any person who delights to stir up strife is a fool (v. 8).

Furthermore, the fruit of the Spirit is a catalog of antitheses to a bellicose, aggressive, warlike attitude: "love, joy, peace, longsuffering, kindness, goodness, faithfulness, gentleness, self-control" (Galatians 5:22–23). So our *first* inclination when we encounter someone in error ought to be the very same kind of tender meekness prescribed for anyone in any kind of sin in Galatians 6:1: "If a man is overtaken in any trespass, you who are spiritual restore such a one in a spirit of gentleness, considering yourself lest you also be tempted." It is the duty of every Christian "to speak evil of no one, to be peaceable, gentle, showing all humility to all men. For we ourselves were also once foolish, disobedient, deceived, serving various lusts and pleasures, living in malice and envy, hateful and hating one another" (Titus 3:2–3). And that attitude is a particular duty for those in spiritual leadership. Brawlers aren't qualified to serve as elders in the church (1 Timothy 3:3). Because "a servant of the Lord must not quarrel but be gentle to all, able to teach, patient, in humility correcting those who are in opposition, if God perhaps will grant them repentance, so that they may know the truth" (2 Timothy 2:24–25).

All those principles should indeed dominate our dealings with others and our handling of disagreements. And if those were the only verses in Scripture that told us how to deal with error, we might be justified in thinking those principles are absolute, inviolable, and applicable to every kind of opposition or unbelief we encounter.

But that's not the case. We're instructed to contend earnestly for the faith (Jude v. 3). Immediately after the apostle Paul urged Timothy to "pursue righteousness, godliness, faith, love, patience, gentleness" (1 Timothy 6:11), he exhorted him to "fight the good fight of faith" (v. 12), and to guard what had been committed to his trust (v. 20).

A CLOSER LOOK AT SPIRITUAL WARFARE

It's vital that we understand why Scripture so frequently employs the language of warfare with regard to the cosmic spiritual conflict of the ages—especially in reference to the battle for truth. This is an idea that permeates Scripture. It is not some savage notion dreamed up by persecuted Christians in the first century that has now outlived its usefulness in this more sophisticated age. It is not a childish word-picture that we have finally outgrown. It is not an accommodation to simple-minded first-century prejudices that is out of place in the twenty-first century. In fact, those who simply wave aside the concept as inherently uncivil, uncouth, and therefore unhelpful in a postmodern culture are placing themselves in great peril.

Whether we like it or not, as Christians we are in a life-or-death conflict against the forces of evil and their lies. It is *spiritual* war. It's not a literal, physical conflict with mortal weaponry. It's not a campaign to increase anyone's wealth or confiscate anyone's treasure. It is not a war over territory or geopolitical dominion. It most assuredly is not an angry jihad for the expansion of Christendom's earthly influence. It's not any kind of magical warfare with unseen beings from the nether realms. It's not a battle for ascendancy between individuals or religious sects, and it most certainly is not a campaign on the part of the church to take over the state. But it is nonetheless a serious war with eternal consequences.

Because this spiritual conflict is first and foremost a theological conflict—a war in which divine truth is set against demonic error—we do need to bear in mind always that our goal is the destruction of falsehoods, not people. In fact, the result, if we are faithful, will be the liberation of people from the strongholds of lies, false doctrines, and evil ideologies that hold them captive. That is precisely how Paul described our battle plan in the cosmic conflict in 2 Corinthians

10:3–5: "For though we walk in the flesh, we do not war according to the flesh. For the weapons of our warfare are not carnal but mighty in God for pulling down strongholds, casting down arguments and every high thing that exalts itself against the knowledge of God, bringing every thought into captivity to the obedience of Christ." So Paul says we are to wage war against every idea that exalts itself against divine truth.

Despite so much militant language, there is nothing mean-spirited about the stance Paul was describing (including when he went on in the next verse to tell the Corinthians he personally was "ready to punish all disobedience when your obedience is fulfilled)." He was set not only for the defense of the truth, but also for an offensive incursion against false belief systems. His strategy, in his own words, involved the demolition those false ideologies, by systematically dismantling their erroneous doctrines, casting down their fallacious arguments, and exposing their lies with the truth.

In other words, truth was his only weapon. He did not assault the false teachers in Corinth the same way they had attacked him—with innuendo, distortions of his teaching, purely personal insults, and webs of deceit. He answered their deception with truth—cutting through the Gordian knot of their lies with "the Sword of the Spirit, which is the Word of God" (Ephesians 6:17). He contended for the truth and against error in absolute earnest. But in all his dealings with false teachers, Paul's aim was the annihilation of their false doctrine, not the false teachers *per se.* The warfare wasn't a merely personal dispute between Paul and his antagonists to see who could win the loyalty of the flock in Corinth; it was a battle for infinitely higher principles than that, and something much more significant than anyone's personal reputation was at stake.

Paul was not always gracious and gentle with the purveyors of false teaching in the same way he was fatherly toward believers who were merely perplexed by the confusion of voices. In fact, I can't think of an instance in the epistles where Paul's interaction with false teachers was dominated by the gentleness of that fatherly spirit. Often he displayed righteous anger against them; he wrote with utter contempt for all they stood for; he even cursed them (Galatians 1:7–8).

On his first missionary journey, immediately after leaving Antioch with Barnabas, Paul came to the first stop in his missionary adventure in Seleucia, on Cyprus. Reaching the city of Paphos, he had his first recorded encounter with a false religious teacher, whose name was Elymas Bar-Jesus. Here is how Paul addressed him: "O full of all deceit and all fraud, you son of the devil, you enemy of all righteousness, will you not cease perverting the straight ways of the Lord? And now, indeed, the hand of the Lord is upon you, and you shall be blind, not seeing the sun for a time" (Acts 13:10–11). God affirmed Paul's confrontational approach by a miraculous judgment against Elymas. "Immediately a dark mist fell on him, and he went around seeking someone to lead him by the hand" (v. 11). What called for such aggressive confrontation? The stakes were very high, because Sergius Paulus was listening to the gospel, and his soul was at stake. In any case such as that, the direct and severe approach to dealing with an overt false teacher is actually preferable to a feigned display of approval and brotherhood (2 John 10–11; cf. Psalm 129:5–8; 2 Timothy 3:5).

Paul was certainly fair with his opponents in the sense that he never misrepresented what they taught or told lies about them. But Paul plainly recognized their errors for what they were and labeled them appropriately. He spoke the truth. In his everyday teaching style, Paul spoke the truth gently and with the patience of a tender father. But when circumstances warranted a stronger type of candor, Paul could speak very bluntly—sometimes even with raw sarcasm (1 Corinthians 4:8–10). Like Elijah (1 Kings 18:27), John the Baptist (Matthew 3:7–10), and even Jesus (Matthew 23:24), he could also employ derision effectively and appropriately, to highlight the ridicu-lousness of serious error (Galatians 5:12). He was a sacred-cow tipper in the mold of Moses or Nehemiah.

Paul didn't seem to suffer from the same overscrupulous angst that causes so many people today to whitewash every error as much as language permits; to grant even the grossest of false teachers the benefit of every doubt; and to impute the best possible intentions even to the rankest of heretics. The apostle's idea of "gentleness" was not the sort of faux benevolence and artificial politeness people today sometimes think is the true essence of charity. We never once see him inviting false teachers or casual dabblers in religious error to dialogue, nor did he approve of that strategy even when someone of Peter's stature succumbed to the fear of what others might think and showed undue deference to false teachers (Galatians 2:11–14). Paul drew the boundaries of godly amiability and Christian hospitality pretty much where the apostle John did. When false teachers seek refuge under the umbrella of your fellowship, John said, don't give them the time of day: "Whoever transgresses and does not abide in the doctrine of Christ does not have God. He who abides in the doctrine of Christ has both the Father and the Son. If anyone comes to you and does not bring this doctrine, do not receive him into your house nor greet him; for he who greets him shares in his evil deeds" (2 John 9–11).

WHAT *DID* JESUS DO?

Let's be candid: refusing even the hospitality of a greeting sounds awfully harsh in this age of diplomacy and *detente,* doesn't it? What are we to make of that passage from John, the apostle of love?

First of all, in the culture of the first-century Hebrew world, a "greeting" was a ceremonial public blessing (Luke 10:5; cf. Matthew 10:12), combined with a stately display of hospitality that included multiplied favors and ritual courtesies (cf. Luke 7:44–46). What was to be withheld from any itinerant false teacher were not casual, common words of passing courtesy, but a solemn pronouncement of blessing similar to the greeting John had opened his epistle to this lady with—"Grace, mercy, and peace will be with you from God the Father and from the Lord Jesus Christ, the Son of the Father, in truth and love" (v. 3). When John told her to refuse anyone whose teaching contradicted the apostolic doctrines, he wasn't instructing her to be unladylike or discourteous; he was cautioning her against undue deference to a peddler of lies.

There's nothing wrong with asking, "What would Jesus do?" That's a fine question. How would Christ Himself respond to the post-evangelical goulash of opinions represented in *Christianity Today*, in the Emerging blogosphere, and in the trendy evangelical megachurches that have held the evangelical movement in thrall for the past few decades? Would He affirm the current mainstream evangelical apathy toward truth and authentic biblical unity? Would He approve of those who, confronted with a plethora of contradictions and doctrinal novelties, simply celebrate their movement's "diversity" while trying to avoid all controversy, embracing every theological renegade, and elevating orthopraxy over orthodoxy? Was Jesus' meek-and-gentle mildness of that sort?

I'm convinced we can answer those questions with confidence if we first ask a slightly different question: What *did* Jesus do? How *did* He deal with the false teachers, religious hypocrites, and theological miscreants of His time? Did He favor the approach of friendly dialogue and collegial disagreement, or did He in fact adopt a militant stance against every form of false religion?

Anyone even superficially familiar with the gospel accounts ought to know the answer to that question, because there is no shortage of data on the matter. As we noted early in this introduction,

Jesus' interaction with the Scribes, Pharisees, and hypocrites of His culture was full of conflict from the start of His earthly ministry to the end. Sometimes the Pharisees provoked the conflict; more often than not, Jesus did. *Hostile* is not too strong a word to describe His attitude toward the religious system they represented, and that was evident in all His dealings with them.

We're going to survey that theme in this book. We'll see that Jesus never suffered professional hypocrites or false teachers gladly. He never shied away from conflict. He never softened His message to please genteel tastes or priggish scruples. He never suppressed any truth in order to accommodate someone's artificial notion of dignity. He never bowed to the intimidation of scholars or paid homage to their institutions.

And He never, never, never treated the vital distinction between truth and error as a merely academic question.

I never could believe in the Jesus Christ of some people, for the Christ in whom they believe is simply full of affectionateness and gentleness, whereas I believe there never was a more splendid specimen of manhood, even its sternness, than the Saviour; and the very lips which declared that He would not break a bruised reed uttered the most terrible anathemas upon the Pharisees.

—CHARLES H SPURGEON

1

When It's Wrong to Be "Nice"

❦

*Then, in the hearing of all the people, He said to His disciples,
"Beware of the scribes . . ."*

Luke 20:45–46

*J*esus' way of dealing with sinners was normally marked by such extreme tenderness that He earned a derisive moniker from His critics: Friend of Sinners (Matthew 11:19). When He encountered even the grossest of moral lepers (ranging from a woman living in adultery in John 4:7–29 to a man infested with a whole legion of demons in Luke 8:27–39), Jesus always ministered to them with remarkable benevolence—without delivering any scolding lectures or sharp rebukes. Invariably, when such people came to Him, they were already broken, humbled, and fed up with the life of sin. He eagerly granted such people forgiveness, healing, and full fellowship with Him on the basis of their faith alone (cf. Luke 7:50; 17:19).

The one class of sinners Jesus consistently dealt with sternly were the professional hypocrites, religious phonies, false teachers, and self-righteous peddlers of plastic piety—the scribes, lawyers, Sadducees, and Pharisees. These were the religious leaders in Israel—spiritual "rulers" (to use a term Scripture often applies to them). They were the despotic gatekeepers of religious tradition. They cared more for custom and convention than they did for the truth. Almost every time they appear in the gospel accounts, they are concerned mainly with keeping up appearances and holding on to their power. Any thought they might have had for authentic godliness always took a backseat to more academic, pragmatic, or self-serving matters. They were the quintessential religious hypocrites.

THE SANHEDRIN AND THE SADDUCEES

The ruling power these men possessed was derived from a large council based in Jerusalem, consisting of seventy-one prominent religious authorities, collectively known as the *Sanhedrin*. Council members included the high priest and seventy leading priests and religious scholars. (The number was derived from Moses' appointment of seventy advisors to assist him in Numbers 11:16.)

The Sanhedrin had ultimate authority over Israel in all religious and spiritual matters (and thus even in some civil affairs). The council's authority was formally recognized even by Caesar (though it was not always respected by Caesar's official representatives or his troops on the ground in Jerusalem). The council was a fixture in first-century Jerusalem, and it constituted the most important ruling body in all of Judaism until the destruction of the temple in AD 70. (The Sanhedrin continued to operate in exile after that for more than 250 years—though for obvious reasons, their power was greatly diminished. Persistent Roman persecution finally silenced and disbanded the council sometime in the fourth century.)

The gospel accounts of Christ's crucifixion refer about a dozen times to the Sanhedrin as "the chief priests, the scribes, and the elders" (e.g., Matthew 26:3; Luke 20:1). The high priest presided over the full council, of course. The *chief priests* were the ranking aristocracy of the high-priestly line. (Some of them were men who had already served as high priest at one time or another; others were in line to serve a term in that office.) Virtually all the chief priests were also Sadducees. The *elders* were key leaders and influential members of important families outside the high-priestly line—and they were predominantly Sadducees too. The *scribes* were the scholars, not necessarily of noble birth like the chief priests and elders, but men who were distinguished mainly because of their expertise in scholarship and their encyclopedic knowledge of Jewish law and tradition. Their group was dominated by Pharisees.

So the council consisted of a blend of Pharisees and Sadducees, and those were rival parties. Although Sadducees were vastly outnumbered by Pharisees in the culture at large, the Sadducees nevertheless maintained a sizable majority in the Sanhedrin, and they held on to the reins of power tightly. The status of their priestly birthright in effect trumped the Pharisees' scholarly clout, because the Pharisees were such devoted traditionalists that they bowed to the authority of the high-priestly line—even though they strongly disagreed with practically everything that made the Sadducees' belief system distinctive.

For example, the Sadducees questioned the immortality of the human soul—denying both the resurrection of the body (Matthew 22:23), and the existence of the spirit world (Acts 23:8). The Saducean party also rejected the Pharisees' emphasis on oral traditions—going about as far as they could in the opposite direction. In fact, the Sadducees stressed the Pentateuch (the five books of Moses) almost to the exclusion of the rest of the Old Testament. As a result, the powerful messianic expectation that pervaded the teaching of the Pharisees was almost completely missing from the Sadducees' worldview.

The two groups also held conflicting opinions regarding *how* ceremonial customs should be observed. Both Sadducees and Pharisees tended to give more attention to ceremonial law than they did to the law's moral ramifications. But the Pharisees generally made ceremonies as elaborate as possible, and Sadducees tended toward the opposite direction. In general, the Sadducees were not as rigid as the Pharisees in most things—except when it came to the issue of enforcing law and order. As long as the Sadducees enjoyed a modicum of power that was recognized by Rome, they were fiercely conservative (and often harsh) when it came to the implementation of civil law and the imposition of punishments and penalties.

But in most respects, the Sadducees were classic theological liberals. Their skepticism with regard to heaven, angels, and the afterlife automatically made them worldly minded and power hungry. They were much more interested in (and skilled at) the *politics* of Judaism than they were devoted to the religion itself.

MEET THE PHARISEES

Nevertheless, it was the Pharisees, not the more doctrinally aberrant Sadducees, who became the main figures of public opposition to Jesus in all four New Testament gospel accounts. Their teaching dominated and epitomized the religious establishment in first-century Israel. They were the spiritual descendants of a group known as the *Hasideans* in the second and third centuries BC. The Hasideans were ascetics, devoted to Jewish law and opposed every kind of idolatry. In the mid-second century BC, the Hasideans had been drawn into the famous revolt led by Judas Maccabeus against Antiochus Epiphanes, and subsequently their teachings had a profound and lasting impact on popular Jewish religious culture. *Hasid* is from a Hebrew word meaning "piety." (The modern

Hasidic sect, founded in the eighteenth century, is not in any direct line of descent from the Hasideans, but their beliefs and practices follow the same trajectory.)

The word *Pharisee* is most likely based on a Hebrew root meaning "separate"—so the name probably underscores their separatism. Indeed, Pharisees had an ostentatious way of trying to keep themselves separate from everything that had any connotation of ceremonial defilement. Their obsession with the external badges of piety was their most prominent feature, and they wore it on their sleeves—literally. They used the broadest possible leather straps to bind phylacteries on their arms and foreheads. (Phylacteries were leather boxes containing bits of parchment inscribed with verses from the Hebrew Scriptures.) They also lengthened the tassels on their garments (see Deuteronomy 22:12) in order to make their public display of religious devotion as conspicuous as possible. Thus they had taken a symbol that was meant to be a reminder to themselves (Numbers 15:38–39) and turned it into an advertisement of their self-righteousness, in order to gain the attention of others.

The historian Josephus was the earliest secular writer to describe the sect of the Pharisees. Born within four or five years of Jesus' crucifixion, Josephus records that he was the son of a prominent Jerusalem priest (a Sadducee) named Matthias.[1] Beginning about age sixteen, Josephus studied with each of the three main sects of Judaism—the Pharisees, the Sadducees, and the Essenes. Not fully satisfied with any of them, he lived in the desert for three years and followed an ascetic teacher (whose rough, spartan lifestyle was in some ways reminiscent of John the Baptist, and undoubtedly very much like the desert-based Essenes who originally hid the Dead Sea Scrolls). But then after his desert sojourn, Josephus returned to Jerusalem and pursued the life of a Pharisee.[2] His life was severely disrupted, of course, by the fall of Jerusalem in AD 70. Josephus subsequently became a Roman loyalist and wrote his history at the behest of the Empire. Most scholars therefore believe he deliberately slanted portions of his history in ways he knew would please the Romans. But he nevertheless wrote as someone with inside knowledge of the Pharisees, and there is no reason to doubt any of the details he gave in his descriptions of them.

Josephus notes that the Pharisees were the largest and strictest of the major Jewish sects. In fact, he says the Pharisees' influence was so profound in early first-century Jewish life that even the Pharisees' theological adversaries, the Sadducees, had to conform to the Pharisees' style of prayer, Sabbath observance, and ceremonialism in their public behavior, or else popular opinion would not have tolerated them.[3]

So the Pharisees' clout was palpable in Israel's daily life during Jesus' lifetime—especially with regard to issues of public piety like Sabbath regulations, ritual washings, dietary restrictions, and other issues of ceremonial purity. These things became the emblems of the Pharisees' influence, and they made it their business to try to enforce their customs on everyone in the culture—even though many of their traditions had no basis whatsoever in Scripture. Most of their conflicts with Jesus centered on precisely those issues, and from the very start of His public ministry, the Pharisees set themselves against Him with the fiercest kind of opposition.

There were some exceptional Pharisees, of course. Nicodemus was a prominent "ruler of the Jews" (John 3:1). He was evidently a member of the Sanhedrin, the governing religious council in Jerusalem (cf. John 7:50). "This man came to Jesus by night" (John 3:3), evidently for fear of what his fellow Pharisees would think if they knew about his sincere interest in Jesus. In stark contrast to most of the Pharisees who approached Jesus, Nicodemus was making a genuine inquiry, not merely putting Jesus to the test. Therefore Christ spoke to him candidly and straightforwardly but without the kind of severity that colored most of Jesus' dealings with Pharisees. (We'll examine Jesus' dialogue with Nicodemus more closely in chapter 3.)

All four gospels also mention a wealthy and influential council member named Joseph of Arimathea, who became a disciple of Christ ("but secretly, for fear of the Jews" says John 19:38). Mark 15:43 and Luke 23:50 both expressly identify Joseph as a member of the Sanhedrin, and Luke says Joseph "had not consented to their decision and deed" when they conspired to murder Jesus. It was of course Joseph who secured Pilate's permission to remove Jesus' body from the cross, and he and Nicodemus hastily prepared the corpse for burial and deposited it in a sealed tomb (John 19:39). There is no record in the New Testament of any direct encounter between Jesus and Joseph of Arimathea during Christ's earthly ministry. Apparently Joseph kept his distance, not even approaching Jesus at night the way Nicodemus had done. This was not because he had any fear of Jesus, but he feared what the other Jewish leaders might say, do, or think of him if they knew he was secretly a disciple of Jesus.

As a rule, then, Jesus' interactions with the Pharisees, Sadducees, scribes, and leading priests were marked by acrimony, not tenderness. He rebuked them publicly and to their faces. He repeatedly said harsh things *about* them in His sermons and public discourses. He warned His followers to beware of their deadly influence. He consistently employed stronger language in His denunciations of the Pharisees than He ever used against the pagan Roman authorities or their occupying armies.

That fact absolutely infuriated the Pharisees. They gladly would have embraced any messiah who opposed the Roman occupation of

Israel and affirmed their pharisaical traditions. Jesus, however, spoke not a word against Caesar while treating the entire religious aristocracy of Israel as if they were more dangerous tyrants than Caesar himself.

Indeed, they were. Their false teaching was far more destructive to Israel's well-being than the political oppression of Rome. In spiritual terms, the self-righteousness and religious traditionalism of the Pharisees represented a more clear and present danger to the vital health of the nation than the tightening political vise that had already been clamped on Israel by Caesar and his occupying armies. That is saying quite a lot, given the fact that in less than half a century Roman armies would completely lay waste to Jerusalem and drive Israel's population into a far-flung exile (the Diaspora) from which the Jewish people have not fully emerged even today.

But as profound and far-reaching as the holocaust of AD 70 was for the Jewish nation, a far greater calamity was looming in the institutionalized self-righteousness of the Pharisees' brand of religion—especially their preference for human traditions over the Word of God. That led to a *spiritual* disaster of eternal and infinite proportions, because most Israelites in that generation rejected their true Messiah—and multitudes of their descendants have continued the relentless pursuit of religious tradition for almost two full millennia, many refusing to give any serious consideration to the claims of Christ as God's Messiah.

The Pharisees' legalistic system was in effect a steamroller paving the way for that tragedy. The apostle Paul (a converted Pharisee himself) was describing pharisaical religion to a T in Romans 10:2–3, when he lamented the unbelief of Israel: "I bear them witness that they have a zeal for God, but not according to knowledge. For they being ignorant of God's righteousness, and seeking to establish their own righteousness, have not submitted to the righteousness of God."

8

The Pharisees did indeed have a kind of zeal for God. On the surface, they certainly did not appear to pose as great a threat as the Roman armies did. In fact, the Pharisees were genuine experts when it came to knowing the *words* of Scripture. They were also fastidious in their observance of the law's tiniest external details. If they purchased seeds for their herb gardens, for example, they would meticulously count the grains in each packet and measure out a tithe (Matthew 23:23).

To the eye of a superficial observer, the religious culture the Pharisees had cultivated in first-century Israel might have appeared to represent a kind of golden age for Jewish law. It was certainly not the same variety of overtly false religion we read about so frequently in the Old Testament—those repeated epochs of backsliding and idolatry with golden calves, Asherah worship, and worse.

No one could accuse a Pharisee of any overtolerance for pagan beliefs, right? They were, after all, strongly opposed to every expression of idolatry and totally committed even to the incidental minutiae of Jewish law. Plus, for safety's sake they had added many surplus rituals of their own making, as extra shields against accidental defilement. If biblical law demanded ceremonial washings for priests offering sacrifices, why not add *extra* washings for everyone, and make them an essential part of common daily routines? That is precisely what they did.

From a human perspective, these things all had the appearance of profound devotion to God. Looked at in that way, the Pharisees might have been thought the *least* likely men of their generation to become Messiah's worst enemies. They were profoundly religious, not careless or profane. They certainly weren't avowed atheists openly undermining people's faith in God's Word. They promoted piety, not licentiousness. They advocated zeal, rigor, and abstinence—not worldliness and indifference to spiritual things. They championed Judaism, not the sort of pagan syncretism their Samaritan neighbors and so many earlier generations of Israelites had dabbled in. Their religion was their whole life.

It even took precedence over God Himself.

And therein lay the problem. The Pharisees had devised a slick disguise, concealing their self-righteousness and hypocrisy under a veneer of religious zeal. They were careful to maintain the appearance of—but not the reality of—sincere devotion to God. More than that, they had so thoroughly blended their manmade religious traditions with the revealed truth of God that they themselves could not even tell the difference anymore. Despite all their studied expertise in the unique variety of Old Testament scholarship they promoted, they insisted on viewing the Scriptures through the lens of human tradition. Tradition therefore became their primary authority and the governing principle in their interpretations of Scripture. Under those circumstances, there was no way for Scripture to correct their *faulty* traditions. The Pharisees thus became the chief architects of a corrupted brand of cultural and traditional (but not truly biblical) Judaism. By Jesus' time it was already a monstrous, burdensome system of rule keeping, ritual, superstition, human custom, sabbatarian legalism, and self-righteous pretense—all closely supervised under the critical eye of the Pharisees.

The Pharisees who blindly followed the party line in the name of tradition were false teachers, no matter how pious or noble they might have appeared to the superficial eye. They were the worst kind of wolves in sheep's clothing—corrupt rabbis wearing the wool robes of a prophet and devouring the sheep of the Lord's flock under the cover of that disguise. They were in fact determined rebels against God and His Anointed One, even though they covered themselves with such a cloying, pretentious display of external piety. Even when confronted with liberating biblical truth, they stubbornly carried on being shills for legalism.

No wonder Jesus dealt so sternly with them.

THE EVIL OF FALSE RELIGION

Men and women who lack a biblical worldview tend to think of religion as the noblest expression of the human character. Popular opinion in the world at large has generally regarded religion as something inherently admirable, honorable, and beneficial.

In reality, no other field of the humanities—philosophy, literature, the arts, or whatever—holds quite as much potential for mischief as religion. Nothing is more thoroughly evil than *false* religion, and the more false teachers try to cloak themselves in the robes of biblical truth, the more truly Satanic they are.

Nevertheless, benign-looking, suavely religious emissaries of Satan are ordinary, not extraordinary. Redemptive history is full of them, and the Bible continually warns about such false teachers—savage wolves in sheep's clothing, "false apostles, deceitful workers, transforming themselves into apostles of Christ. And no wonder! For Satan himself transforms himself into an angel of light. Therefore it is no great thing if his ministers also transform themselves into ministers of righteousness" (2 Corinthians 11:13–15).

Delivering his farewell speech at Ephesus, the apostle Paul told the elders of that young but already beleaguered church, "I know this, that after my departure savage wolves will come in among you, not sparing the flock. *Also from among yourselves* men will rise up, speaking perverse things, to draw away the disciples after themselves" (Acts 20:29–30, emphasis added). He was warning them that false teachers would arise not only from within the church, but that they would creep unnoticed into the *leadership* of the church (cf. Jude 4). It undoubtedly happened in Ephesus, and it has happened again and again in every phase of church history. False teachers robe themselves in the garments of God. They want people to believe that they represent God, that they know God, that they have special insight into divine truth and wisdom, even though they are emissaries of hell itself.

In 1 Timothy 4:1–3, Paul prophesied that the church of the last days would be assaulted by false teachers with a Pharisaical approach to asceticism, which they would use as a cloak for licentiousness:

> Now the Spirit expressly says that in latter times some will depart from the faith, giving heed to deceiving spirits and doctrines of demons, speaking lies in hypocrisy, having their own conscience seared with a hot iron, forbidding to marry, and commanding to abstain from foods which God created to be received with thanksgiving by those who believe and know the truth.

Notice how Scripture emphatically says false teachers who like to wear a cloak of self-righteousness and hide under the pretense of orthodoxy are evil, envoys of the devil, teachers of demonic doctrines. Again, nothing is more thoroughly diabolical than false religion, and we are warned repeatedly and explicitly not to take false teaching lightly because of its close resemblance to the truth.

Never were false teachers more aggressive than during the earthly ministry of the Lord Jesus Christ. It was as if all hell amassed its heaviest assault ever against Him during those three years. And we can certainly understand that. To thwart the gospel and to try to frustrate the plan of God, Satan unleashed everything he had against Jesus Christ, ranging from Satan's own direct efforts to tempt Him (Matthew 4:1–11; Luke 22:40–46) to demons who confronted Him while feigning homage to Him (Mark 5:1–13)—and everything else in between, including the infiltration of Judas, the false disciple, whom Satan himself influenced, indwelt, and empowered to commit the ultimate act of treachery (Luke 22:3).

But the steadiest and most sustained attack against Jesus—and the main campaign of vocal opposition that finally hounded Him to the cross—was the incessant antagonism of the Pharisees, goaded on by the Sanhedrin.

They, in turn, were being directed by Satan. They were undoubtedly oblivious to this fact, but Satan was using them as pawns in his relentless campaign against the truth.

It seems almost unthinkable that the fiercest opposition to Christ would come from the most respected leaders of society's religious sector. But it's true. Look at the broad scope of Jesus' earthly ministry as the gospel writers recorded it, and ask, "Who were the chief agents of Satan who attempted to thwart His work and oppose His teaching? Where did the main resistance to Christ come from?" The answer is obvious. It wasn't from the culture's criminal underworld or its secular underclass. It wasn't from society's outcasts—the tax collectors, lowlifes, thugs, prostitutes, and thieves. Instead, the chief emissaries and agents of Satan were the most devout, the most sanctimonious, the most respected religious leaders in all of Israel— led in that effort by the very strictest of all their major sects, the Pharisees.

That whole strategy was without a doubt orchestrated and set in motion by Satan himself. In fact, Paul's whole point in 2 Corinthians 11:14–15 is that secret subterfuge is and always has been the devil's primary tactic. Therefore it should come as no surprise to us that enemies of the gospel have always been (and still are) most formidable when they are religious. The more successful they are at convincing people they are within the circle of orthodoxy, the more effective they will be at undermining the truth. The more deeply they can infiltrate the community of true believers, the more damage they can do with their lies. The closer they can get to the sheep and gain their trust, the more easily they can devour the flock.

DANCES WITH WOLVES

Any literal shepherd tasked with feeding and leading a flock of lambs would be thought deranged if he regarded wolves as potential pets to be domesticated and amalgamated into the fold. Suppose he actively sought and tried to befriend young wolves, presuming he could teach them to mingle with his sheep—*insisting* against all wise counsel that his experiment might succeed, and if it does, the wolves will acquire the sheep's gentleness and the sheep will learn things from the wolves, too. Such a shepherd would be worse than useless; he himself would pose an extreme danger to the flock.

Nearly as bad would be a shepherd whose vision is myopic. He has never seen a wolf clearly with his own eyes. He therefore believes the threat of wolves is grossly exaggerated. Even though his sheep keep disappearing or getting torn to shreds by *something*, he refuses to believe it is wolves that are harming his flock. He declares that he is tired of hearing shrill wolf-warnings from others. He begins telling the story of "The Boy Who Cried Wolf" to everyone who will listen. Finally concluding that other people's "negativity" toward wolves poses a greater danger to his flock than the wolves themselves, he takes out his reed and plays a gentle tune to lull the lambs to sleep.

Then, of course, there is the "hireling, he who is not the shepherd, one who does not own the sheep." He "sees the wolf coming and leaves the sheep and flees; and the wolf catches the sheep and scatters them. The hireling flees because he is a hireling and does not care about the sheep" (John 10:12–13).

Self-seeking hirelings, myopic shepherds, and wannabe wolf

tamers are all too prevalent in the church today. So are wolves in sheep's clothing. Frankly, some of the postmodern lamb's wool costumes aren't even the least bit convincing. But some pastors seem to have no hesitancy about unleashing these eager wolves among their flocks. Many are like the near-sighted shepherd in my parable—convinced that warnings about the threat of wolves are potentially more dangerous than actual wolves.

Contemporary evangelicalism in general seems to have no taste whatsoever for any kind of doctrinal friction—much less open conflict with spiritual wolves. The Evangelical Manifesto I cited in the introduction to this book clearly reflects that point of view, expressing many more words of concern about evangelical public relations than it ever does for evangelical doctrinal soundness. The document confidently asserts that "the Evangelical message, 'good news' by definition, is overwhelmingly positive, and always positive before it is negative."[4] That's a considerable overstatement—especially given the fact that Paul's systematic outline of the gospel in Romans begins with the words, "For the wrath of God is revealed from heaven" (Romans 1:18) and then goes on for almost three full chapters expounding on the depth and universality of human "ungodliness and unrighteousness," which is what unleashed God's wrath in the first place. Only after he has made the bad news inescapable does Paul introduce the gospel's good news. He follows the very same pattern in abbreviated form in Ephesians 2:1–10.

As we are going to see, Jesus Himself was not *always* positive before being negative. Some of His longest discourses, including all of Matthew 23, were entirely negative.

The recent Evangelical Manifesto gives a nod of commendation to "those in the past for their worthy desire to be true to the fundamentals of faith," but then it seems to suggest that militancy in defense of the core truths of Christianity is always to be avoided. In fact, the main reason the manifesto gives for listing "conservative fundamentalism" as one of two opposite corruptions of the true Protestant spirit (the other being "liberal revisionism") is that certain fundamentalists have resisted the liberalizing tendency with "styles of reaction that are personally and publicly militant to the point where they are sub-Christian."[5]

Granted, self-styled fundamentalists have often behaved in shameful ways. It's quite true that jealous infighting between certain larger-than-life "fundamentalist" personalities has frequently been both too public and too personal—and decidedly sub-Christian. In fact, the pugnaciousness of some fundamentalist leaders shattered their movement and left classic fundamentalism without many influential voices today. But to be clear: the problem with that style of militancy was never *merely* that it was too personal or too public—but that it was utterly misdirected and increasingly grounded in ignorance rather than understanding. Many at the forefront of that movement seemed to have little understanding of what was truly fundamental and what was peripheral. In other words, they weren't fundamentalists at all in the original sense of that term. They had an uncanny knack for straining at gnats while swallowing camels. That's not authentic fundamentalism, but a corruption of it. In fact, it is one modern embodiment of the pharisaical spirit.

The answer to fundamentalism's failure certainly is not for evangelicals to forswear conflict altogether and greet wolves with a welcoming smile and amicable dialogue. That is unquestionably the direction the evangelical current is running. The Evangelical Manifesto makes remarks like those about the dangers of fundamentalism while tacitly acknowledging that the evangelical movement itself is seriously muddled and urgently in need of reformation. Of the "three major mandates" the Manifesto lists, reaffirming our identity comes first.[6] Yet nowhere does the document suggest any strategy for dealing with the many aberrant opinions (including countless echoes of "liberal revisionism") that are currently demanding evangelical acceptance. Indeed, the whole Manifesto seems deliberately muted so as not to give anyone the impression that alternative points of view are shut out from the evangelical conversation. "Our purpose is not to attack or to exclude but to remind and to reaffirm."[7] After all, "different faiths and the different families of faith provide very different answers to life, and these differences are decisive not only for individuals but for societies and entire civilizations. Learning to live with our deepest differences is therefore of great consequence both for individuals and nations."[8] I doubt that either Paul or Jesus would sign that.

The problem is that the needed reformation *within* evangelicalism won't occur at all if false ideas that undermine our core theological convictions cannot be openly attacked and excluded. When peaceful coexistence "with our deepest differences" becomes priority one and conflict *per se* is demonized as inherently sub-Christian, any and every false religious belief can and will demand an equal voice in the "conversation."

That has actually been happening for some time already. Listen, for example, to what some of the leading voices in and around the Emergent movement have said. Tony Campolo is a popular speaker and author who has a major influence in evangelical circles. He believes evangelicals should be in dialogue with Islam, seeking common ground. In an interview conducted by Shane Claiborne, Campolo said:

> I think that the last election aggravated a significant minority of
> the evangelical community, believing that they did not want to
> come across as anti-gay, anti-women, anti-environment, pro

war, pro capital punishment, and anti-Islam. There is going to be one segment of evangelicalism, just like there is one segment in Islam that is not going to be interested in dialogue. But there are other evangelicals who will want to talk and establish a common commitment to a goodness with Islamic people and Jewish people particularly.[9]

Brian McLaren is perhaps the best-known figure in the Emergent conversation. He thinks the future of the planet—not to mention the salvation of religion itself (including Christianity)—depends on a cooperative search for the real meaning of Jesus' message. In McLaren's assessment, this means an ongoing dialogue between Christians and followers of all other religions. This, he is convinced, is of the utmost urgency:

> In an age of global terrorism and rising religious conflict, it's significant to note that all Muslims regard Jesus as a great prophet, that many Hindus are willing to consider Jesus as a legitimate manifestation of the divine, that many Buddhists see Jesus as one of humanity's most enlightened people, and that Jesus himself was a Jew, and without understanding his Jewishness, one doesn't understand Jesus. A shared reappraisal of Jesus' message could provide a unique space or common ground for urgently needed religious dialogue—and it doesn't seem an exaggeration to say that the future of our planet may depend on such dialogue. This reappraisal of Jesus' message may be the only project capable of saving a number of religions, including Christianity.[10]

Indiscriminate congeniality, the quest for spiritual common ground, and peace at any price all naturally have great appeal, especially in an intellectual climate where practically the worst gaffe any thoughtful person could make is claiming to know what's true when so many other people think something else is true.

Besides, dialogue *does* sound nicer than debate. Who but a fool wouldn't prefer a calm conversation instead of conflict and confrontation?

In fact, let's state this plainly once more: Generally speaking, avoiding conflicts is a good idea. Warmth and congeniality are normally preferable to cold harshness. Civility, compassion, and good manners are in short supply these days, and we ought to have more of them. Gentleness, a soft answer, and a kind word usually go farther than an argument or a rebuke. That which edifies is more helpful and more fruitful in the long run than criticism. Cultivating friends is more pleasant and more profitable than crusading against enemies. And it's ordinarily better to be tender and mild rather than curt or combative—especially to the *victims* of false teaching.

But those qualifying words are vital: *usually, ordinarily, generally.* Avoiding conflict is not *always* the right thing. Sometimes it is downright sinful. Particularly in times like these, when almost no error is deemed too serious to be excluded from the evangelical conversation,[11] and while the Lord's flock is being infiltrated by wolves dressed like prophets, declaring visions of peace when there is no peace (cf. Ezekiel 13:16).

Even the kindest, gentlest shepherd sometimes needs to throw rocks at the wolves who come in sheep's clothing.

WAS JESUS ALWAYS "NICE"?

The Great Shepherd Himself was never far from open controversy with the most conspicuously religious inhabitants in all of Israel. Almost every chapter of the Gospels makes some reference to His running battle with the chief hypocrites of His day, and He made no effort whatsoever to be winsome in His encounters with them. He did not invite them to dialogue or engage in a friendly exchange of ideas.

As we are going to see, Jesus' public ministry was barely under-way when He invaded what they thought was their turf—the temple grounds in Jerusalem—and went on a righteous rampage against their mercenary control of Israel's worship. He did the same thing again during the final week before His crucifixion, immediately after His triumphal entry into the city. One of His last major public discourses was the solemn pronunciation of seven woes against the scribes and Pharisees. These were formal curses against them. That sermon was the farthest thing from a friendly dialogue. Matthew's record of it fills an entire chapter (Matthew 23), and as noted earlier, it is entirely devoid of any positive or encouraging word for the Pharisees and their followers. Luke distills and summarizes the entire message in three short verses: "Then, in the hearing of all the people, He said to His disciples, 'Beware of the scribes, who desire to go around in long robes, love greetings in the marketplaces, the best seats in the synagogues, and the best places at feasts, who devour widows' houses, and for a pretense make long prayers. These will receive greater condemnation'" (Luke 20:45–47).

That is a perfect summary of Jesus' dealings with the Pharisees. It is a blistering denunciation—a candid diatribe about the seriousness of their error. There is no conversation, no collegiality, no dialogue, and no cooperation. Only confrontation, condemnation, and (as Matthew records) curses against them.

Jesus' compassion is certainly evident in two facts that bracket this declamation. First, Luke says that as He drew near the city and observed its full panorama for this final time, He paused and wept over it (19:41–44). And second, Matthew records a similar lament at the end of the seven woes (23:37). So we can be absolutely certain that as Jesus delivered this diatribe, His heart was full of compassion.

Yet that compassion is directed at the victims of the false teaching, not the false teachers themselves. There is no hint of sympathy, no proposal of clemency, no trace of kindness, no effort on Jesus' part to be "nice" toward the Pharisees. Indeed, with these words Jesus formally and resoundingly pronounced their doom and then held them up publicly as a warning to others.

This is the polar opposite of any invitation to dialogue. He *doesn't* say, "They're basically good guys. They have pious intentions. They have some valid spiritual insights. Let's have a conversation with them." Instead, He says, "Keep your distance. Be on guard against their lifestyle and their influence. Follow them, and you are headed for the same condemnation they are."

This approach would surely have earned Jesus resounding outpouring of loud disapproval from today's guardians of evangelical protocol. In fact, His approach to the Pharisees utterly debunks the cardinal points of conventional wisdom among modern and postmodern evangelicals—the neoevangelical fondness for eternal collegiality, and the Emerging infatuation with engaging all points of view in endless conversation. By today's standards, Jesus' words about the Pharisees and His treatment of them are breathtakingly severe.

Let's turn back to the very beginning of Jesus' ministry and observe how this hostility between Him and the Pharisees began and how it developed.

I think many readers will be surprised to discover that it was Jesus who fired the first shot. And it was a shockingly powerful broadside.

The stern and holy Christ, the indignant, mighty Messiah, the Messenger of the Covenant of whom it is written: "He shall purify the sons of Levi, and purge them as gold and silver, that they may offer unto the Lord an offering of righteousness," is not agreeable to those who want only a soft and sweet Christ. [What we see instead is] the fiery zeal of Jesus which came with such sudden and tremendous effectiveness that before this unknown man, who had no further authority than his own person and word, this crowd of traders and changers, who thought they were fully within their rights when conducting their business in the Temple court, fled pellmell like a lot of naughty boys.

—R. C. H. Lenski[12]

2

Two Passovers

❧

They found Him in the temple, sitting in the midst of the teachers, both listening to them and asking them questions.

Luke 2:46

When He had made a whip of cords, He drove them all out of the temple.

John 2:15

*J*esus' earliest recorded encounter with Jerusalem's leading rabbis was the mildest, most benign of all His recorded face-to-face meetings with them. It occurred when He was still a boy of twelve, visiting Jerusalem with His parents for the Passover feast. Of all the gospel writers, Luke alone has anything to say about Jesus' childhood or adolescence, and this is the only episode Luke recorded from the birth of Jesus until His baptism: "His parents went to Jerusalem every year at the Feast of the Passover. And when He was twelve years old, they went up to Jerusalem according to the custom of the feast" (Luke 2:41–42).

The name *Passover* referred to that night at the end of Israel's bondage in Egypt when the death angel went through all the land of Egypt and killed the firstborn in every Egyptian home—but passed over the Israelites' dwellings, because they had marked their front doorposts and lintels with the blood of a sacrificial lamb (Exodus 12:23–27).

Passover was commemorated annually with the sacrifice of a lamb and a major feast. It was the biggest one-day event on the Jewish calendar, always celebrated on 14 Nisan. That was the first month of the Hebrew religious year, and it fell at the peak of springtime. (Because it was based on a lunar calendar rather than a 365-day year, the date varies according to modern calendars, but it ranges from mid-March to early April).

The day after Passover each year began a weeklong celebration known as the Feast of Unleavened Bread (Leviticus 23:6–8). Combined, then, these two holidays spanned eight full days. During that week, all of Jerusalem would be jammed with pilgrims who came to offer sacrifices, partake of the feasts, and participate in other festivities.

PASSOVER IN JERUSALEM—SCENE ONE

At twelve in that culture, Jesus was on the doorstep of manhood. The following year He would be *bar mitzvah*—a son of the commandment. He would then be formally regarded as an adult, personally accountable to the law, and eligible to take part publicly in Jewish worship. Until then, however, He was still a child—and not only in the eyes of His culture. He was a real child in every sense undergoing all the normal processes of biological, mental, and social development. In other words, Jesus as a child was not some kind of paranormal prodigy. The gospel record makes this inescapably clear.

In fact, this brief window into His childhood is one of the Bible's most vivid portrayals of Christ in His full humanity. In the second and third centuries after Christ, spurious writings occasionally appeared, purporting to contain firsthand accounts of Jesus' childhood. Sometimes known as the "infancy gospels," these were gnostic fabrications filled with fanciful and often ridiculous stories. They usually portrayed the boy Jesus as a sort of transcendental *wunderkind.* They paint a grotesque picture of a powerful but petulant boy who performed all kinds of implausible childish wonders—making sparrows from clay and causing them to fly; stretching wooden beams in His father's carpentry shop so that they fit; and healing His playmates—or striking them dead, depending on His mood. One account has Him causing the next-door neighbors to go blind. The boy-christ of the gnostic gospels also was known for rebuking any teachers who had the audacity to try to instruct Him.

The one authentic biblical account of Jesus' childhood stands in stark contrast to all such tales. What we see in Luke 2 is a very normal boy with true-to-life parents.

Joseph and Mary went annually to Jerusalem to celebrate Passover (v. 41). But it is likely that Luke 2 is describing Jesus' first-ever Passover in Jerusalem. It was customary for boys in their last year of childhood to experience their first feast at the temple. The preparation for *bar mitzvah* included instruction in the law, including familiarity with Jewish customs, rituals, feasts, and sacrifices. The Passover week afforded an intensive initiation into all of these, so it was common for boys in their final year of childhood to have the privilege of accompanying their parents to Jerusalem for that week of celebration. (Matthew 21:15 says that at Christ's triumphal final entry into Jerusalem there were "children crying out in the temple and saying, 'Hosanna.'" Matthew uses a masculine noun for "children." Normally boys still in their childhood would not be found in large numbers in the temple grounds. But Jesus' entry into Jerusalem was less than a week before Passover, and twelve-year-old boys would be there from all over Israel, anticipating their first significant worship experience in the temple.) It seems that when Jesus Himself was a boy on the precipice of manhood, His family followed that same custom.

Luke says nothing about the actual Passover celebration or the Feast of Unleavened Bread, but he picks up the story when it was time for the family to return to Galilee:

"When they had finished the days, as they returned, the Boy Jesus lingered behind in Jerusalem. And Joseph and His mother did not know it; but supposing Him to have been in the company, they went a day's journey, and sought Him among their relatives and acquaintances. So when they did not find Him, they returned to Jerusalem, seeking Him" (Luke 2:43–45).

Jesus' separation from His parents was rooted in a very simple misunderstanding on their part. The gospel account by no means suggests that Jesus was being mischievous or rebellious. He was simply engrossed in the goings-on at the temple—the very thing He was there to participate in. On the day they were scheduled to depart, however, Jesus' parents were preoccupied with preparations for the journey home. When they left, He lingered—not out of disrespect or defiance, but simply because (like all children) He was utterly absorbed in something that had arrested His attention. His true humanness never shows more clearly than it does in this account.

Because so many pilgrims descended on Jerusalem during that week, all the roads and inns would be jammed, and large numbers of people from each community would travel to and from the feast together. From a town the size of Nazareth, there may have been a hundred or more people in Jesus' parents' party, some walking, some riding slow beasts of burden. A band that large would likely stretch over a mile's distance, and the women generally traveled in a group or several small groups together, rather than being spread out among the men.

So it is easy to understand how this confusion arose. Mary and Joseph no doubt each presumed Jesus was with the other parent. He certainly would not have been a mischief-prone child, so neither parent gave any thought to investigating His whereabouts until the end of the first day's travel, when they suddenly discovered He was not with the group at all.

Any parent can easily imagine the feelings of horror that would have seized them as soon as they realized they had left Him behind. It was, of course, a full day's journey *back* to Jerusalem. They doubtless returned as quickly as possible, most likely that very night. If so, they would have arrived around daybreak or shortly after, exhausted and fretful. They began searching all of Jerusalem looking for Jesus—doubtless expecting that He was likewise searching for them. They would have started with places they knew were familiar to Him, and when that yielded no result, they would have combed every alleyway and corner of the city, growing more desperate as the hours went by. "Three days," Luke says—probably counting from the time of their original departure at the end of the feast. At the very least, then, they were frantically scouring all of Jerusalem for a day and a half, checking and rechecking all the places they had been with Him.

Except, perhaps, the most obvious place.

"Now so it was that after three days they found Him in the temple, sitting in the midst of the teachers, both listening to them and asking them questions. And all who heard Him were astonished at His understanding and answers" (vv. 46–47).

This is a unique picture of Jesus, seated among Israel's leading rabbis, politely listening to them, asking questions, and amazing them with His comprehension and discernment. Still a child in every sense, He was already the most amazing student they had ever had the privilege to teach. He had evidently kept these teachers fully engaged for three days, and when Joseph and Mary finally came upon the scene, Jesus' attention was still so focused on the lesson that He had not yet even thought to go looking for them.

Because He was still a child—the *perfect* child—it is only reasonable to assume that Jesus maintained the role of a respectful student. We're not to think He was rebuking, challenging, even instructing those rabbis. In fact, Luke seems to include this brief vignette about Jesus' childhood precisely to stress the full humanity of Christ—how He grew "in wisdom and stature, and in favor with God and men" (v. 52). Again, Luke is saying that every aspect of Jesus' development into full manhood (intellectually, physically, spiritually, and socially) was *ordinary*, not extraordinary. That means even though He was God incarnate, with all the full attributes of God in His infinite being, in some mysterious way His divine omniscience (while available to Him whenever it suited His Father's purpose) was normally shrouded. His conscious mind was therefore subject to the normal limitations of human finitude. In other words, as Luke says here, Jesus truly *learned* things. Although He knew everything exhaustively and omnisciently as God, He did not always maintain full awareness of everything in His human consciousness (as we see in Mark 13:32). The questions He asked those rabbis were part of the learning process, not some backhanded way of showing the rabbis up. He was truly learning from them and processing what they taught Him. This experience surely provided our Lord's first personal insight into their approach to Scripture and their religious system, which He would later denounce.

No hint is given as to the subject matter of the lesson, but three days isn't even enough for a thorough survey of the Old Testament, so it is certainly not necessary to assume the temple rabbis were delving into mystifyingly deep theological subjects. They were most likely discussing matters related to their interpretation of Israel's history, the law, the psalms, and the prophets. Luke says Jesus was listening and asking questions, and what amazed these tutors was His grasp of the information they were giving Him and His answers (v. 47). So they were obviously quizzing Him as they went, and they were astonished at both His attention span and His ability to perceive spiritual truth.

It would have been an amazing lesson to eavesdrop on, and it is the only time in all the gospel accounts where we see Jesus sitting at anyone's feet to learn. No doubt throughout His childhood He *did* have other teachers as well, and Luke seems to acknowledge this in his description of how Jesus matured (v. 52), but Luke 2:46 remains the only brief window into Jesus' student career that we are given anywhere in Scripture. And it is the only record in all the gospels of any extended friendly exchange between Jesus and any group of leading rabbis.

The lesson came to a rather abrupt halt when Joseph and Mary finally found Jesus. Their anxiety and exasperation are certainly easy to understand from any parent's point of view: "When they saw Him, they were amazed; and His mother said to Him, 'Son, why have You done this to us? Look, Your father and I have sought You anxiously'" (v. 48).

This was probably not the first time—and it certainly would not be the last—that Jesus' innocent motives would be misunderstood and misconstrued. Nor should His reply to Joseph and Mary be read as an insolent retort. He was truly amazed that they hadn't known exactly where to look for Him. "He said to them, 'Why did you seek Me? Did you not know that I must be about My Father's business?'" (v. 49).

Mary, of course, was referring to Joseph when she said, "your father." Jesus, however, was calling God "My Father." (Plainly Jesus already had a clear sense of who He was and where His true accountability lay.) But at the moment, Jesus' parents were so overwhelmed with relief to have found Him, so amazed to find Him at the feet of these prominent rabbis, and so fatigued from the whole ordeal that "they did not understand the statement which He spoke to them" (v. 50).

Luke ends this singular glimpse at Jesus' childhood with this wrap-up: "Then He went down with them and came to Nazareth, and was subject to them, but His mother kept all these things in her heart. And Jesus increased in wisdom and stature, and in favor with God and men" (vv. 51–52). That is the end of Luke 2, and it is a perfect summary of Jesus' boyhood.

At first glance, it's not easy to understand how Jesus, as God incarnate, with all the attributes of deity, could possibly increase in wisdom or gain favor with God. But this is a statement about Jesus' *humanity.* As God, He is of course perfect in every way and therefore eternally unchanging (Hebrews 13:8). Divine omniscience by definition does not allow for any increase in wisdom. But this text is saying that in the conscious awareness of His human mind, Jesus did not always avail himself of the infinite knowledge He possessed as God (cf. Mark 13:32). He did not lose His omniscience or cease being God, but He voluntarily suspended the use of that quality—so that as a boy, He learned things the same way every human child learns. Furthermore, in his growth from boyhood to manhood, He gained the admiration of others and the approval of God for the way He lived as a human subject to God's law (Galatians 4:4).

Luke 2:52 is therefore not a denial of Jesus' deity; it is an affirmation of His true humanity. The stress is on the normalcy of His development. In His progress from childhood to manhood He endured everything any other child would experience—except for the guilt of sin.

PASSOVER IN JERUSALEM—SCENE TWO

Fast-forward more than fifteen years. Jesus is now a fully mature adult about thirty years old, and He is back in Jerusalem for another Passover. This time John is the only evangelist who records the event: "Now the Passover of the Jews was at hand, and Jesus went up to Jerusalem" (John 2:13). Jesus' public ministry will last a little more than three years total, and thus it spans four Passovers. His reputation will quickly begin to spread during this first Passover week, and His crucifixion will occur on Passover Day exactly three years later.

Scripture gives us no information whatsoever about Jesus' life after the end of Luke 2 until He comes to be baptized by John in the Jordan River.[1] So John is recording the very earliest close-up look at Jesus in a public, urban context. In fact, this Passover is really the first major public event of our Lord's ministry. Although Jesus will work and live mostly in Galilee, He chooses the biggest event of the year in Jerusalem to make His public debut. As we see from the narrative that unfolds, Jesus makes no attempt to come across as "positive" before provoking a confrontation:

> He found in the temple those who sold oxen and sheep and doves, and the money changers doing business. When He had made a whip of cords, He drove them all out of the temple, with the sheep and the oxen, and poured out the changers' money and overturned the tables. And He said to those who sold doves, "Take these things away! Do not make My Father's house a house of merchandise!" (vv. 14–16)

The abruptness of Jesus' appearance at the temple is a literal fulfill-ment of Malachi 3:1–2: "'And the Lord, whom you seek, will sud-denly come to His temple, even the Messenger of the covenant, in whom you delight. Behold, He is coming,' says the LORD of hosts. 'But who can endure the day of His coming? And who can stand when He appears? For He is like a refiner's fire and like launderers' soap.'"

Jerusalem was again jammed with pilgrims, not only from all over the land of Israel, but also from Jewish communities throughout the Roman world. The population of the city might more than double during a typical Passover week. Of course, merchants throughout the city profited immensely from the revenue that came in from pilgrims during the holidays.

The temple priests even had their own extremely profitable franchise set up right there on the temple grounds. A portion of the massive outer court (known as the court of the Gentiles) had been turned into a bustling bazaar, filled with licensed animal-merchants and money changers. With multitudes coming to celebrate Passover from all corners of the empire, it was impossible for some of them to bring their own oxen, lambs, or doves for sacrifice. Furthermore, paschal lambs had to be "without blemish, a male of the first year" (Exodus 12:5). Other sacrificial animals likewise all had to be flawless. The law was clear about this: "Whatever has a defect, you shall not offer, for it shall not be acceptable on your behalf" (Leviticus 22:20). Priests would therefore carefully inspect every animal brought to the altar, and if they found a defect, they would pronounce the animal unsuitable. For obvious reasons it would be terribly inconvenient for any family to carry a sacrificial animal more than three days journey from Galilee only to have it declared unfit for sacrifice. And for many, the journey to Jerusalem was too far even to think of bringing animals for sacrifice along. So the temple merchants sold preapproved animals—but at a very dear premium.

The money changers' tables were likewise supposed to be a service for pilgrims and worshippers, because offerings to the temple had to be made with Jewish coins. Roman coins had impressions of Caesar (Luke 20:24), which were deemed idolatrous. Other foreign coinage was likewise unacceptable for temple offerings, either because it was minted from impure metal or because imagery stamped on it made the coins unacceptable for an act of worship. Therefore only one particular kind of half-shekel coin could be used.

The Old Testament prescribed a half-shekel offering from every male twenty years old and older, to be offered with each national census (Exodus 30:13–14). The half-shekel tax was specifically to be used for the maintenance of the temple (v. 16), and by the first century, with Herod's massive rebuilding of the whole temple grounds, this had become an annual donation, required of every devout Hebrew man. A half-shekel coin was roughly equivalent to two days' pay for the average laborer.

Obviously, foreigners needed to exchange their money for authentic half-shekel coins in order to make the donation, and temple authorities appear to have cornered the market for all Hebrew currency exchange in Jerusalem. (The Romans had no doubt granted them this monopoly as a way of placating the Sanhedrin.) The result was that they charged a usurious exchange rate for the coins. In fact, the Greek word for money changers is *kollubistes,* derived from the name of a coin called the *kollubos,* which was probably what they charged for the exchange rate. The name of the coin derives from a root that means "clipped," so the name *kollubistes* carries an unflattering connotation: "money clippers."

Under Old Testament law, Jews were not permitted to charge interest to their own countrymen, whether "on money or food or anything that is lent out at interest" (Deuteronomy 23:19). So a high exchange rate on half-shekel coins was bad enough under any circumstances. But the fact that this was being done with the offerings of worshippers, on the temple grounds, under the temple authorities' oversight and with their encouragement, was positively evil. If the animals had been sold at fair market prices and if money had been exchanged without interest fees, this might have been a legitimate service to sponsor in the temple's outer court. But in effect, temple authorities were housing and profiting from a den of thieves (cf. Mark 11:17)—exploiting the very people they ought to have been ministering to.

It's not hard to imagine what all this activity did to the ambience of the temple grounds, either. Bleating sheep, bawling oxen, haggling merchants, and indignant pilgrims all raised their voices together amid the miasma of manure from all those animals. It was a hive of noise, dissonance, filth, and pandemonium. It was certainly no atmosphere for worship. It was carnal chaos, the first sight to greet every pilgrim arriving on the temple mount.

Jesus' response actually reflects an amazing degree of patience and deliberation. (But not the kind of patience that invites friendly dialogue before issuing a reproof; and not the sort of deliberation that figures out a way to be positive before doing something negative.) He carefully, painstakingly braided some cords together to make a whip or a scourge (like a cat-o'-nine-tails). Small cords would be lying around in abundance—cheap strands used to tether the animals. There's something wonderfully ironic—but fitting—in the realization that the symbol of the Lord's displeasure was fashioned by Him from instruments of bondage brought to the site by the offenders themselves. He thus used the tools of the sinners' unjust trade to measure out justice against them.

Jesus' response is amazingly bold, especially when we consider that at this point He was largely unknown, acting out publicly against the most powerful confederacy in Judaism, intruding on their turf (or so *they* thought), and setting Himself against a large number of unscrupulous profitmongers who probably would not hesitate to use violence against Him.

It seems unlikely that *He* inflicted any physical injury on *them*. A whip of small cords was a common and harmless tool used for driving large animals. (Such a makeshift whip would probably not be capable of inflicting any actual pain on oxen or sheep; it was actually a very mild means of driving them compared to a typical oxgoad.) There's no suggestion that He flogged the merchants or money changers. Verse 15 says, "He drove them all out of the temple, with the sheep and the oxen." Most likely He used the whip to drive the animals, and He used the animals as a motive for the merchants to chase after them. Thus He cleared the area in short order.

Still, Jesus' decisiveness and power were impressive and must have been incredibly intimidating. His anger is evident; His zeal is grand and imposing; and the force of divine authority in His words is unmistakable. He accomplished exactly what He set out to do, and if any beast or scoundrel offered physical resistance, Scripture doesn't mention it.

Jesus was clearly acting as a prophet and reformer in the classic style of Israel's Old Testament men of God. Even more than that, by speaking of God as "My Father" (rather than using the common expression "our Father") He implicitly declared Himself *more* than a prophet and reformer—the very Son of God. He unapologetically invoked His Father's name and authority, and He issued curt commands with emphatic finality that discouraged any comeback. He was not making suggestions or requests, much less asking for friendly dialogue.

He even turned over the money changers' tables and poured their coins onto the ground. There must have been great tumult all around, but in the midst of it, Jesus appears unruffled—fierce in His anger, perhaps, but resolute, single-minded, stoic, and wholly composed. He is the very picture of self-control. (This is truly *righteous* indignation, not a violent temper that has gotten out of hand.)

The merchants and money changers, by contrast, were instantly sent scrambling. "He drove them *all* out of the temple" (v. 15, emphasis added). With the revisions Herod had made to the temple grounds, this means they fled the temple mount completely. And what bedlam went with them! Animal merchants frantically chased their sheep and oxen, whose herding instincts would have made the whole evacuation seem very much like a stampede— probably down the southern steps, sending waves of pilgrims coming *up* those steps, scurrying to get out of the way. The money changers would have instinctively scrambled to gather whatever coins were sent flying when the tables were overturned. But as animals and people fled the scene, the money changers must have realized how exposed they now were. With their tables overturned, there was nothing to shield them from Jesus' wrath or from the shame they incurred in the eyes of the pilgrims they were ripping off. So they took flight as well. Bird merchants dutifully grabbed up crates of doves and fled in obedience to those powerful words: "Take these things away! Do not make My Father's house a house of merchandise!" (v. 16).

Jesus' complete control of the situation was such that no actual riot broke out. There's no mention of any injury to either man or beast. The most "violent" action described here is the overturning of tables.

If there had been any actual brawling or lasting commotion, the Romans kept a military garrison stationed adjacent to the temple in Fort Antonia, complete with a watchtower that enabled lookouts to observe what was happening in the temple courts. They would have been there in minutes to deal with any serious trouble. But that wasn't necessary. Calm immediately settled in—actually a stark, refreshing contrast to the endless commotion of the animal bazaar and the barking of the bankers.

John, one of the earliest disciples Jesus called, was undoubtedly present on this day, and he therefore writes this account as an eyewitness. So he describes his own thoughts when He says, "Then His disciples remembered that it was written, 'Zeal for Your house has eaten me up'" (v. 17). That is a reference to Psalm 69:9: "Zeal for Your house has eaten me up, and the reproaches of those who reproach You have fallen on me." That verse in turn exactly parallels Psalm 119:139: "My zeal has consumed me, Because my enemies have forgotten Your words." Both passages apply perfectly to this incident. Both texts describe a zealous fury that is not the selfish pique of someone who has suffered a personal insult. Instead, it is a deep outrage that comes from the realization that *God* is being dishonored. Again we see clearly that Jesus was moved by *righteous* indignation—springing from the purest motives of a chaste and virtuous heart. This had nothing to do with the brand of out-of-control rage we often associate with human anger.

A CROSS-EXAMINATION—SCENE THREE

Jesus' assault on the money changers was a bold first-strike incursion into the very heart of the Sanhedrin's power base. He did this without warning and without any prior entreaty to them. It was a prophetic action in the style of Elijah. And the temple authorities understood this immediately. They been struggling for several years with the political problem of what to do about John the Baptist—who himself came in the spirit and power of Elijah (Luke 1:17). "They feared the people, for all counted John to have been a prophet indeed" (Mark 11:32). That clearly figured into why they did not instantly seize Jesus or charge Him with a crime. Instead, they demanded proof of His prophetic credentials. John writes: "So the Jews [the Jewish rulers and their deputies][2] answered and said to Him, 'What sign do You show to us, since You do these things?'" (John 2:18).

Those who came to interrogate Jesus were undoubtedly officers of the temple guard. This was a small but powerful security force operating under the authority of the Sanhedrin (cf. Acts 5:24; John 7:32, 45–46; 18:3, 12, 18, 22; 19:6). Their primary task was the maintenance of order in and around the temple, and they were an intimidating presence there. Any disturbance in the temple court would have drawn a group of them instantly. Since Jesus' words and actions in cleansing the temple contained an implicit claim of prophetic authority, they demanded a sign—a miracle—as proof of that authority. It was a formal demand with all their legal authority behind it. Their likely motive was to intimidate Him into submission. They probably never dreamed He would have any kind of answer to their demand for a sign.

As a matter of fact, He had already given them a major sign. The act of cleansing the temple itself was a dramatic initial fulfillment of that passage in Malachi 3:1–5—and therefore a clear demonstration of Jesus' messianic authority. Furthermore, over the course of His ministry, He would perform countless miraculous signs and wonders (Matthew 11:5; John 21:25) in every conceivable sort of public venue, often in the presence of ruling elders. They *kept* demanding more and bigger signs anyway (John 6:30; Matthew 12:38; 16:1; Mark 8:11), underscoring the hard-hearted stubbornness of their unbelief. Near the end of Jesus' ministry, John would say, "Although He had done so many signs before them, they did not believe in Him" (John 12:37).

Perhaps that is why here, during His initial confrontation with the Sanhedrin, Jesus gave them no miraculous sign. (Though it is clear from verse 23 that He did numerous miracles during the feast week following that Passover.) Instead, on this occasion, He made His very first subtle prophecy about the greatest sign of all: "Jesus answered and said to them, 'Destroy this temple, and in three days I will raise it up'. . . . [and] He was speaking of the temple of His body" (John 2:19–21).

In other instances where the Pharisees demanded cosmic signs and wonders, Jesus likewise indicated that His own resurrection from the dead would be the ultimate sign to them. "An evil and adulterous generation seeks after a sign, and no sign will be given to it except the sign of the prophet Jonah. For as Jonah was three days and three nights in the belly of the great fish, so will the Son of Man be three days and three nights in the heart of the earth" (Matthew 12:39–40). That statement, just like His words here about destroying the temple, was purposely cryptic. No one understood what He was saying at the time, but the resurrection made the meaning of both prophecies clear.

The temple authorities were visibly stunned by Jesus' reply. To them, His statement seemed like the words of a madman. "It has taken forty-six years to build this temple, and will You raise it up in three days?"

They missed the subtlety of Jesus' true meaning, of course, and assumed that He was speaking about the temple edifice atop mount Moriah. They were literally standing in the shadow of that temple, which was the most impressive building in all of Israel. Built by Herod, it was a monumental, pristine, gleaming-white, gold-trimmed structure made of imported marble rather than the native off-white limestone—so that it not only stood higher than any other edifice in Jerusalem; it also stood out.

Herod the Great had built the temple as part of an extensive construction campaign conceived by him as the means by which he would perpetuate his name and reputation. He had already built spectacular palaces in Tiberias, Caesarea, and Masada. He also built basilicas, villas, aqueducts, amphitheaters, and whole cities all over the western Mediterranean region—including a number of impressive Roman-style temples honoring pagan gods. The trademarks of his style were innovative architecture and very large scale. Indeed, Herod *would* have been remembered mainly as one of history's greatest builders—if he had not brought such infamy on himself by slaughtering all the male children in Bethlehem after Jesus was born (Matthew 2:16)—an act which, by all accounts, was consistent with his ruthless style of leadership. (Of course, another reason Herod's name is synonymous with villainy is that his son and successor, Herod Antipas, was complicit in the death of Christ. The Herods all made themselves enemies of the gospel from the very beginning—and that fact is what we remember them best for, rather than Herod's monuments to his ego.) Still, the architectural achievements of Herod the Great were unsurpassed by anyone else before the modern era and impressive by any measure.

Jerusalem's temple was Herod's grandest and most majestic project. The previous temple, built by Zerubbabel some five hundred years before Christ, was small and dilapidated. Compared to the many Roman temples that dotted that part of the world, Zerubbabel's temple seemed embarrassingly modest. So even though the Jews hated Herod, they accepted his proposal to build a new temple, designed to be grander in size and opulence than any other temple in the ancient world. Herod agreed to quarry all the stone for the new temple prior to the demolition of Zerubbabel's structure, and a plan was put in place so that sacrifices could continue uninterrupted even during the construction of the new edifice. All the hands-on construction work on the temple building was done by priests as well.

The most ambitious aspect of the whole temple project was Herod's plan to expand the usable area atop the temple mount. His engineers dug trenches all around the hill and then built retaining walls surrounding a large rectangular area. The top was leveled and the large southern slope was built up with the resulting landfill to create a rectangular plateau. (The Western Wall in Jerusalem today is part of the base for that platform. Those famous, enormous, square-cut stones are part of the original retaining wall built by Herod's workmen.) Thus the top of the temple mount was made to accommodate a temple and courtyard more than twice the size of Zerubbabel's temple. The main temple building was considerably taller. And the whole complex was breathtakingly opulent. The eastern side of the temple building itself was decorated with gold ornaments. Massive gold plates covered the doors, and beaten gold laminate overlaid most of the major design elements on the building. This reflected the sun for most of the day and made the temple the dominant structure in the city, visible from every major approach to Jerusalem. As John 2:20 says, the project had already been underway for forty-six years when Jesus had this first confrontation with the Pharisees—and the work on the temple grounds would not be completely finished for at least three more decades.

Naturally, then, the temple authorities were incredulous when they thought Jesus was suggesting He could accomplish over a weekend what it had taken numerous skilled workmen forty-six years—and counting—to accomplish. Of course, He could have done that easily. He was, after all, the One who spoke the whole universe into existence in the first place (John 1:3, 10). But as the disciples realized years later, after the resurrection, He was actually speaking of something even more profound than a mere brick-and-mortar construction project. He was talking about His bodily resurrection. Nevertheless, this probably did not even strike the temple guard as a serious reply.

Amazingly, the temple authorities did not take Jesus into custody. Clearly, Jesus' point about the defilement of the temple hit its target squarely. The people in the temple courtyard certainly knew they were victims of the swindling merchants' greed. Their sympathies would certainly have been with Jesus. Whatever commotion His actions caused seems to have died down quickly, and by the time the security force arrived, they were alone against Jesus with a backdrop of worshippers who certainly saw Jesus' point, whether the temple authorities themselves would acknowledge it or not. So the temple rulers evidently did not press the issue any further in this instance. The confrontation between Jesus and the temple guard appears to have ended as abruptly as John's account of it does and without further incident, because in verse 23, John describes Jesus "in Jerusalem at the Passover, during the feast," doing signs and wonders.

This whole episode was obviously a great embarrassment to the Sanhedrin. Jesus exposed the chicanery of their on-site business dealings. He declared them guilty of defiling the temple. He did this openly in broad daylight while the Sanhedrin had home-field advantage. He did not cower and back away when a team of their thugs arrived to challenge Him. And in the end, they were the ones forced to back down, because Jesus' point was too clear and too obvious to refute. If they arrested Him, even on a misdemeanor charge of disturbing the peace, that would necessitate a trial. Witnesses would be deposed. Testimony would be given. And they were already clearly too exposed to want to drag this incident out any further. So it appears they had to let Him walk away.

But they never forgot or forgave this incident. Three years later, on the night of His arrest, at His initial trial before the Sanhedrin, when no one could bring any legitimate charge against Him, the chief priests finally suborned perjury against Him. And the testimony given by the false witnesses harked back to this very first public skirmish between Jesus and the hypocrites. Matthew 26:60–61 describes what happened: "At last two false witnesses came forward and said,

'This fellow said, "I am able to destroy the temple of God and to build it in three days."' Of course they were twisting both His words and His true meaning. Nevertheless, He would finally give them their sign and the ultimate proof of His authority just a few days later, by rising from the grave.

In Jesus' thinking this first conflict with the Sanhedrin likewise loomed large. As we shall see in the closing chapter of our study, He cleansed the temple once more at the end of His ministry, early in that final week before the Crucifixion. These two public assaults, exhibiting His divine authority and righteous indignation, are like bookends on the public ministry of Christ. They give context and meaning to all His other encounters in between with the religious elite of Israel.

For those who would prefer a meek, perpetually friendly, sentimental messiah reaching out to other religious leaders and engaging in scholarly dialogue with them instead of challenging them, this may seem to establish a troubling precedent at the very start of His dealings with the Jewish leaders. But by His own avowal, the Prince of Peace is no peacemonger when it comes to hypocrisy and false teaching. "Do not think that I came to bring peace on earth. I did not come to bring peace but a sword" (Matthew 10:34). There was certainly no question about that now in the minds of the Sanhedrin, and most of them utterly hated Him from the start because of the way He humiliated them.

To add irony upon irony, Jesus' first one-on-one encounter with a member of the Sanhedrin would be a secret meeting with a completely different tone and tenor from this one. It will start with an overture of peace—but not from Jesus. The next encounter would be initiated by one of the leading Pharisees, Nicodemus.

There are several things which may help to make the life fair in the eyes of men, but nothing will make it amiable in the eyes of God, unless the heart be changed and renewed. Indeed, all the medicines that can be applied, without the sanctifying work of the Spirit, though they may cover, they can never cure the corruptions and diseases of the soul. . . . Such civil persons go to hell without much disturbance, being asleep in sin, yet not snoring to the disquieting of others; they are so far from being awaked that they are many times praised and commended. Example, custom, and education, may also help a man to make a fair show in the flesh, but not to walk after the Spirit. They may prune and lop sin, but never stub it up by the roots. All that these can do, is to make a man like a grave, green and flourishing on the surface and outside, when within there is nothing but noisomeness and corruption.

—GEORGE SWINNOCK[3]

3

A Midnight Interview

❧

"That which is born of the flesh is flesh, and that which is born of the Spirit is spirit. Do not marvel that I said to you, 'You must be born again.'"

John 3:6–7

From that first pre-Passover run-in with Israel's religious leaders through the end of His earthly ministry, Jesus taught and healed chiefly among the common people, who "heard Him gladly" (Mark 12:37). Scribes, Pharisees, and Sadducees often hung around the edges, watching through critical eyes, occasionally challenging Jesus' teaching or expressing outrage at His refusal to observe all their ceremonial rules. But from this point on, practically all Jesus' recorded encounters with the Pharisees involved conflicts.

A FEW FRIENDLY PHARISEES

A survey of all the Gospels produces very few exceptions to that pattern. But they are worth mentioning.

For example, all three Synoptic Gospels record the raising of Jairus's daughter from the dead (Matthew 9:18–26; Mark 5:22–43; and Luke 8:41–56). Jairus was a ruler in the Capernaum synagogue, doubtless a disciple of Pharisees—possibly even a Pharisee himself. More likely, however, he was a layman who served as an elder in that small community. In any case, he is a very rare example of a ruling Jewish leader whom Jesus blessed rather than condemning. Jairus came to Jesus in an hour of desperation, "for he had an only daughter about twelve years of age, and she was dying" (Luke 8:42).

The little girl actually *did* die while Jairus was bringing his request to Jesus (v. 49), and Jesus then raised her from the dead. The only note of negativity in that whole episode comes from Jairus's friends and fellow mourners, in response to Jesus' reassurance that the girl would be made well: "And they ridiculed Him, knowing that she was dead" (v. 53). Jairus, of course, was "astonished" when Jesus raised his daughter from the dead (v. 53)—and he was doubtless moved with the profoundest gratitude. What became of him after that is not recorded, but Jesus' words to him just prior to raising the girl from the dead—"Do not be afraid; only believe" (Mark 5:36)—are nothing if not tender, positive, and reassuring. So it seems fair to infer that Jairus did indeed believe in Christ—one of a small handful of Jewish religious leaders who gave evidence of faith in Jesus while His ministry among the common people was flourishing.

The rich young ruler was likewise a religious official of some sort (see Matthew 19:16–26; Mark 10:17–27; and Luke 18:18–27). He might well have been a Pharisee. After all, one of the Pharisees' characteristic traits was their love of money (Luke 16:14), and that was certainly this young man's besetting sin. But he approached Jesus with a question that certainly *sounded* sincere. Even his greeting rang with authentic respect: "Good Teacher, what shall I do to inherit eternal life?" (Luke 18:18).

Jesus' reply—though not what the young man had hoped to hear—was without any tone of reproach or scolding. In fact, Mark 10:21 expressly tells us that Jesus "loved him," reminding us that Jesus' frequent anger with the Jewish religious leaders, His hatred for their hypocrisy, and His opposition to their errors were by no means inconsistent with authentic love for *them*. Those who think it is inherently unloving to confront, admonish, or correct need to re-examine Jesus' approach: "As many as I love, I rebuke and chasten. Therefore be zealous and repent" (Revelation 3:19).

On at least three occasions (all recorded by Luke) Jesus had dinner in the homes of Pharisees (Luke 7:36–50; 11:37–54; 14:1–14). If those events began cordially, they nevertheless all ended with Jesus denouncing the Pharisees' doctrine and practice, so they don't really constitute major deviations from the pattern of Jesus' contentious interactions with Israel's religious leaders.

In fact, the Luke 11 incident ended with Jesus pronouncing a series of woes against the Pharisees and religious lawyers. Luke's closing words in that narrative pretty well describe the flavor of *most* of Jesus' face-to-face conversations with Israel's religious leaders: "As He said these things to them, the scribes and the Pharisees began to assail Him vehemently, and to cross-examine Him about many things, lying in wait for Him, and seeking to catch Him in something He might say, that they might accuse Him" (Luke 11:53–54).

NIC AT NIGHT

The account of Nicodemus in John 3 is certainly the most unusual of all Jesus' encounters with Pharisees—and the only significant example of an extended friendly dialogue between Jesus and a Pharisee. In fact, it stands out as the longest personal conversation Jesus had with any religious leader in all the gospel accounts. Notice, however: what makes this meeting so unusual is Nicodemus's response to Jesus. Jesus was no less blunt with Nicodemus than He ever was with any Pharisee. But Nicodemus evidently came to Jesus truly wishing to learn, rather than with the typical pharisaical agenda of self-aggrandizement at Jesus' expense. And the result was a markedly different sort of exchange.

Nicodemus seems to have approached Jesus shortly after that first temple cleansing—perhaps later that same week, during the Feast of Unleavened Bread. It is clear from the gospel narrative that Nicodemus's interest in Christ was genuine, insofar as it went. Still, it fell short of authentic saving faith—and Jesus made that clear in his first words to Nicodemus.

It had been a busy week of public ministry for Jesus. It is the first time on record that He performed numerous miracles, and He did them publicly. Interestingly, John's account of that week doesn't focus on the miracles at all. In fact, John mentions them only once in passing, without even saying what kind of miracles they were: "Many believed in His name when they saw the signs which He did" (2:23). Presumably the signs John speaks of were healings and demonic deliverances, because such miracles became a staple of Jesus' public ministry (Mark 1:34). But John does not pause to describe them here. His main point in mentioning these initial miracles was to record that Jesus gained both fame and followers that week, *and yet Jesus remained somewhat reserved—even aloof—toward His many would-be disciples.*

John writes: "Now when He was in Jerusalem at the Passover, during the feast, many believed in His name when they saw the signs which He did. But Jesus did not commit Himself to them, because He knew all men, and had no need that anyone should testify of man, for He knew what was in man" (John 2:23–25).

That's the close of John 2, and it leads immediately into the account of Nicodemus. As a transition between the two passages, it is significant for a couple of reasons. First, it establishes a context that explains why Jesus dealt with Nicodemus the way he did. Second, it is one of many powerful affirmations of Jesus' deity that John weaves into his gospel. Here John is highlighting the proof of Jesus' divine omniscience. Jesus knew the hearts of men, which only God can know (1 Samuel 16:7; 1 Kings 8:39; Revelation 2:23).

Incidentally, although John gave no detailed account of the miracles he mentioned in John 2:23, that first torrent of public miracles was dramatic further proof of Jesus' deity. This sudden outpouring of "signs" must have utterly amazed and thrilled the apostle. He and Andrew had been disciples of John the Baptist in the wilderness east of the Jordan River when Jesus called them (John 1:35–39). John the Baptist had never done any miracles (John 10:41); yet people came to hear him in large numbers from all over Judea and the surrounding areas (Matthew 3:5). The Baptist declared that he was not the Messiah but merely the forerunner (John 1:23; cf. Isaiah 40:3–5). He was the herald sent to announce Jesus as the Lamb of God who would take away the sin of the world (John 1:29). As soon as John and Andrew understood that, they left John's circle of disciples and followed Jesus. The events described in John 2–3 probably occurred within days or (at most) weeks afterward.

So when Jesus began to do miracles, the disciples must have been ecstatic. Here was undeniable proof that Jesus was the true Messiah! They believed that when Messiah came, He would quickly take authority over all earthly kingdoms and establish His millennial rule worldwide, with Israel as the seat of that kingdom. As a matter of fact, they retained that expectation even after the resurrection, virtually until the ascension of Christ (Acts 1:6).

Such a hope was not far-fetched. Christ will indeed establish His kingdom on earth one day. Old Testament prophecies are full of detailed promises about the millennial kingdom that are not yet fulfilled. The establishment of our Lord's throne in Israel only awaits His second coming.

But the disciples expected all things to be fulfilled in one advent. From the start of Jesus' public ministry, they naturally regarded Jesus' immediate popularity among the common people as a tremendous sign of progress in that direction. They no doubt assumed that Jesus would soon *also* gain the support of Israel's religious leaders, and after that, the institution of His kingdom could not be far behind.

From the disciples' perspective, then, Jesus' restraint toward the appreciative crowds—not to mention his guarded (some might say *antagonistic*) interaction with a religious bigwig like Nicodemus— must have been mystifying. In retrospect, John could certainly see why Jesus remained standoffish, and he even underlined it as clear evidence of Jesus' omniscience.

Here is a practical lesson from this account: a positive response to Jesus should never be taken as proof of authentic trust in Him. There is a shallow, fickle brand of "belief" that is not saving faith at all. From the first public miracle He performed until this very day, there have always been people who "accept Christ" without truly loving Him, without submitting to His authority, and without abandoning their self-confidence and trust in their own good works. That is precisely what John describes at the end of John 2, and that becomes his transition into the Nicodemus narrative. Nicodemus was (at this point) one of those almost-believers to whom Jesus did not automatically commit himself.

John makes a clever play on words in the closing three verses of chapter 2. The expression "many *believed* in His name" in verse 23 and the expression "Jesus did not *commit Himself* unto them" in verse 24 both use the same Greek verb. John is saying that many people responded to Jesus with a kind of enthusiasm that fell short of wholehearted faith, so He didn't completely trust them, either. In other words, they *said* they believed Him, but He didn't believe them. He had no faith in their faith.

John, of course, didn't write his gospel with chapter divisions. The verse numbers and the break in the flow of the narrative after John 2:22–25 would not be there at all if we were reading from John's original manuscript. He moves naturally from the fact that Jesus knew the hearts of men to the account of Nicodemus, which actually illustrates precisely what John was saying. In fact, the story of Nicodemus is a vivid example of how *perfectly* Jesus knows the human heart. Nicodemus, meanwhile, demonstrates how easy it is to respond positively to Jesus and yet fall short of authentic faith.

Nicodemus comes on the scene quietly, late at night. Fear of what his fellow council-members might think (or do to him) seems to be his motive for coming under cover of darkness. That becomes completely clear in John 19:38–39, where Nicodemus appears in tandem with Joseph of Arimathea, preparing the body of Jesus for burial after the crucifixion. The apostle John says that "Joseph of Arimathea [was] a disciple of Jesus, but secretly, for fear of the Jews" (v. 38). The next verse begins: "And Nicodemus . . ." The two of them were apparently friends and spiritual companions—the only two members of the Sanhedrin who were sympathetic to Christ during His earthly ministry—"but secretly, for fear."

RARE AFFIRMATION FROM A PHARISEE

When Nicodemus first met Jesus in John 3, however, the Pharisee was not yet truly a believer. He was clearly intrigued by Christ. He showed him the utmost respect. In fact, Nicodemus's greeting was an unqualified acknowledgment of Christ's prophetic authority— an affirmation unheard of by any other Council member either before or after this. He said, "Rabbi, we know that you are a teacher come from God, for no one can do these signs that you do unless God is with him" (v. 2).

The title "Rabbi" was an expression of honor. Coming from a ruling Pharisee like this, it was a signal that Nicodemus regarded Jesus as an equal. Of course Nicodemus intended that as a great compliment.

AN IMPOSSIBLE DEMAND FROM JESUS

Jesus' reply was abrupt and to the point, a demonstration of the prophetic authority Nicodemus had just acknowledged: "Truly, truly, I say to you, unless one is born again he cannot see the kingdom of God" (v. 3 NASB). Ignoring the verbal honor Nicodemus had paid to Him, changing the subject away from His own ability to do miracles, Jesus made a statement that was plainly intended as a remark about Nicodemus's spiritual *inability* and blindness.

It was a breathtaking reply, especially given Nicodemus's stature as a religious leader. Nicodemus was no doubt accustomed to being shown great honor and deference. *Jesus' first recorded words to him instead conveyed the clear and deliberate implication that this leading Pharisee was still so far from the kingdom of heaven that he was unable to see it at all.* If Nicodemus had been motivated solely by pride, or merely looking for affirmation, he would certainly have been offended by Jesus' reply.

But Nicodemus was clearly being drawn to Christ by the Holy Spirit, because his answer to Jesus was surprisingly unruffled. There's no hint of resentment, no insults directed at Jesus, and no iciness. He continues to show Jesus the respect due a dignified rabbi by asking a series of questions designed to draw the meaning out of Jesus' words—words that must have hit him like a hard slap in the face.

Nicodemus had devoted his life to a rigid observance of the Pharisees' traditions, which he no doubt firmly believed were fully in accord with the law of God. He might have expected commendation from Jesus for his personal piety. He might have hoped he could help reconcile Jesus and the Sanhedrin after the Temple-cleansing incident. That was, after all, Jesus' only public conflict with Israel's religious leaders so far. Nicodemus may well have heard about John the Baptist's advocacy of Jesus. He had obviously heard about (possibly even witnessed) the miracles. In fact, the language Nicodemus used (*"we* know that You are a teacher come from God") suggested that he had discussed Jesus' prophetic credentials with others who agreed that He must be from God. Clearly, Nicodemus approached Jesus with high hopes and eager expectations.

How Jesus' reply must have stunned him! Nicodemus had honored Christ by calling Him Rabbi; Jesus suggested in return that Nicodemus was not even a spiritual beginner yet. He had no part in the kingdom whatsoever. Jesus wasn't being unkind or merely insulting; He was being truthful with a man who desperately needed to hear the truth. Nicodemus's soul was at stake.

"Born again?" Nicodemus did not instantly seem to grasp that Jesus was talking about *regeneration*—the new birth, the spiritual awakening of a dead soul. But it was clear enough that Jesus was calling him to make a whole new start. That was a lot to ask of someone like Nicodemus, who (like any good Pharisee) believed he was accumulating merit with God by a lifetime of careful attention to the law's tiniest ceremonial details. What did Jesus want him to do? Cast all that aside like so much garbage?

That, of course, is precisely how the apostle Paul would later describe his own conversion from Pharisaism in Philippians 3:7–9: "What things were gain to me, these I have counted loss for Christ. Yet indeed I also count all things loss for the excellence of the knowledge of Christ Jesus my Lord, for whom I have suffered the loss of all things, and count them as rubbish, that I may gain Christ and be found in Him, not having my own righteousness, which is from the law, but that which is through faith in Christ, the righteousness which is from God by faith."

Jesus chose the perfect language to convey all that to Nicodemus: "You must be born again" (John 3:7). With that simple expression, Jesus demolished Nicodemus's entire worldview and value system. His Jewish birth and upbringing; his attainments as a leading Pharisee; the care with which he kept himself from ceremonial defilement; the respect he had earned in the eyes of his countrymen; all the merit he thought he had stored up for himself—Jesus reduced it all at once to utter worthlessness. Whatever else Jesus meant, this much was plain: Jesus was demanding that Nicodemus forsake everything he stood for, walk away from everything he had ever done as a Pharisee, abandon hope in everything he ever trusted, and start all over from the beginning.

Nicodemus's reply has often been misunderstood: "How can a man be born when he is old? Can he enter a second time into his mother's womb and be born?" (v. 4). Don't imagine that Nicodemus was so naive as to think Jesus was telling him he literally needed to be physically reborn. Nicodemus must have been a highly skilled teacher himself, or he would not have attained his position. He was clearly a perceptive man—perhaps the most discerning of all the Sanhedrin. So we must give him credit for a modicum of intelligence. His question to Jesus should no more be interpreted as a literal reference to physical birth than Jesus' original remark to him. How well Nicodemus understood Jesus' point isn't spelled out for us in detail, but it is clear that he got the gist of the idea that he needed a whole new start.

Thus his rejoinder to Jesus merely picked up on Jesus' imagery and employed it to show Jesus that he understood the impossibility of what Jesus had prescribed for him. He was a mature man—patriarchal enough in both age and wisdom to serve as one of Israel's chief elders. Membership in the Sanhedrin was an honor not often bestowed on young men. So when Nicodemus asked, "How can a man be born when he is *old*?" he was pointing out that men his age don't simply decide to start over at the beginning. And when he asked, "Can he enter a second time into his mother's womb and be born?" it's only reasonable to assume he was remarking about the utter impossibility of causing *himself* to be "reborn" in any sense. He certainly understood far more than he is usually given credit for.

A CRYPTIC REFERENCE FROM THE OLD TESTAMENT

To anyone who lacked Nicodemus's familiarity with the Old Testament, Jesus' next reply might have only compounded the confusion. Jesus answered, "Most assuredly, I say to you, unless one is born of water and the Spirit, he cannot enter the kingdom of God. That which is born of the flesh is flesh, and that which is born of the Spirit is spirit. Do not marvel that I said to you, 'You must be born again'" (John 3:5–7).

In fact, many Bible students who examine this passage are confused by it. Some have suggested that when Jesus spoke of "water," he was speaking of baptism—and some of them then interpret this to be a statement about the necessity of water baptism as a prerequisite for regeneration. But John's baptism could not have been a means of regeneration, because it signified an already-repentant heart, which is a *fruit* of regeneration. Christian baptism (likewise a symbol, not a means, of regeneration) had not even been instituted yet. So the idea of baptism is utterly foreign to this passage.

Some commentators suggest that "water" is a reference to the amniotic fluid that signals the onset of physical birth, and they therefore believe Jesus was describing two distinct births in verse 5—physical birth ("water"), and spiritual birth ("the Spirit"). A closer look, however, shows that verse 5 simply restates verse 3 in different words. Notice the parallelism: "Unless one is *born again,* he cannot see the kingdom of God" (v. 3); and "Unless one is *born of water and the Spirit,* he cannot enter the kingdom of God" (v. 5). To be "born again" is the same thing as being "born of water and the Spirit." The parallelism is deliberate, and the phrase "born of water and the Spirit" is simply Jesus' explanation of the *second* birth. In order to understand the expression "water and the Spirit," we have to ask how Nicodemus would have understood it.

There are two famous passages in the Old Testament where the words *water* and *Spirit* are brought together in a way that makes sense of this passage. One is Isaiah 44:3, which uses a poetic parallelism to equate the two terms, by making water a symbol of the Holy Spirit: "I will pour water on him who is thirsty, and floods on the dry ground; I will pour My Spirit on your descendants." The Holy Spirit is frequently depicted in the Old Testament being poured out like water (cf. Proverbs 1:23; Joel 2:28–29; Zechariah 12:10). So to a Jewish teacher steeped in the language of the Old Testament, the idea of being "born of water and the Spirit" would evoke the idea of an outpouring of God's Spirit—which is precisely what Jesus was saying.

But the key Old Testament text on this—the one I'm convinced Jesus was alluding to, and the one that almost certainly came to Nicodemus's mind—was an important and familiar passage: Ezekiel 36:25–27. There the Lord is affirming the promise of the new covenant to Israel, and He says, "I will sprinkle clean water on you, and you shall be clean; I will cleanse you from all your filthiness and from all your idols. I will give you a new heart and put a new spirit within you; I will take the heart of stone out of your flesh and give you a heart of flesh. I will put My Spirit within you and cause you to walk in My statutes, and you will keep My judgments and do them."

That passage speaks of regeneration, the spiritual awakening of a dead soul. And that is the very truth Jesus was pressing upon Nicodemus. He was confronting this leading Pharisee with the truth that he needed a whole new heart—new *life;* not just a cosmetic makeover or another ritual added to an already-oppressive system of pharisaical spiritual disciplines, but a wholesale spiritual renewal so vast and dramatic that it can only be described as a second birth. With Ezekiel 36 as context, Jesus' juxtaposition of *water* and *Spirit* makes perfect sense. He was intentionally pointing Nicodemus to the familiar truth of that key promise about the new covenant.

To borrow a precisely parallel New Testament expression, "water" and "Spirit" are best understood as a reference to "the washing of regeneration and renewing of the Holy Spirit" (Titus 3:5). In all likelihood, Nicodemus, thoroughly familiar with Ezekiel's prophecy, now understood exactly what Jesus was telling him.

ANOTHER DIFFICULT SAYING FROM JESUS

Jesus continued by further emphasizing that spiritual rebirth is wholly a work of God, not the result of human effort: "That which is born of the flesh is flesh, and that which is born of the Spirit is spirit" (v. 6). Jesus was merely stating a truth which, on reflection, ought to be self-evident. Flesh begets flesh. Living beings all reproduce "each according to its kind" (Genesis 1:24). By the very nature of things, therefore, *spiritual life* cannot be the fruit of human achievement, a fact that contradicts every form of works-religion, including the fundamental belief system of the Pharisees.

On top of that, Jesus added, because spiritual rebirth is a work of the Spirit, it is beyond the control of either human works or human willpower: "The wind blows where it wishes, and you hear the sound of it, but cannot tell where it comes from and where it goes. So is everyone who is born of the Spirit" (v. 8). The *effects* of the wind may be observed, but its boundaries cannot be discerned by human senses, and the wind itself can neither be harnessed nor directed by human efforts or ingenuity. The Holy Spirit's ministry operates in a similar fashion. He is sovereign and moves where He wishes, not at the whim of any human agenda. His workings are not contained in—or automatically dispensed through—any religious rituals or ceremonial protocols. In fact, the Spirit isn't moved by what *we* do at all, but by His own sovereign will.

To a typical Pharisee, what Jesus was saying to Nicodemus would likely have come across as highly offensive. Jesus was attacking the very core of Nicodemus's belief system, plainly implying that Nicodemus was lost, spiritually lifeless, and ultimately no better off in his rigid Pharisaism than an utterly immoral Gentile without God. (Indeed, as we shall observe throughout this study, Jesus said that very thing to the Pharisees quite often.)

This was a direct answer to Nicodemus's questions ("How can a man be born when he is old? Can he enter a second time into his mother's womb and be born?"). Jesus was telling Nicodemus, in language Nicodemus was sure to grasp, that not only was He not speaking of any superficial or fleshly self-reformation, but He was in fact calling for something Nicodemus was powerless to do *for himself.* This punctured the heart of Nicodemus's religious convictions. To a Pharisee like him, the worst imaginable news would be that there was nothing he could possibly do to help himself spiritually.

Jesus had basically equated this distinguished Pharisee with the most debased and dissipated kind of sinner. He had described Nicodemus's case as utterly hopeless. Talk about harsh!

But that is, after all, the very starting point of the gospel message. Sinners are "dead in trespasses and sins . . . by nature children of wrath . . . having no hope and without God" (Ephesians 2:1, 3, 12). This is one of the universal effects of Adam's sin on his offspring

(Romans 5:12). We are born with sinful tendencies and fallen hearts, and we all sin. "All have sinned and fall short of the glory of God" (Romans 3:23). "There is none righteous, no, not one" (v. 10). "All we like sheep have gone astray" (Isaiah 53:6).

Furthermore, Scripture says we are hopeless to redeem ourselves, atone for our own sin, reform our hearts and minds, or earn any kind of merit in the eyes of God. Romans 8:7–8 says, "The carnal mind is enmity against God; for it is not subject to the law of God, nor indeed can be. So then, those who are in the flesh cannot please God." That describes the fallen condition of all humanity, not merely a special, notorious class of particularly sinful people. Even the very best of people, apart from Christ and His holy Spirit, are helplessly in bondage to sin. Even those who in the eyes of the world manage to seem respectable, altruistic, or "good" by comparison are not *really* good at all by the divine standard. (As Jesus told the rich young ruler in Matthew 19:17, "No one is good but One, that is, God.") Therefore sinners in their fallen state are under God's condemnation, with no hope of redeeming themselves.

Let's face it: the idea that the entire human race is fallen and condemned is simply too harsh for most people's tastes. They would rather believe that most people are fundamentally good. Virtually every popular arbiter of our culture's highest, noblest values—from Oprah Winfrey to the Hallmark Channel—tells us so constantly. All we need to do, they say, is cultivate our underlying goodness, and we can fix everything wrong with human society. That's not terribly different from what the Pharisees believed about themselves.

But Scripture says otherwise. We are hopelessly corrupted by sin. All who do not have Christ as Lord and Savior are in bondage to evil, condemned by a just God, and bound for hell. Jesus not only strongly implied those very things in his opening words to Nicodemus; before He had finished fully explaining the gospel that evening, He made

His meaning explicit: "He who does not believe is condemned already" (John 3:18).

THE GOSPEL DISTILLED FOR NICODEMUS

Nicodemus's response was utter astonishment: "How can these things be?" (v. 9). It was not that he didn't understand what Jesus was saying. I think he got the message plainly enough. But it overthrew his deepest convictions and left him virtually speechless. That question ("How can these things be?") is the last thing we hear from Nicodemus in the narrative of John 3. He had nothing further to say.

No wonder. Jesus was about to deliver His most direct, personal, scolding barb at Nicodemus yet: "Are you the teacher of Israel, and do not know these things?" (v. 10). Everything Jesus had said to Nicodemus so far had a clear basis in the Old Testament. Nicodemus was one of the top biblical scholars in the nation. *How could he not know these things?* It sounds like a put-down. The average Pharisee would have taken it that way and lashed back at Jesus with insults, accusations, or otherwise contemptuous retorts.

Not Nicodemus. He was completely silenced by the rebuke. In fact, he more or less fades into the background of John's narrative. He is not mentioned again until chapter 7, where he appears in a meeting of the Sanhedrin, says a word in defense of Jesus, and is promptly shouted down (John 7:44–53).

The focus of John 3 then turns exclusively to Jesus, who delivers one of his most important discourses ever—an extended lesson on gospel truth. It is one of the most familiar and often-quoted passages in all the New Testament. Its centerpiece, of course, is perhaps the most beloved verse in the Bible, a beautiful single-verse summary of the gospel message: "For God so loved the world that He gave His only begotten Son, that whoever believes in Him should not perish but have everlasting life" (John 3:16).

But the surrounding context of John 3:16 stands in rather stark contrast to the familiar sweetness of that verse. Jesus' discourse taken as a whole is an extended indictment of the spirit of Pharisaism. As Nicodemus listened in total silence, Jesus proceeded to draw a clear contrast between believers and unbelievers, the humble and the hypocrites, the truly reborn and the merely religious. And it was all too clear in His judgment that the Pharisees—Nicodemus included—were on the wrong side of that divide. Nicodemus had nothing to do but listen.

John 3:11–21 is rich enough that if space permitted we could devote at least a full chapter or two to unpacking it—and that still wouldn't begin to plumb its depths. In keeping with the theme of this book, however, we'll just take note of two or three obvious ways Jesus' discourse would have stepped hard on Nicodemus's toes.

First, notice that Jesus directly implicated Nicodemus as an unbeliever: "Most assuredly, I say to you, We speak what We know and testify what We have seen, and *you do not receive Our witness*. If I have told you earthly things and *you do not believe,* how will you believe if I tell you heavenly things?" (vv. 11–12, emphasis added). To postmodernized ears, that sounds extraordinarily harsh. Contemporary evangelicals typically bristle at the thought of challenging anyone's profession of faith. Religious television networks are overrun with teachers who profess to be Christians but whose doctrine and lifestyle show no real fruit of salvation. People like that have flourished and even begun to dominate the non-Christian public's perception of what Christianity is, mainly because more sound and solid evangelical leaders are reluctant to call them by name and say plainly that they are charlatans and false teachers. To oppose another minister publicly just doesn't seem "nice." The thought of being *perceived* as harsh or negative is more odious to some Christians than actually *being* undiscerning. So false teachers are given free reign to promote their false teachings and flaunt their extravagant lifestyles.

Nicodemus's ignorance about his need for regeneration was proof of his unbelief. He had studied the Old Testament in an academic way, and from the standpoint of his fellow Pharisees, he was one of the top experts on the subject. But he had never bothered to apply its teaching to his own heart, and therefore Jesus was perfectly blunt with him: "You do not believe."

Second, don't miss the point of the Old Testament allusion Jesus makes in verses 14–15: "As Moses lifted up the serpent in the wilderness, even so must the Son of Man be lifted up, that whoever believes in Him should not perish but have eternal life." The reference is to an incident that occurred during Israel's wandering in the wilderness during the Exodus. Numbers 21 records that the people grew discouraged; they began to despise the manna God provided daily for their sustenance, and in frustration they rebelled against both God and Moses. "And the people spoke against God and against Moses: 'Why have you brought us up out of Egypt to die in the wilderness? For there is no food and no water, and our soul loathes this worthless bread'" (Numbers 21:5).

God unleashed a plague of poisonous snakes into the camp, "and they bit the people; and many of the people of Israel died" (v. 6). In response, the people repented and begged Moses to intercede with the Lord on their behalf. The Lord commanded Moses to make a bronze serpent, set it on a pole in the midst of the camp, and tell the people "that everyone who is bitten, when he looks at it, shall live" (v. 8). The whole story was an illustration of justification by faith, and that was the point Jesus was making here.

But consider the difficulty of that analogy from Nicodemus's perspective. As a ruler of Israel, he had always thought of himself in the role of Moses. Jesus Himself said, "The scribes and the Pharisees sit in Moses' seat" (Matthew 23:2). But the analogy suggested that Nicodemus needed to see himself in the place of the sinning Israelites. Even the Old Testament imagery Jesus used was a contradiction of the Pharisees' spiritual self-image. To a casual observer (especially to anyone trained in the rules of postmodern discourse and the canons of political correctness), it might seem as if Jesus was deliberately trying to provoke Nicodemus, smacking him hard again and again, demeaning his pharisaical pride in every conceivable way. In reality, Jesus was not being mean-spirited, but precisely the opposite. Nicodemus needed to recognize his spiritual poverty and see his need for a Savior. And Jesus cared more for the truth than He cared about how Nicodemus felt about it. Sometimes the truth isn't "nice"—but it's always focused and unyielding.

That was certainly the case here. Before Nicodemus could receive any help from Jesus, he needed to see how desperate his situation was. "Those who are well have no need of a physician, but those who are sick" (Matthew 9:12). And when a patient has a life-threatening illness that urgently needs treatment, the physician needs to give him the bad news candidly. That was the case with Nicodemus.

So notice, third, the way Jesus ended his discourse on the gospel by bringing the emphasis right back to the problem of human depravity and God's condemnation of unbelievers:

> He who believes in Him is not condemned; but he who does not believe is condemned already, because he has not believed in the name of the only begotten Son of God. And this is the condemnation, that the light has come into the world, and men loved darkness rather than light, because their deeds were evil. For everyone practicing evil hates the light and does not come to the light, lest his deeds should be exposed. But he who does

the truth comes to the light, that his deeds may be clearly seen, that they have been done in God. (John 3:18–21)

This, too, is contrary to most contemporary ideas about how to do personal evangelism. Today's evangelicals generally think if we offend someone by pressing the claims of the gospel too firmly or too plainly, we've done something terribly wrong. The reality is quite the opposite: if you think the gospel can be proclaimed in a way that is always appealing and never upsetting to unbelievers, you have the wrong idea about what the gospel message says.

That is why Jesus left the issue with Nicodemus on a note of condemnation. John 3:16, of course, is famous for its stress on the love of God and the giving of Christ so that "whoever believes in Him should not perish but have everlasting life." That's the central truth of the gospel message and the promise that makes it good news. But it is *not* good news for those who remain in unbelief. Therefore Jesus' conversation with Nicodemus ended on a harsh and sobering note about the severe condemnation that rests on all unbelievers and hypocrites. Since Jesus had already implicated Nicodemus in verse 12 with the words "you do not believe," this was a very direct and personal challenge aimed squarely at him and the pharisaical belief system he represented.

THE REST OF THE STORY

As a matter of fact, Jesus' discourse on the gospel in John 3 ends on such a negative note that if this were the only place we encounter Nicodemus in all of Scripture, we might conclude that he left without saying any more and remained in unbelief all his life.

Scripture gives us two more glimpses of the man, however. It is clear that despite Jesus' severity and directness with him—or perhaps because of it—Nicodemus retained an interest in Jesus throughout the Lord's earthly ministry. And at some point he *did* believe, making the passage from death unto life. How and when this happened is not spelled out for us, but each of the biblical vignettes of Nicodemus shows him increasingly bold in separating himself from the rest of the Sanhedrin.

John 7 describes a meeting of the Sanhedrin in which the rest of the Pharisees were inveighing against Jesus and those who followed Him ("This crowd that does not know the law is accursed"—v. 49). They wanted Him arrested and brought before them, and it is clear that their one goal is to silence Him by whatever means they can. But one voice of dissent speaks on Jesus' behalf from within the Sanhedrin, and it is Nicodemus: "Does our law judge a man before it hears him and knows what he is doing?" (v. 51).

For that, Nicodemus incurred the scorn of his fellow Pharisees, who shot back: "Are you also from Galilee? Search and look, for no prophet has arisen out of Galilee" (v. 52). Clearly, they were not willing to entertain even a hint of possibility that Jesus might be from God—even though His miracles clearly affirmed His authority; even though they could not refute one word of His teaching; and even though they had no legitimate charge with which to indict Him. But as Jesus Himself said, "everyone practicing evil hates the light and does not come to the light, lest his deeds should be exposed" (John 3:20).

There is every reason to conclude that Nicodemus, who originally came to Jesus under cover of darkness, was eventually drawn to the True Light and became a genuine believer. The last time we meet Nicodemus in Scripture is in John 19:39, where he and Joseph of Arimathea hastily prepared the Savior's body for burial. It was an act that could well have cost him everything, at the very moment when the rest of the Sanhedrin had whipped public fury against Jesus into a murderous rage. He clearly had become a different man than he was when he first approached Jesus as an unbelieving Pharisee.

In the long term, then, Jesus' apparent harshness with Nicodemus was fully vindicated. Blunt, unvarnished directness was precisely what Nicodemus needed. No one else in all of Israel would dare speak that way to a religious leader of Nicodemus's stature. But Jesus was telling him the most important thing he could possibly hear, in a voice that rang with authority.

All the Pharisees and religious leaders in Israel needed a similar wake-up call, and that explains the tone of Jesus' dealings with them throughout the gospel accounts. Remember that Nicodemus came to Jesus near the start of our Lord's public ministry. Sadly, however, apart from this one conversation with Nicodemus, *all* Jesus' public interactions with the Pharisees ended badly, with the Pharisees being offended or angry. From this point on, every Pharisee and religious figure Jesus will deal with responds with hostility, outrage, indignation, and in the end, the ultimate act of violence.

Might Jesus have gained a more positive response from the Pharisees if He had shown them the kind of deference they demanded? What if He had sought common ground with them and focused only on what He could affirm in their belief system? There was, after all, a lot to affirm; the Pharisees weren't flirting with gross paganism like the Baal worshipers in Elijah's time. What if Jesus had stressed where they were *right* rather than constantly attacking what was *wrong* in their teaching? Is it possible that the Sanhedrin would have been more open to Jesus if He had not constantly used them as the epitome of all that was wrong with Israel spiritually?

Jesus knew something evangelicals today often forget: Truth doesn't defeat error by waging a public relations campaign. The struggle between truth and error is spiritual warfare, and truth has no way to defeat falsehood except by exposing and refuting lies and false teaching. That calls for candor and clarity, boldness and precision—and sometimes more severity than congeniality.

The fact that Nicodemus was the only Pharisee to listen to Christ without being so offended that he turned completely against Him is no indictment of the way Jesus dealt with Israel's chief religious leaders. Rather, it is a gauge of how truly evil their whole system was. From here on, that becomes one of the central themes of all four gospel accounts.

God chooses not milksops destitute of backbone, to wear his glory upon their faces. We have plenty of men made of sugar, nowadays, that melt into the stream of popular opinion; but these shall never ascend into the hill of the Lord, nor stand in his holy place, nor wear the tokens of his glory.

—CHARLES H. SPURGEON[1]

4

This Man Speaks Blasphemies

❧

*Now it happened on a certain day, as He was teaching, that
there were Pharisees and teachers of the law sitting by, who had
come out of every town of Galilee, Judea, and Jerusalem.*

Luke 5:17

*S*cripture gives much more detail about the second half of Jesus'
ministry than about those early months, but a pattern of increasing
conflict is nevertheless evident throughout. Most of our Lord's early
ministry took place in Galilee, where (at first) He was out from under
the constant scrutiny of the Jerusalem-based Sanhedrin. The Gospels
are sparse in the details they record about those months. We know that
this is when Jesus gathered most of His closest disciples (Matthew
4:18–22; Mark 1:16–20). Three Gospels record that He cast out
demons, did countless miracles, and ministered constantly to large
crowds during that first year (Matthew 4:23–24; Mark 1:39–45; Luke
5:15). Beyond that, the biblical record gives only a few specifics.

But as Jesus gained fame and followers, the religious leaders at
some early point seem to have taken measures to keep Him under

surveillance wherever He went. All of a sudden, every time He appeared in public—even in the remotest corners of Galilee—Pharisees always seemed to be present. His conflicts with scribes and Pharisees soon began to increase steadily in both frequency and intensity.

A key thing to notice is that so far, the scribes and Pharisees have done nothing overt to provoke any conflict with Jesus. *He* incited that first clash with them in Jerusalem by driving the money changers from the Temple without a single word of warning or prior announcement. The only personal interaction recorded between Jesus and an individual Pharisee up to this point was the dialogue with Nicodemus, who came on friendly terms—and Jesus rebuked him. For many months, that pattern continued. Every open conflict Jesus had with the Pharisees was instigated by Him, including the first major Galilean conflict between Jesus and the Jewish leaders—in which case He publicly embarrassed some Pharisees based on His knowledge of what they were *thinking*. Matthew, Mark, and Luke all describe the incident, but Luke's account is the fullest, so we'll focus most of our attention there.

This is also the first appearance of the Pharisees in Luke's gospel. Luke has a lot to say about the Pharisees and their opposition to Christ, but here is where he first introduces them. The setting is sometime after Jesus has returned to Galilee following that first Passover in Jerusalem. We can't tell precisely how much time has elapsed, but a careful harmony of the Gospels suggests that nearly a year and a half passed after that first temple cleansing before Jesus encountered overtly hostile Pharisees in Galilee.[1]

JESUS' MOVE TO CAPERNAUM

Jesus had remained in Jerusalem for an unspecified time teaching, healing, and gathering disciples after the Passover feast. John 4:1 says word eventually came to the Pharisees that Jesus was making more disciples than John the Baptist, so it sounds as if He lingered in Jerusalem for more than just a few days after Passover. On the other hand, John 4:45 indicates that many of those early disciples were Galileans who had come to Jerusalem for the feast. It seems unlikely that large crowds of people from Galilee would stay long in Jerusalem after the feast week was over. So Jesus' ministry there may have consumed no more than a couple of weeks. In any case, sometime in that interval after Passover is when the meeting with Nicodemus occurred.

Jesus then returned to Galilee via Samaria (John 4:3–4), taking a route no Pharisee would have taken. The Samaritans were considered unclean, and merely traveling through their land was thought by the Pharisees to be spiritually defiling. That was, of course, just one of many pharisaical taboos Jesus would break. But while traveling through Samaria, He had his famous encounter with the woman at the well in Sychar. That account consumes all of John 4. Christ led her to salvation—and she subsequently brought many in Sychar to Christ. Many of the villagers came to saving faith (John 4:39–42). Throughout this chapter, Jesus' conflict with the scribes, Pharisees, and Sanhedrin is merely subtext in John's narrative. But it nevertheless looms large in the background. Knowledgeable Jewish readers would know that Jesus' decision to travel through Samaria—and especially His ministry to a Samaritan woman with a sordid marital history (John 4:16–19)—would deeply offend any sensible Pharisee. (As a matter of fact, that shocked even Jesus' closest disciples—v. 27.)

After two days' ministry in Sychar, Jesus finally returned to Galilee (v. 43), the region where He grew up. No doubt because of the miracles He did wherever He went, His reputation quickly spread throughout the region. That opened opportunities for Him to preach and teach in the many synagogues scattered throughout Galilee (Luke 4:14–15). He seems to have had an extended itinerant ministry that took Him all over the Galilee region. Synagogues convened only on the Sabbath, so the fact that Jesus ministered in many of them suggests that this itinerant phase of His ministry lasted for many weeks' time. So it was a long, circuitous journey back from Jerusalem.

At last He came to His hometown synagogue, to minister there as He had all over the region. Nazareth was a small, rural town, so He would have been well-known to virtually everyone in the synagogue there, having grown up in their midst and attended that very synagogue every week of His young life. Luke expressly says it was His custom to go there on the Sabbath (4:16). Coming back now as a rabbi who was gaining renown and already accumulating many followers from all over Galilee, He no doubt piqued their curiosity by His mere presence.

But on that very first Sabbath back in His hometown, He caused a furor. He was handed the scroll of Isaiah, and He began to read from Isaiah 61. (Of course, the chapter and verse divisions did not exist in Jesus' time, but the place where He began reading is Isaiah 61:1 in modern Bibles.) He started at the beginning of the passage and suddenly stopped midsentence before he finished verse 2, closed the scroll, sat down, and declared that the prophecy He had just read was now fulfilled (v. 21). While the people were marveling and murmuring about the grace with which He spoke—amazed that one from their own midst could speak with such authority and aplomb—He interrupted with a shocking challenge for them:

He said to them, "You will surely say this proverb to Me, 'Physician, heal yourself! Whatever we have heard done in Capernaum, do also here in Your country.'" Then He said, "Assuredly, I say to you, no prophet is accepted in his own country. But I tell you truly, many widows were in Israel in the days of Elijah, when the heaven was shut up three years and six months, and there was a great famine throughout all the land;

but to none of them was Elijah sent except to Zarephath, in the region of Sidon, to a woman who was a widow. And many lepers were in Israel in the time of Elisha the prophet, and none of them was cleansed except Naaman the Syrian." (vv. 23–27)

Notice: He portrayed Himself as a prophet comparable to Elijah— a Messenger from God not even accepted by His own people. He cast the people in the role of unbelievers—like the disobedient Israelites in Elijah's day who had bowed the knee to Baal. He spoke of God's sovereignty in bypassing all of Israel to minister to a single Gentile outcast, and strongly implied that they were in the same boat as the reprobate Israelites who were bypassed by Elijah's ministry.

The point He was making was not lost on the people of Nazareth. It would have been clear to anyone familiar with the Old Testament account of Elijah. He was in effect telling a synagogue full of religious people that they needed to be saved. Being an Israelite and the physical offspring of Abraham was no guarantee of divine blessing. Without faith, it is impossible to please God (Hebrews 11:6), and He shows mercy to whom He will show mercy (Exodus 33:19; Romans 9:15). Those truths were implicit in Jesus' reference to the Israelites of Elijah's era. It stunned the people of His own hometown, because he was clearly putting them in the same category as Baal-worshiping apostates.

The whole mood in Nazareth changed instantly: "All those in the synagogue, when they heard these things, were filled with wrath" (Luke 4:28). They drove Him out of the synagogue, to the outskirts of the city, and to the very edge of a cliff or rock ledge, where they intended to throw Him off.[2] This was the first recorded major attempt on His life, and it came from the very community where He had grown up!

But just before they reached the edge of the rock precipice, Jesus miraculously eluded the mob. Simply "passing through the midst of them, He went His way" (v. 30). They were evidently confounded— temporarily blinded or supernaturally put into a state of confusion— and Jesus walked away from them without a struggle and with no pursuers.

In fact, He walked away from Nazareth completely. In the next verse, Luke says, "Then He went down to Capernaum, a city of Galilee, and was teaching them on the Sabbaths" (v. 31). In other words, He established his home base in Capernaum, on the north shore of the Sea of Galilee, some thirty miles from Nazareth. Matthew 4:13 says, "Leaving Nazareth, He came and *settled* in Capernaum" (NASB, emphasis added). After this, when we read a reference to "His own city" (Matthew 9:1), it's talking about Capernaum. Mark 2:1 says when Jesus was in Capernaum, He was "at home" (NASB).

Most of Jesus' closest disciples also called Capernaum home. It was where Zebedee, father of James and John, had his fishing business. It was where Peter and Andrew hailed from. It was if anything an even more insignificant and obscure village than Nazareth, but it was perfectly situated for One who delights to use "the foolish things of the world to put to shame the wise, . . . the weak things of the world to put to shame the things which are mighty; and the base things of the world and the things which are despised . . . [so] that no flesh should glory in His presence" (1 Corinthians 1:27–29).

JESUS' REPUTATION GROWS

Soon crowds of people flocked to Capernaum to see and hear Jesus. They were astonished at the authority with which He taught (Luke 4:32). With that same authority, He cast out demons (vv. 33–36) and healed the sick—starting with Peter's mother-in-law (vv. 38–42).

Multitudes began to come from all over the region to be healed and delivered, and "He laid His hands on every one of them and healed them" (v. 40).

He had to steal away into a deserted place in order to get away from the demands of the crowds. They pursued Him even there, "and tried to keep Him from leaving them; but He said to them, 'I must preach the kingdom of God to the other cities also, because for this purpose I have been sent'" (vv. 42–43). So with Capernaum as His base, he continued the ministry He had begun prior to that tumultuous Sabbath in Nazareth, ministering in synagogues all over Galilee.

Multitudes continued to follow Jesus wherever He went. The crowds were so vast and so crushing on the shores of Galilee that the only way Jesus could preach to them without being utterly surrounded and swallowed up by a sea of humanity was to sit in a boat and do His teaching from just offshore. He cleansed lepers, healed all kinds of diseases, and taught the ever-increasing multitudes. Since there was never an infirmity He could not heal or a possessed person He could not deliver, the crowds continued to grow and pursue Him more aggressively than ever. "So He Himself often withdrew into the wilderness and prayed" (Luke 5:16).

What Luke describes is a tireless, nonstop campaign of daily teaching and public ministry. Crowds pursued Jesus constantly, daily, from sunup to sundown. In the rural regions of Galilee, even a few hundred people would constitute a massive throng—certainly large enough to overwhelm a village the size of Capernaum. But the swarms of people continued to grow until they numbered in the thousands. All four Gospels record the feeding of five thousand—an astonishing number, given the fairly sparse population of the region. And more amazing yet, the Gospels all indicate that such large crowds gathered relentlessly on a daily basis, even following Jesus into the wilderness,

making it virtually impossible for Him to find any kind of soli-
tude. It was reminiscent of John the Baptist's wilderness ministry (cf.
Matthew 3:5; 4:25)—except with miracles.

Naturally, news of Jesus' Galilean ministry reached all the way to
Jerusalem, and came to the attention of the Sanhedrin.

ENTER THE PHARISEES

When Luke first mentions the "Pharisees and teachers of the law,"
they are watching Jesus from the sidelines. They have come to
Capernaum, not as part of the normal crowd seeking to benefit from
Jesus' ministry, but as critical observers, looking for reasons to condemn Him and if possible thwart him before He became any more
popular. It is clear that they had formed this agenda ahead of time,
because they arrived "on a certain day . . . out of every town of
Galilee, Judea, and Jerusalem" (Luke 5:17).

Jesus was in Capernaum, in a house. Mark seems to suggest that
it was the house where Jesus himself lived (Mark 2:1). As usual, the
press of the crowds was suffocating, and Jesus was preaching from
within the house to as many people as could gather within earshot.
Mark describes the scene: "Many were gathered together, so that
there was no longer room, not even near the door; and He was speaking the word to them" (v. 2). Luke adds, "And the power of the Lord
was present to heal them" (Luke 5:17).

Here's a pattern you will notice in almost every confrontation
between Jesus and Pharisees: in one way or another, His deity is
always at the heart of the conflict. It is as if He deliberately provokes
them with claims, statements, or actions that He knows they will
object to, and then He uses the resulting conflict to demonstrate that
all the authority He claimed did indeed belong to Him.

On this occasion, the issue at stake was the forgiveness of sins.

Remember that Jesus had been performing public healings for several weeks all over Galilee. There was no question about His ability to heal any disease or deliver the spiritually downtrodden from any kind of demonic bondage. Demons and disease alike always fled at His Word—sometimes even at His presence. "Wherever He entered, into villages, cities, or the country, they laid the sick in the marketplaces, and begged Him that they might just touch the hem of His garment. And as many as touched Him were made well" (Mark 6:56). In Jesus' own words, this was the proof of all His claims and the confirmation of all His teaching: "The blind see, the lame walk, the lepers are cleansed, the deaf hear, the dead are raised, the poor have the gospel preached to them" (Luke 7:22).

On this particular day, however, Jesus was presented with a particularly difficult case—a tragic and incurable affliction so debilitating that the sick man had to be carried on a stretcher by four other men. The crowd was so concentrated and so tightly drawn to Jesus in order to hear, it would have been well nigh impossible for one healthy man to squeeze through and get next to Jesus, much less four men carrying a paraplegic on a stretcher.

Here was a man so desperately in need of healing that four others—perhaps friends and neighbors, possibly even relatives—had gone to all this trouble to carry him to Capernaum in order to seek help from this healer they had all heard about. But when they got there, there was no hope of even seeing Jesus, because the spiritually starved multitudes essentially had Him barricaded in a house, from which His voice could only faintly be heard teaching.

It may well be that forgiveness was the very topic He was teaching about. The subject was certainly in the air. Immediately before this, after teaching from Peter's boat, Jesus had instructed Peter to launch out into the deep and let down his nets (Luke 5:4). To any fisherman such a strategy would sound foolish. Fish were best netted at night, in shallow waters, while they were feeding. Peter had fished all night and caught nothing (v. 5). During daylight hours, the fish would migrate to much deeper, cooler waters, where it would normally be impossible to reach them with nets. "Nevertheless," Peter said, "at Your word I will let down the net." When the haul of fishes was so great that the nets began to break, Peter was instantly smitten with the realization that he was in the presence of divine power—and the first thing he was aware of was the weight of his own guilt. "He fell down at Jesus' knees, saying, "Depart from me, for I am a sinful man, O Lord!" (v. 8).

Forgiveness was also one of Jesus' favorite subjects to preach about. It was one of the key themes in His Sermon on the Mount. It was a focus of the Lord's Prayer and the subject He expounded on at the end of that prayer (Matthew 6:14–15). It's the central theme that dominates all of Luke 5. If forgiveness was not the very subject Jesus was preaching on, it was nevertheless about to become the topic of the day.

Now imagine the Pharisees, sitting somewhere on the periphery, watching and listening for things to criticize as these four men carrying the stretcher arrived on the scene.

WHO CAN FORGIVE SINS BUT GOD?

If they wanted to see Jesus in action, these Pharisees had certainly come on the right day. Here was a hopelessly paralyzed man who had been brought from some distance by four other men whose journey from another village could not have been an easy one. And when they arrived, they must have seen instantly that they had no hope of getting close to Jesus by any conventional method. Even if they waited until Jesus left the house, the crowds were much too thick and too electrified to make way for five men to penetrate all the way to the center of the vast throng that surrounded Jesus wherever he went.

The fact that the man was carried on a pallet rather than seated in some kind of cart suggests that he was probably a quadriplegic, totally paralyzed in all his limbs—perhaps as a result of some injury to his neck. He was a classic object lesson about the fallen human condition. He was unable to move; utterly reliant on the grace and goodness of others, completely impotent to do anything whatsoever for himself.

Here was an infirmity that would require a true and obvious miracle for healing. This was not like the invisible ailments (sore backs, migraines, and stomach ailments) we often see "cured" by people who claim to possess gifts of healing today. His muscles would be atrophied and shriveled to nothing from nonuse. If Jesus could heal him, it would be instantly obvious to all that a true miracle had taken place.

The sheer desperation of the man and his four friends can be measured by what they did when they realized they would not be able to get close to Jesus. They went up to the roof. In order for four men to ascend with a stretcher, there must have been an external stairway leading to a veranda or walkway. Even at that, it would be a difficult ascent. But this was evidently a substantial house, with a typical Mediterranean-style upper-level patio adjacent to a tiled section of roof. That afforded the men exactly the opportunity they needed. They carried the man upstairs, determined approximately where Jesus was below them, and began removing the tiles over that part of the roof.

What a dramatic entrance this was! It no doubt startled the crowd when the roof began to open up. The gap in the roof needed to be large enough for the man and his stretcher—which likely meant that not only the external roof tiles but also some of the underlying lattice-work supporting the tiles had to be carefully removed. A tile roof was no cheap or temporary covering, and there's simply no way to open a hole in a tile roof like that without lots of debris and dust falling into the crowd below. We would normally expect both the crowd and the landlord to be annoyed by the actions of these men.

But in Jesus' eyes, this was clear evidence of great faith. All three Synoptic Gospels record this incident, and all three say Jesus *"saw* their faith" (v. 20; Matthew 9:2; Mark 2:5). He saw faith reflected in their persistence and determination, of course. After all the work they had done to lay their friend at Jesus' feet, it was obvious to everyone what they were there for: they had brought the man for physical healing. Anyone who thought about it could see it required some degree of faith in Jesus' healing ability to go to all that work.

But the text is suggesting that Jesus saw something even deeper. Because He is God incarnate, He could also see into their hearts, perceive their motives, and even know their thoughts—just as He had seen into the heart of Nicodemus, and just as He had discerned the halfhearted faith of those early admirers of His ministry in Jerusalem to whom He had refused to commit himself (John 2:23–25).

What He saw as these men lowered their friend from the ceiling was true faith—repentant faith. Not one of the gospel accounts suggests that either the paralyzed man or his friends said a word. There was no verbal testimony from the man about his repentance. There was no statement of contrition. There was no confession of sin. There was no affirmation of faith in God. There was no verbal cry for mercy. There didn't need to be; Jesus could see into the man's heart and mind. He knew that the Holy Spirit had done a work in the paralyzed man's heart. The man had come to Jesus with a broken and contrite spirit. He wanted to be right with God. He did not even need to say that. Jesus knew it because as God, He knows all hearts.

Here was an opportunity for Jesus to display His deity. Everyone could see the man's *affliction;* only Jesus could see his *faith.* Without any comment either from the paralytic man at Jesus' feet or from the four men peering through the hole in the roof, Jesus turned to the paralytic man and said, "Man, your sins are forgiven you" (v. 20).

He freely forgave him. He fully justified him. With those words, the man's sins were obliterated from his account, wiped off the divine books. On His own personal authority, Jesus instantly absolved that man of all the guilt of all his sins forever.

With that claim, Jesus gave the scribes and Pharisees exactly what they were waiting for: an opportunity to accuse Him. And make no mistake: Jesus' words to the paralytic would be deeply shocking to the Pharisees' religion by any measure. In the first place, if He were not God incarnate, it would indeed be the very height of blasphemy for Him to pretend He had authority to forgive sins. In the second place, the Pharisees' religion was strongly oriented toward works—so that in their view, forgiveness must be *earned*. It was unthinkable to them that forgiveness could ever be granted immediately and unconditionally by faith alone.

According to Matthew, some of the scribes who were there reacted "at once" (Matthew 9:3). But curiously, in this instance, they did not rise up and shout out a verbal protest. It was still early enough in Jesus' ministry, and they constituted a small enough minority on the fringe of this crowd in Jesus' own community that their initial reaction seems surprisingly subdued. If their shock registered at all, it was only on their faces. Luke says they "began to reason, saying, 'Who is this who speaks blasphemies? Who can forgive sins but God alone?'" (5:21). Matthew makes it clear that they said these things "within themselves"—not aloud (9:2). Mark likewise says, "The scribes were sitting there and reasoning in their hearts, 'Why does this Man speak blasphemies like this? Who can forgive sins but God alone?'" (Mark 2:6–7). In their minds collectively they were all thinking the same thing. *This is blasphemy of the worst kind. Who but God can legitimately forgive sins?*

The question was merely rhetorical; they weren't really wondering what the answer might be. They knew full well that no one can forgive sins except God. Their doctrine on that point was sound enough. You and I can individually forgive whatever wrongs are done to us as far as our own personal claims for justice are concerned, but we don't have the authority to absolve anyone from guilt before the throne of God. No man can do that. No priest can do that. No one can do that but God alone. Anyone who usurps that prerogative is either God or a blasphemer. In fact, for someone who is not God, this would indeed be the supreme act of blasphemous idolatry—putting himself in the place of God.

WHO IS THIS?

Jesus had deliberately put Himself at the center of a scenario that would force every observer to render a verdict about Him. That's true not only of the people who were eyewitnesses in Capernaum that day but also for those who simply read this account in Scripture. And the choice is clear. There are only two possible conclusions we can make with regard to Christ: He is either God incarnate, or He is a blasphemer and a fraud. There is no middle ground, and that is precisely the situation Jesus was aiming for.

There are a lot of people even today who want to patronize Jesus by saying He was a good person, an outstanding religious leader, an important prophet, a profound ethicist, a paragon of integrity, kindness, and decency—a *great* man, but still merely a man—not God incarnate. But this one episode in His public ministry is sufficient to erase that choice from the list of possibilities. He is either God or the ultimate blasphemer. He purposely erased every possible middle-way alternative.

Jesus did not scold the Pharisees for thinking that only God can forgive sin. They weren't wrong about that. Nor did He write their concern off as a misunderstanding of His intention. That's what He would have done if He were indeed a good man not claiming to be God incarnate, and not really claiming any special authority to forgive sin or justify sinners. If that were the case, He ought to have immediately said, "Whoa, whoa, whoa! You misunderstood me. I'm not saying *I* can forgive the man, I simply meant to say that *God* will forgive the man." Any good, noble, godly man would want to correct such a misconception and set the record straight, affirming that only God can forgive sin. He didn't do any of that.

Instead, He rebuked them for "think[ing] evil" about Him (Matthew 9:4). They were wrong to assume the worst about Him when in fact He had already often displayed the power of God convincingly and publicly by healing diseases that no one but God could heal and by casting out demons that only God has power over. Instead of thinking *No mere man can forgive sin. He just blasphemed,* they ought to have been asking themselves, *Can it possibly be that this is no mere man?*

All three Synoptics stress that Jesus read their thoughts (Matthew 9:4; Mark 2:8; Luke 5:22). Just as He knew the heart of the paralytic and understood that the man's first concern was for the salvation of his soul, He knew the hearts of the Pharisees and understood that their only motive was to find a way to accuse Him. The fact that He knew what they were thinking ought to have been another clue to them that He was no mere man.

But they were already thinking well past that. As far as they were concerned, this was a case of blasphemy pure and simple, and no other option even seems to have occurred to them. Moreover, if they could make *that* accusation stick, they could call for Him to be stoned. Open blasphemy was a capital crime. Leviticus 24:16 was emphatic about that: "Whoever blasphemes the name of the LORD shall surely be put to death. All the congregation shall certainly stone him, the stranger as well as him who is born in the land. When he blasphemes the name of the LORD, he shall be put to death."

WHICH IS EASIER?

Before the scribes and Pharisees could even give voice to what they were thinking, Jesus Himself pressed the issue. "He answered and said to them, 'Why are you reasoning in your hearts? Which is easier, to say, "Your sins are forgiven you," or to say, "Rise up and walk"?'" (Luke 5:22–23).

They were thinking, *This man is blaspheming because he claims to do what only God can do.* Notice that Jesus did not even hint that they might have misunderstood His intentions. He did not double back and try to qualify His own statement. Nor did He challenge their belief that only God can forgive sin. As a matter of fact, they were exactly right about that.

Of course, only God can infallibly read human hearts, too. In Ezekiel 11:5, God Himself says, "I know the things that come into your mind." He speaks again in Jeremiah 17:10: "I, the LORD, search the heart, I test the mind." No human has the ability to see perfectly into the mind of another like that. "The LORD does not see as man sees; for man looks at the outward appearance, but the LORD looks at the heart" (1 Samuel 16:7). Jesus had just displayed knowledge both of the paralytic's mind and their own secret thoughts about Him. Shouldn't that have made them pause and reflect on who this was that they were dealing with?

That is precisely what Jesus was challenging them to consider. He proposed a simple test: "Which is easier, to say, 'Your sins are forgiven you,' or to say, 'Rise up and walk'?" (Luke 5:23). While it is certainly true that only God can forgive sins, it is likewise true that only God can perform the kind of regenerative miracle necessary to restore the atrophied muscles and brittle bones of a quadriplegic to perfect wholeness in a split second—so that he could literally rise up and walk on command. The question was not whether Jesus could make this man *better*, but whether He could instantly make him whole and healthy.

Even with the best methods of modern medicine, if someone happens to recover the ability to move after suffering a catastrophic injury of the sort that causes severe paralysis, it usually takes months of therapy for the brain to rediscover how to send accurate signals through the injured nerve paths to the disabled limbs. Regardless of how long this man had been paralyzed, we might expect at the very least that he would need some time to learn how to walk again. But Jesus' healings always bypassed all such therapy. People born blind were given not only their sight but also the instant ability to make sense of what they saw (John 9:1–38; Mark 8:24–25). When Jesus healed a deaf person, he also immediately healed the resultant speech impediment—no therapy required (Mark 7:32–35). Whenever He healed lame people, He gave them not only regenerated muscle tissue, but also the strength and dexterity to take up their beds and walk (Matthew 9:6; Mark 2:12). It strikes me as ironic that when modern faith healers and charismatic charlatans nowadays claim to heal people, the patient usually falls over immobile, or in uncontrollable convulsions. Jesus' healings had exactly the opposite effect. Even a man infirm and bedridden for thirty-eight years could immediately pick up his pallet and walk away (John 5:6–9).

That is just what this man needed: an act of divine, creative power such as only God can perform.

Notice carefully the way Jesus framed His question: "Which is easier to *say*?" He was picking at their thought process. They were indignant because he had granted this man forgiveness. They had never challenged his right to heal. Obviously, both forgiveness and healing are impossible for any mere man to *do*. No mere man has the power either to heal at will or to absolve sin at will. Healing is actually a perfect metaphor for forgiveness in that regard. In fact, the two things are inseparable, because sickness is a result of the curse brought on creation by sin. Sickness is merely a symptom; sin is the ultimate cause. (That's not to suggest that every sickness is the immediate consequence of a specific sin, of course. In John 9:3 Jesus expressly says there are other reasons for this or that individual's ailments. But the existence of illness and infirmity in a universe that was originally created perfect is nevertheless ultimately a result of the curse of sin.) So the power to heal all sickness presupposes the power to forgive any sin. Both are humanly impossible. But Jesus could do either or both with equal authority.

Still, which is easier to *say*? Obviously, it's easier to tell someone his sins are forgiven, because no one can see if it actually happened. The kind of forgiveness Jesus granted this man is a divine transaction. It occurs in the mind of God and the courtroom of heaven. It is a decree only God can make, and there's no immediate earthly evidence of it. It's easy to *say;* humanly impossible to *do*.

So Jesus in effect says, "You're questioning whether I can forgive that man's sin, aren't you? And you think it's very easy to say, 'Your sins are forgiven.' In fact, you think my saying it is blasphemy and that I have overstepped a boundary no man should ever come near."

The fact that Jesus knew their hearts so perfectly and yet refused to avert the public conflict they sought is significant. He knew full well that the Pharisees would be offended if He declared this man's sins forgiven, and yet He was not deterred from doing it. In fact, He did it as publicly as possible. He surely *could* have healed this man's infirmity without provoking that kind of open conflict with the Pharisees. He could have also dealt privately with the issue of the man's guilt, rather than making such a pronouncement within earshot of everyone. Jesus was surely aware that many people in a crowd that size would not be able to understand what He was doing or why He did it. At the very least, He could have taken time to pause and explain why He had a right to exercise divine authority. Any or all of those things would have at least avoided the perception that He was deliberately inflaming the Pharisees.

Those are the kinds of things a typical, solicitous evangelical in these postmodern times might insist *ought* to be done. Shouldn't we avoid public controversy at all costs, especially in circumstances like these, with so many simple villagers present? Friction between Jesus and the religious elite of Israel could not possibly be edifying to the common fishermen and housewives of Capernaum, could it? A wise person would do everything in his power to avoid offending these Pharisees—right? What possible good could come from turning this man's deliverance into a theater of public controversy?

But Jesus had no such scruples. The point He was making was vastly more important than how the Pharisees or the people of Capernaum felt about it. Therefore, "'[So] that you may know that the Son of Man has power on earth to forgive sins'—He said to the man who was paralyzed, 'I say to you, arise, take up your bed, and go to your house'" (Luke 5:24).

Now, it is not at all easy to say to someone like this, "Arise, take up your bed, and go." Because if you say that and he doesn't do it straightaway, you have just revealed that you have no authority to do what you are claiming. Unlike the phony healings featured on religious television by today's celebrity faith healers, Jesus' miracles involved serious and visible infirmities. He healed people who had suffered from appalling long-term maladies. He healed every imaginable kind of ailment—congenital disabilities and physical deformities included. He healed people as they came to Him—in their home-towns and on their public streets—not from the safety of a stage surrounded by screeners and security guards. He performed countless healings—far more than those specifically described in Scripture (John 21:25)—healing everyone who ever came to Him for relief from any infirmity (Matthew 4:24; 12:15; 19:2; Mark 5:56; Luke 6:18–19). And He healed up close, in the presence of many eye-witnesses whose testimony could not possibly be impeached.

Impostors, fake healers, staged miracles, and counterfeit healings were as common in Jesus' time as they are today. So it is significant that no one ever seriously questioned the reality of Jesus' miracles—including the Pharisees. They always attacked Him on other grounds. They questioned the source of His power. They accused Him of wrongfully healing on the Sabbath. They would certainly have claimed He was merely using sleight of hand if a credible case for that accusation could have been made. But nothing in the gospel record suggests that the Pharisees or anyone else ever even tried accusing Him of fakery. How could they, given the nature and the abundance of His miracles?

Now His entire reputation hinged on an impossibility. He would demonstrate in the most graphic way possible that He has authority to do what only God can do.

THE CRITICS SILENCED

Luke's account is notable for its straightforward simplicity. The writing style mirrors the startling suddenness of the miracle. Everything from this point on in the narrative happens so quickly that Luke covers it all in two short verses. Of the paralytic, Luke says, *"Immediately he rose up before them, took up what he had been lying on, and departed to his own house, glorifying God"* (5:25 emphasis added).

A lot happened in that one instant. The man's bones, fragile from nonuse, hardened perfectly. His muscles were restored at once to full strength and functionality. His joints and tendons became sturdy and mobile. All the elements of his physiology that had atrophied were regenerated. His nervous system switched back on and immediately became fully functional. Neuron fibers that had long ago ceased to feel anything sprang instantly back to life. One moment he felt nothing in those useless extremities; the next moment he felt all the strength and energy that comes with perfect health. Arms that one minute before had needed to be borne by four men and a stretcher suddenly were able to carry the stretcher back home.

The man's departure seems awfully abrupt. But Jesus' command consisted of three simple imperatives: "Arise, take up your bed, and go to your house" (v. 24). And that is precisely what the man did. If he paused to thank Jesus, he did not stop for long. We know for a fact that he was deeply grateful. But he was also understandably eager to get home and show his loved ones what God had done for Him.

Luke doesn't say how far away his home was, but it must have been a wonderful walk. And here's where we see his profound gratitude: all the way home he was "glorifying God" (v. 26).

The Bible sometimes understates the obvious things: "glorifying God." That's what the angels did in heaven when they announced the birth of the Messiah (Luke 2:14–15). It's easy to envision this man running, leaping, clapping, and dancing all the way home. If his four friends went home with him, he probably outran them all. They must have been a little fatigued from carrying him to Capernaum; he was newly reborn, freshly invigorated, and relieved of every burden he had ever borne except that now-useless stretcher.

"Glorifying God" would also have involved lots of noise—laughing, shouting, and singing hallelujahs. I imagine he could hardly wait to run to his front door, throw it open with a shout of gladness, burst in with his new arms held wide, and celebrate his new wholeness with his wife, his kids, or whatever family he had at home.

But the *best* part was not that he could skip home; the best part was that he was cleansed of his sin. I don't know what all he had dared to hope for when he and the four erstwhile pallbearers started out that morning. But I'm fairly certain he did not expect what he got. All his sins were forgiven and he had been created new. No wonder he glorified God.

The miracle had a corresponding effect on the people of Capernaum. "They were all amazed, and they glorified God and were filled with fear, saying, 'We have seen strange things today!'" (v. 26). The Greek expression Luke used means "seized with astonishment." The noun in that phrase is *ekstasis,* which of course is the root of the English word *ecstasy.* It literally speaks of a mind jolt—a powerful shock of amazement and profound delight. In this case, however, to translate the word as *ecstatic* would not really capture the people's reaction as Luke pictures it. It was more like stunned shock—mixed with fear and wonder.

Like the formerly paralyzed man, they glorified God. The praise of the crowd, however, is of a different character from the healed man's worship. He was moved by deep personal gratitude and a heart freshly delivered from guilt. They were simply in awe of the strangeness of what they had seen. We know from subsequent events that most of Capernaum's admiration for Jesus would turn out to be a fickle sort of esteem. Many in that crowd were halfhearted disciples and hangers-on who would quickly fall away when Jesus' teaching became harder.

But most peculiar is the fact that Luke says nothing more about the Pharisees. With a kind of stealth that will soon become a pattern, they simply lapse into utter silence and fade out of the story. The man who was healed went home one way, glorifying God and rejoicing in his newfound robe of righteousness. The religious leaders of Israel slunk away in the opposite direction—silently seething with anger, resentful that Jesus had pronounced the paralytic forgiven, unable even to rejoice in the man's good fortune, and silently plotting their next attempt to discredit Jesus. We know that was their response, because when they show up again, they will be a little more angry, a lot more exercised, and a lot less open to any serious consideration of Jesus' claims. This first Galilean controversy seems to mark the start of a pattern of increasingly hostile public conflicts with Jesus whereby their hearts would be completely hardened against Him.

This occasion also fairly summed up the spiritual reasons for the Pharisees' intense hatred of Jesus. They could not stand the compassion that would forgive a sinner on the spot. The idea that Jesus would instantly and freely justify a paralytic—someone who by definition was unable to work—contradicted everything they stood for. Jesus' exercise of divine authority also rankled them. It was not so much that they really believed Him guilty of blasphemy—after all, He answered that charge by repeatedly and convincingly proving He had full power to do what only God can do. But they had their own idea of what God should be like, and Jesus simply didn't fit the profile. Besides all that, He was a threat to their status in Israel (John 11:48)—and the more He humiliated them in public this way, the more their own influence diminished. From here on, that reality loomed as an urgent crisis in all their thoughts about Him.

After this episode, critical Pharisees become commonplace in all the gospel narratives. They soon began to dog Jesus' steps everywhere He went, seizing every reason they could find to accuse Him, opposing Him at every turn, even resorting to lies and blasphemy in their desperation to discredit Him.

Clearly, they had already written Him off completely. If they would not acknowledge Him when they saw a dramatic miracle like the instant healing of this paralytic, nothing would penetrate their hardened, self-righteous hearts. They were already well down the path that would make them the chief conspirators in His murder.

Jesus, of course, embodied *all* the attributes of God—kindness, longsuffering, and mercy on the one hand; wrath, righteousness, and judgment on the other. All those qualities are discernible in some measure in the way He dealt with the Pharisees over the course of His ministry. But because the gospel was at stake and His own lordship was constantly under attack from these men who were the most influential spiritual leaders in the nation, His tenderness never overshadowed His severity in any of His dealings with them.

Their course was fixed, apparently sometime before this first Galilean encounter with Him. Their hearts were already set to be unyielding to His authority, oblivious to His teaching, opposed to His truth, insensitive to His righteousness, and impervious to His rebukes. They had essentially written Him off already.

He would soon write them off as well.

*B*rethren, the Savior's character has all goodness in all perfection; he is full of grace and truth. Some men, nowaday, talk of him as if he were simply incarnate benevolence. It is not so. No lips ever spoke with such thundering indignation against sin as the lips of the Messiah. "He is like a refiner's fire, and like fuller's soap. His fan is in his hand, and he will throughly purge his floor." While in tenderness he prays for his tempted disciple, that his faith may not fail, yet with awful sternness he winnows the heap, and drives away the chaff into unquenchable fire. We speak of Christ as being meek and lowly in spirit, and so he was. A bruised reed he did not break, and the smoking flax he did not quench; but his meekness was balanced by his courage, and by the boldness with which he denounced hypocrisy. "Woe unto you, Scribes and Pharisees, hypocrites; ye fools and blind, ye serpents, ye generation of vipers, how can ye escape the damnation of hell?" These are not the words of the milksop some authors represent Christ to have been. He is a man—a thorough man throughout—a God-like man—gentle as a woman, but yet stern as a warrior in the midst of the day of battle. The character is balanced; as much of one virtue as of another. As in Deity every attribute is full orbed; justice never eclipses mercy, nor mercy justice, nor justice faithfulness; so in the character of Christ you have all the excellent things.

—CHARLES H. SPURGEON[3]

5

Breaking the Sabbath

❧

*He not only broke the Sabbath, but also said that God was His
Father, making Himself equal with God.*

John 5:18

$\mathcal{M}$atthew, Mark, and Luke all record that the healing of the
paralytic was followed immediately by the call and conversion of
Matthew. He of course became one of the Twelve and is the author
of the gospel that bears his name. But until Jesus called him to dis-
cipleship, Matthew would have been one of the most hated and despicable men in the entire Galilean region. He was a tax collector (a
publican, to use the familiar terminology of the King James Version).
He was therefore regarded by the entire community as a traitor to
the Jewish nation. He was the polar opposite of the Pharisees—in
just about every conceivable way.

Mark refers to Matthew as "Levi the son of Alphaeus" (Mark
2:14). That, together with the fact that the gospel he wrote is thoroughly Jewish in style and content, indicates that Matthew was a
Hebrew by birth. But he worked for Rome. He was a willing agent

of Caesar. He was basically in league with Israel's enemy in order to facilitate their evil occupation of the promised land and make money for himself by oppressing Israel's people. Rome's system of taxation was utterly corrupt, too. Tariffs were ambiguously assessed and inconsistently levied through a method that seemed more like extortion than anything else. Tax collectors were overwhelmingly crooked, well-known for using their office to line their own pockets. Officially, Rome looked the other way and allowed them to do that. After all, corruption greased the wheels of their aggressive revenue-producing machine. And Matthew was a big cog in the Galilean component of that apparatus.

Everything about Matthew would have been odious to faithful Israelites. As a matter of fact, publicans were the lowest and most despised of all the social outcasts in all the land. They were considered the most despicable of sinners, and they often lived up to that reputation in every conceivable sense. Pharisees and common people alike viewed them with the utmost scorn.

A SHORT TIMELINE

Not only do all three Synoptic Gospels place the call of Matthew immediately after the healing of the paralytic; both Matthew and Luke indicate that what follows happened immediately, on that same day. *"As Jesus passed on from there,* He saw a man named Matthew sitting at the tax office" (Matthew 9:9 emphasis added). *"After these things* He went out and saw a tax collector named Levi, sitting at the tax office" (Luke 5:27). Apparently, as soon as the paralyzed man picked up his pallet and left for home, Jesus went out of the house where the healing had taken place and started toward the lake shore. In a village as small as Capernaum, situated right at water's edge, that could not be more than a few blocks. Mark indicates that Jesus' plan was to continue teaching the multitudes, and the waterfront obviously afforded a better, more suitable venue than a house for that. As "He went out again by the sea" (Mark 2:13), somewhere along the way "He saw Levi the son of Alphaeus sitting at the tax office" (v. 14).

The tax office was obviously well situated so that Matthew could amass maximum revenue. Tradesmen trying to save time and bypass the hazardous Galilean road system regularly shipped goods by water across the Sea of Galilee. Capernaum was one of the best places on the north shore to connect with the *Via Maris*—a major thoroughfare between Damascus and the Mediterranean. Matthew was perfectly positioned at that unusual crossroads so that he could intercept and tax traffic in all directions, whether by water or by land. He could also keep an eye on the lucrative fishing trade in Capernaum and assess regular tariffs on the fishermen.

That means Matthew was perhaps the least likely person in all of Capernaum to become one of Jesus' twelve closest followers. The other disciples, mostly fishermen from Capernaum, undoubtedly knew him well, and they must have despised the way he had made himself wealthy off their livelihood.

"FOLLOW ME!"

But on that day, as Jesus passed the tax office, He caught Matthew's eye and gave him a simple two-word greeting: "Follow Me!" All three accounts of this incident record just that; no more. Matthew was obviously a man already under conviction. He had borne the weight of sin and guilt long enough, and upon hearing that simple command from Jesus, "he left all, rose up, and followed Him" (Luke 5:28).

For a man in Matthew's position, leaving everything behind so quickly was a dramatic turnaround comparable to the paralytic's sudden ability to walk and carry his own stretcher. Matthew's heart change was a *spiritual* rebirth, but no less miraculous than the paralytic's instant physical healing. As far as Matthew's career was concerned, this was a total and irreversible change of course. You could not walk away from a Roman tax commission and then have second thoughts and ask for your office back two days later. But Matthew did not hesitate. His sudden repentance is one of the most dramatic conversions described anywhere in Scripture.[1]

In a village the size of Capernaum (fewer than two hundred yards from water's edge to the northern perimeter of the village), it is virtually certain that Matthew's office was very near the house where Jesus healed the paralytic. Given the commotion of the crowd, it would be impossible for the events of that day to escape Matthew's notice. He must have perked up when Jesus declared the paralytic man's sins forgiven. He was, after all, a publican and social outcast. We can discern from his immediate response to Jesus that he was utterly fed up with the life of sin. He was probably feeling the spiritual barrenness that goes with ill-gotten material wealth. And it is clear that he was sensing the weight of his own guilt under the Holy Spirit's conviction. Jesus had just granted a forlorn quadriplegic the very thing Matthew's own soul craved: forgiveness, cleansing, and a pronouncement of justification. Coming from Someone like Jesus who obviously had the authority to back up His decrees, that would definitely have caught Matthew's attention. Clearly, before Jesus even walked by and spoke to Him, Matthew was being drawn to faith because of what he had seen that day.

Matthew's perspective was the polar opposite of the Pharisees'. He yearned to be free from his sin; they would not even admit that they were sinners. No wonder Matthew's response to Jesus was so immediate.

WHY DOES HE CONSORT WITH
PUBLICANS AND SINNERS?

Matthew decided to host a celebratory reception for Jesus that very day. Like all new converts, he desperately wanted to introduce as many of his friends as possible to Jesus without delay. So he opened his home and invited Jesus as guest of honor. Luke says "a great number of tax collectors and others" came to the banquet (Luke 5:29). The "others" would of course be the kind of lowlifes who were willing to socialize with a group of publicans. In other words, this gathering would not have included any of the regulars from the local synagogue.

That a rabbi would be willing to fraternize at a party with such people was utterly repugnant to the Pharisees. It was diametrically opposed to all their doctrines about separation and ceremonial uncleanness. Here was yet another pet issue of the Pharisees, and Jesus was openly violating their standards, knowing full well that they were watching him closely. From their perspective, it must have seemed as if He was deliberately flaunting His contempt for their system.

Because He was. Remember an important fact we stressed in the previous chapter: all the friction that has taken place out in the open thus far between Jesus and Israel's religious elite has been entirely at *His* instigation. As far as we know from Scripture, they had not yet voiced a single unprovoked criticism or public accusation against Him.

Even now, the Pharisees were not yet bold enough to complain to Jesus directly. They sought out His disciples and murmured their protest to them. Again, all three Synoptics stress that the Pharisees took their grievance to the disciples. It was a craven attempt to blind-side Jesus by provoking a debate with His followers instead. I like the way Luke says it: "The Pharisees and their scribes began grumbling at His disciples" (Luke 5:30 NASB).

But Jesus overheard (Matthew 9:12; Mark 2:17), and He answered the Pharisees directly, with a single statement that became the definitive motto for His interaction with the self-righteous Sanhedrin and their ilk: "It is not those who are healthy who need a physician, but those who are sick; I did not come to call the righteous, but sinners" (Mark 2:17 NASB). For sinners and tax collectors seeking relief from the burden of their sin, Jesus had nothing but good news. To the self-righteous religious experts, He had nothing to say at all.

Harsh? By postmodern standards, this was a terribly strident thing to say. And (as many people today would quickly point out) there was virtually no possibility that a comment like this would help sway the Pharisees to Jesus' point of view. It was likelier to increase their hostility against Him.

And yet it was the *right* thing for Him to say at this moment. It was the truth they needed to hear. The fact that they were not "open" to it did not alter Jesus' commitment to speaking the truth—without toning it down, without bending it to fit His audience's tastes and preferences, without setting the facts of the gospel aside to speak to their "felt needs" instead.

The Pharisees evidently had no answer for Jesus. None of the gospels record anything further that they said.[2] Here again, they simply lapse into silence and fade into the background of the narrative.

Their strategy when embarrassed like this seemed to be that they would fall back, regroup, rethink their strategy, and simply look for a different way to accuse Him. Each time, they would come back more determined and a little more bold.

Their attempts to discredit Jesus were by no means over. In fact, the Pharisees had only *begun* to fight.

THE CONFLICT CRYSTALLIZES

Sometime not long after that momentous day in Capernaum, Jesus made another journey into Judea. John is the only one of the gospels to mention that Jesus went to Jerusalem (again, to celebrate one of the annual feast days) near the midpoint of His three-year ministry. The incident is recorded in chapter 5 of John's gospel. If at first glance that appears too early to be halfway through Jesus' ministry, that is because John actually condenses the entire first Galilean phase of Jesus' public ministry—approximately a full year—into a handful of verses at the end of chapter 4.

John 4:43 marks Jesus' return to Galilee via Samaria. John 4:45–54 then describes the healing of a nobleman's son, which took place in Capernaum while Jesus was in Cana during the early part of His itinerant work. It is the *only* incident John mentions from those months in Galilee. Then the very next verse (John 5:1) says, "After this there was a feast of the Jews, and Jesus went up to Jerusalem." That trip to Jerusalem resulted in Jesus' next major showdown with the Sanhedrin.

John frequently catalogues events in Jesus' life by the feast days. He mentions six of them, and this is the only one he does not identify by name.[3] The phrase "a feast of the Jews" could be describing that year's Passover feast. More likely, this was the Feast of Tabernacles— the harvest festival.[4]

The question of which feast this was is of no importance to the actual meaning of the narrative. But this is nevertheless a crucial passage, marking a major turning point in Jesus' conflict with the Sanhedrin. After this incident, they were not content merely to discredit Him; they were determined to put Him to death (John 5:18). From that point on, their challenges to His authority would be open, brazen, and increasingly shrill.

Likewise, the rebukes and admonitions Jesus aimed their way would become more and more severe from this point forward.

This incident, in some ways an echo of the previous one, started with the healing of a man who had been completely bedridden for thirty-eight years (v. 5). The miracle took place at the pool of Bethesda, near the Sheep Gate at the northeastern corner of the Temple grounds. It was very close to the place where the sheep market was—where Jesus had driven out the money-changers approximately eighteen months before. John writes,

> Now there is in Jerusalem by the Sheep Gate a pool, which is called in Hebrew, Bethesda, having five porches. In these lay a great multitude of sick people, blind, lame, paralyzed. . . .[5] Now a certain man was there who had an infirmity thirty-eight years. When Jesus saw him lying there, and knew that he already had been in that condition a long time, He said to him, "Do you want to be made well?" The sick man answered Him, "Sir, I have no man to put me into the pool when the water is stirred up; but while I am coming, another steps down before me." Jesus said to him, "Rise, take up your bed and walk." And immediately the man was made well, took up his bed, and walked. (John 5:2–3, 5–9)

As noted, this was poignantly reminiscent of the miracle the Pharisees' delegation had seen Jesus do in Capernaum. The exact nature and extent of this man's disability is not given. He does not appear to have been completely paralyzed like the man in Capernaum. (In verse 7 the man himself suggests that he had some ability to move, though only slowly and with great difficulty.) He might have had a serious arthritic condition, a degenerative muscle disease, some kind of palsy, or a long-term disability from a major injury.

Whatever the precise nature of the man's affliction, it was severe enough to make it impossible for the man to move freely on his own. He was therefore essentially bedridden, and he had been like that for what seemed like a lifetime—thirty-eight years. Such a man would be unemployable and most likely poor. A spring-fed pool of warm mineral water was the cheapest, most effective therapy all the best medical expertise of that era could offer for a disability such as his.

But there was a problem: whoever had brought him to Bethesda didn't stay with him, and thus he was unable even to get in the water when the spring began to flow. He was the very picture of helplessness.

This pool was a magnet for the sick and infirm. Its five covered colonnades sheltered "a great multitude of sick people, blind, lame, paralyzed" (v. 3). Every one of them would undoubtedly have been glad to be healed. But on this occasion, Jesus bypassed them all and quietly singled out this one lone man. He approached him individually and spoke to him privately. He asked a question whose answer would seem to be obvious: "Do you want to be made well?" (v. 6).

The man's reply reveals what was on his mind. He was frustrated and discouraged. Evidently, at the very moment when Jesus approached him, the fellow was lying there pondering the bitter irony of his situation. He was within a few feet of the scant relief available to him, and yet it was no benefit to him whatsoever, because when the soothing waters were flowing, he could not get into the pool before being crowded aside by others. It was an exasperating indignity for him, and he was clearly brooding about it when Jesus approached him. I like D. A. Carson's comment about the man's reply to Jesus (v. 7): "[It] reads less as an apt and subtle response to Jesus' question than as the crotchety grumblings of an old and not very perceptive man who thinks he is answering a stupid question."[6]

The man seems to have believed that it was important to be first into the pool as soon as the waters were agitated (see endnote 5 of this chapter). He wasn't looking for someone to hold his arm to steady and support him while he got into the pool as best he could. Instead, the phrase he used in verse 7 could be literally translated, "I have no one to *cast* me into the pool when the water is stirred up." He may have been hinting that if Jesus was really interested in a lame man's well-being, He should stand by until the waters were stirred again, and then quickly fling the man into the pool!

That was as good as a *yes* answer to Jesus' question, because without another word, Jesus said to him, "Rise, take up your bed and walk" (v. 8). It was practically the same form of expression Jesus had used with the paralytic in Capernaum: three imperatives, all commands the poor man had no ability in himself to obey. But with the command came miraculous power from on high, and *"immediately"* (v. 9) the man's thirty-eight-year-long affliction came to an end. He simply picked up his pallet and walked away. Jesus, meanwhile, quietly blended in with the crowd (v. 13).

In the scope of Jesus' whole ministry, this might have seemed a fairly unremarkable healing. It wasn't accompanied by any sermon or public discourse. Jesus simply spoke privately and very briefly with this one infirm man in a context so crowded that few people, if any, were likely to notice. There was no fanfare prior to the healing, and John's description of the incident gives us no reason to think the man's healing *per se* resulted in any public spectacle. Jesus had healed countless people before, and in that light, everything about this incident was more or less routine for the ministry of Jesus.

Except for one detail. John closes verse 9 by noting, "And that day was the Sabbath." At first glance, that may appear to be an incidental background fact. But it is actually the turning point of the narrative, sparking a conflict that will mark yet another escalation of hostility between Jesus and the chief religious leaders of Israel. By the end of this day, their contempt for Him will have been ratcheted up to such a level of pure hatred that from now on they will not rest—or let Him rest—until they have completely eliminated Him.

Remember that matters concerning obedience on the Sabbath were the Pharisees' home turf. Jesus knew full well that they were almost fanatical about it. They had invented all kinds of restrictions for the day of rest, adding their own super-strict rules to Moses' law in the name of tradition. They treated their manmade customs as if they were binding law, equal in authority to the revealed word of God.

Of course, they did the same thing with all the law's ceremonial precepts, going far beyond what Scripture required. They made every ritual as elaborate and every ordinance as restrictive as possible. They believed this was a pathway to greater holiness. But the Sabbath was a weekly event, the very heartbeat of Israel's religious life and a symbol of theocracy. As such it was a constant reminder that true authority under Moses' law came from God through the priesthood—not by governmental decrees from an earthly king or Caesar. So the high-handed authority the Pharisees claimed over that day was the one great tradition they guarded most fiercely.

They insisted that *everyone* must rigidly observe their Sabbatarian principles. In Jerusalem especially, the entire population was basically required to observe the Sabbath in the manner of the Pharisees. On this issue even the Sadducees yielded to the Pharisees' traditions. Bear in mind that the Sadducees' own scruples about Sabbath observance were not nearly as strict as the Pharisees', but the whole issue was so volatile that for the sake of peace (and also to safeguard their own reputations among the common people who were under the Pharisees' influence), the Sadducees had to follow the Pharisees' conventions when it came to Sabbath observance. The Sadducean high priest himself capitulated—in public at least—to the Pharisees' ultrastrict Sabbatarianism. And in Jerusalem, even pagan Roman soldiers showed as much deference as possible to the Pharisees' restrictions on that one day each week. Ultrastrict Sabbatarian legalism thus became the defining cultural emblem of life and religion in Israel.

Jesus, however, refused to bow to the Pharisees' manmade rules. He broke their Sabbaths openly, repeatedly, and deliberately. He taught that "the Sabbath was made for man, and not man for the Sabbath" (Mark 2:27). He then followed that statement by boldly telling the Pharisees, "Therefore the Son of Man is also Lord of the Sabbath" (v. 28).

The first major conflict over these matters broke out in the wake of this quiet Sabbath healing at the pool of Bethesda. Almost as soon as the healed man picked up his bed (for the first time in thirty-eight years) and began to walk away, he met some religious leaders who accused him of breaking the Sabbath. Before the day was over, Jesus would justify His own breaking of the Pharisees' Sabbath restrictions by saying He is God's Son and therefore perfectly free to do what God Himself does on the Sabbath.

This one incident pretty much determined the issues and set the tone that would dominate Jesus' controversy with the Sanhedrin for the rest of His earthly life. From this day forward, the vast majority of conflicts between Jesus and the Pharisees will involve the question of who truly has authority over the Sabbath. Their Sabbath traditions and His divine authority will thus become the twin issues upon which all the Pharisees' conflicts with Jesus now crystallize. Virtually every public controversy He will have with them from here on will be sparked either by His refusal to bow to their legalism, His claims of equality with God, or both. His clear stance on *both* points of the controversy is perfectly summarized in the declaration that *He* is Lord of the Sabbath.

Now observe how this first Sabbath conflict arose.

NOT LAWFUL TO CARRY YOUR BED

No one could walk through Jerusalem carrying *anything* on the Sabbath (much less a cot or stretcher large enough for a grown man) without catching the critical eye of some Pharisee. Especially this close to the Temple. Predictably, before the formerly disabled man had traveled very far from the Pool of Bethesda, a band of religious authorities stopped him and challenged his right to carry his own sickbed on the day of rest. (John refers to the man's interlocutors as "the Jews," which in John's gospel almost always signifies recognized, high-ranking religious authorities. So these men were probably members of the Sanhedrin council.) "It is the Sabbath," they curtly told him; "it is not lawful for you to carry your bed" (John 5: 10).

The man explained that he had just received a miraculous healing, and that "He who made me well said to me, 'Take up your bed and walk'" (v. 11).

Do not miss the fact that these religious authorities were more concerned about manmade Sabbath traditions than they were with the well-being of a man who had suffered for such a long time. They were acting like middle-school hall monitors rather than mature human beings. So much for their claims of moral superiority. Even most of the people the Pharisees always looked down on would have responded better than they did. Anyone with an ounce of feeling and a basic sense of humanity would naturally rejoice with the man over his good fortune. Simple curiosity would prompt most of us to ask for more details about what had happened and how such a marvelous healing after so long an affliction had suddenly come to pass. It takes a peculiar brand of hyperreligious self-righteousness for anyone to behave as callously as these Jewish authorities did. They totally ignored the glorious triumph of the healing and demanded to know precisely who had healed him, so that they could take up their grievance with whoever *told* this man it was okay to carry his bed.

But Jesus had already slipped away into the multitudes. The brief encounter at Bethesda had been so unexpected and was all accomplished so quickly that the man had not even had time to find out who it was that healed him.

JESUS EQUATING HIMSELF WITH GOD

Apparently the man was somewhere between Siloam and the Temple when he was stopped and challenged. That would mean he walked only a very short distance before being accused of Sabbath-breaking. It is not entirely clear whether he was already headed toward the Temple. He may have quickly changed direction and gone there as a way of visibly demonstrating piety after being accosted and threatened. In any case, "Afterward, Jesus found him in the temple and said to him, 'See, you have been made well. Sin no more, lest a worse thing come upon you'" (v. 14).

We're not told anything about the spiritual state of this man. Jesus did not declare his sins forgiven, as He had in the case of the paralytic at Capernaum. Nor did Christ comment on the man's faith, as He often did when healing people (e.g., Matthew 9:22; Mark 10:52; Luke 7:50; 17:19). The fact that he was in the Temple is the only clue we have that he had any spiritual interest at all. Again, his motive for going there in the first place is unclear.

But Jesus' solemn warning to the man suggests that his original illness may have been a direct consequence of (or a divine chastisement for) some sin he had engaged in. The verb tense Jesus used literally means "don't keep sinning." Of course, Scripture makes it clear that we are not to assume all sickness or catastrophe means God is chastening someone for a specific sin (John 9:3; Luke 13:2–3; Job

32:3). Still, it is equally clear that sometimes God *does* punish sin by those means (Deuteronomy 28:58–61; 1 Corinthians 11:30). If this man's affliction was indeed a chastening for sin, then the "worse thing" Jesus said might happen to this man could even be a reference to eternal judgment. If so, then Jesus' admonition was a call to repentance, and that would indicate that the man had not yet come to faith in Christ. Jesus did sometimes heal people of their physical maladies before they came to saving faith (cf. John 9:35–38; Luke 17:11–19).

But what especially calls this man's faith into question is the way he reacted after meeting Jesus in the Temple and discovering the identity of the One who had healed him. If he expressed any praise or thanksgiving—or made any answer to Jesus at all—John doesn't mention it. Instead, the text says "The man departed" (John 5:15).

He not only departed the presence of Jesus; he went straight to the Jewish authorities who had confronted him and basically turned Jesus in. It's difficult to imagine any noble motive for him to go groveling to the religious leaders. In the worst case, the man was being sinfully self-serving; in the best case, he was being naively stupid. He could not possibly have had any affection for (or relationship with) the Jewish leaders who had challenged him. They would have treated him as unclean prior to his healing, and they *did* treat him with callous disregard immediately afterward. But he wanted no quarrel with them. And he may have had an undue fear of their disapproval, fearing perhaps that they might really stone him. If so, he may have been merely overeager to clear himself of any blame.

On the other hand, he had every reason to know that the religious leaders were extremely angry about the supposed Sabbath violation. When they originally demanded to know who healed him, it must have been patently obvious to him that they were not looking to congratulate Jesus for His benevolence. If he was so intimidated by them and fearful of the repercussions of their displeasure, it is difficult to explain why he would go out of his way to find them again and bring them fresh intelligence about Jesus.

Whatever reason he had for it, the man headed straight for the religious authorities who had accused him, and he reported that Jesus was the one they were seeking. Predictably, they "persecuted Jesus, and sought to kill Him, because He had done these things on the Sabbath" (v. 16). As soon as the man confirmed who had healed him, these religious leaders made a beeline to Jesus and began to accuse and threaten Him with stoning.

Under Moses' law, any deliberate and egregious violation of the Sabbath was grounds for stoning (Exodus 31:14; 35:2). One of the earliest recorded Old Testament stonings involved a violation of the Sabbath (Numbers 15:32–36). So the religious authorities now believed they had a convenient, biblically defensible motive for stoning Jesus. The Sanhedrin had the power of life and death in religious matters, even under Roman rule, and they frequently employed it to deal with cases of wanton blasphemy and deliberate sacrilege. It is unlikely that the Romans would sanction the execution of someone who violated the Sabbath accidentally or in a merely superficial way. (And this case was a misdemeanor by any measure). But if the religious leaders could build a credible case that Jesus was a malicious and chronic blasphemer, they could put Him to death without any serious challenge from Rome.

This incident that began at Bethesda seems to have planted that notion in their minds, and that is why the Sabbath quickly becomes the central motif in their conflict with Him. It also explains the obvious change in their strategy from here on out. They become more bold and outspoken in their accusations. They are no longer trying merely to discredit Him; they are bent instead on destroying Him. They begin watching Him with an especially close scrutiny on the Sabbaths. In fact, after this, whenever Jesus heals on the Sabbath, there are always Pharisees present who will challenge Him.

But even though He knew full well that every such occasion would provoke open conflict with them, Jesus never once backed off or abstained from healing openly on the Sabbath. If anything, He seized those opportunities and did His healings as publicly and as conspicuously as possible. Sometimes he announced to the Pharisees beforehand that he intended to work a miracle, practically daring them to condemn the act *before* He did it (cf. Matthew 12:10; Luke 14:3). He did this, of course, not out of any love for contention, but because it was the best way to highlight the error and injustice that was embedded in the Pharisees' system.

As a matter of fact, on the occasion of this very first Sabbath controversy in Jerusalem, Jesus responded to the religious leaders' condemnation by saying something that was practically guaranteed to offend them more than ever—and which did in fact raise their anger with Him to an unprecedented fever pitch.

There were, of course, many good biblical and rational reasons why Jesus' healing on the Sabbath was no violation of Moses' law. Nor was it a sin to tell the man to pick up his bed and go home. First and foremost, "the Sabbath was made for man, and not man for the Sabbath" (Mark 2:27). The Sabbath was given as a *rest* from one's daily labor (Deuteronomy 5:14). It was supposed to be a delight (Isaiah 58:13), not an onerous burden to people. It was always lawful to do good on the Sabbath (Matthew 12:12). Moreover, both common sense and the Pharisees' own tradition taught that certain kinds of work were perfectly acceptable on the Sabbath. Even to "loose [an] ox or donkey from the stall, and lead it away to water it" was officially no Sabbath violation, because it would be cruel to deny the beast the necessities of life. Circumcisions, required by Moses' law to be performed on the eighth day, could be carried out with no restriction even if that day happened to be a Sabbath (John 7:21–23). By what possible debauched notion of mercy would it be considered acceptable to water an ox or circumcise a baby on the Sabbath but a capital crime to loose a man from a burden he had borne some thirty-eight years?

Jesus *could* have made any or all of those arguments, and in subsequent conflicts over Sabbath propriety with the Pharisees, He made all of them and more.

But on this occasion, the very first time the issue arose, Jesus answered the religious leaders with a reply that was practically guaranteed to fan the flames of their contempt for Him to a higher degree than ever. He said simply: "My Father has been working until now, and I have been working" (John 5:17). In other words, God Himself is not bound by any Sabbath restrictions. He continues His labors day and night (Psalm 121:4; Isaiah 27:3). Jesus was claiming the same prerogative for Himself. It was tantamount to saying He was Lord of the Sabbath. It was indeed a claim that only God incarnate could righteously make.

The religious leaders got the message instantly. They were already persecuting Him and insinuating that He ought to be stoned, even before He made that comment. But now their mood took a turn for the worse: "Therefore the Jews sought all the more to kill Him, because He not only broke the Sabbath, but also said that God was His Father, making Himself equal with God" (John 5:18).

The accusation was true enough. He was indeed equating Himself with God. The point is a familiar one. It is the same issue that prompted them to think he was guilty of blasphemy in Capernaum: "Who can forgive sins but God alone?" (Luke 5:21). On that occasion, He had answered with a demonstration of His authority to heal a man whose cure clearly required divine creative power. That put them to silence. But now He was being much more explicit, by claiming God as His Father. It had long been traditional for Jewish people to refer to God as "our Father" in prayer (1 Chronicles 29:10; Isaiah 63:13). But for Jesus to call God *"My* Father" (especially in a context where He was likening Himself to God) was to suggest that He was of the same essence as God the Father—thus "making Himself equal with God."

This, by the way, is only the third time in the chronology of gospel accounts where it is recorded that Jesus used that expression publicly. The first time was when he was twelve years old, when He said to His parents, "Did you not know that I must be about My Father's business?" (Luke 2:49). The second time was when He first cleansed the Temple, saying, "Do not make My Father's house a house of merchandise!" (John 2:16). After this, He frequently speaks of God as "My Father."

On this occasion, however, He was in effect unveiling for the first time so explicitly in public the truth that He was God's only-begotten Son—not just a prophet or brilliant rabbi, but fully God incarnate. As soon as He used that expression here, all hell broke loose against Him. The majority of Israel's religious leaders, already His sworn enemies, "sought all the more to kill Him."

And yet, even here, Jesus' deadliest opponents, apparently fearful of His powerful presence and uncertain of what the public would think (cf. Matthew 24:46), suddenly faded into the background again.

Jesus, by contrast, stood resolutely against them and expounded fearlessly on the ramifications of His own deity in a discourse that runs from John 5:19 through the end of the chapter. Not only did He claim to be equal with God in His *person,* as the religious leaders correctly inferred from the statement in verse 17, but He also claimed equality with the Father in His *works:* "Whatever [the Father] does, the Son also does in like manner" (v. 19). He then described a surpassing intimacy in His own *knowledge* of the Father, and strongly hinted that the Father's whole purpose is to glorify the Son: "The Father loves the Son, and shows Him all things that He Himself does; and He will show Him greater works than these, that you may marvel" (v. 20). He also equated His own *sovereignty* with that of the Father: "As the Father raises the dead and gives life to them, even so the Son gives life to whom He will" (v. 21). He told them the Father had already handed the duty of divine judgment off to Him: "The Father judges no one, but has committed all judgment to the Son" (v. 22, cf. v. 27). And He proclaimed that the Son is worthy of honor equal to that of the Father: "All should honor the Son just as they honor the Father. He who does not honor the Son does not honor the Father who sent Him" (v. 23).

So He was indeed making Himself equal with God. He even went on to ascribe to Himself resurrection power: "Most assuredly, I say to you, the hour is coming, and now is, when the dead will hear the voice of the Son of God; and those who hear will live" (v. 25; cf. vv. 28–29). He said he possesses self-existence, an important attribute of deity, exactly like the Father:[7] "As the Father has life in Himself, so He has granted the Son to have life in Himself" (v. 26). He declared that everything He does is always in perfect harmony with the Father's will: "I can of Myself do nothing. As I hear, I judge; and My judgment is righteous, because I do not seek My own will but the will of the Father who sent Me" (v. 30).

Incidentally, when Jesus disclaimed the notion that He was merely doing His own will, He certainly was not contradicting anything He had just affirmed about His perfect equality with God.[8] Rather, He was declaring that He knew God's will perfectly, and suggesting (by implication, yet clearly enough) that the religious leaders of Israel who were opposing Him had no clue what God's will was.

And yet, Jesus said, "If I bear witness of Myself, My witness is not true." So he finished the discourse of John 5 by citing four un-impeachable witnesses whose testimony proved that He was authen-tic: John the Baptist (vv. 33–35); the miracles and other good works

Jesus had consistently done (v. 36); the Father Himself (v. 37); and the Scriptures (vv. 38–39, 46–47).

Jesus knew full well that none of those witnesses would sway them. For one thing, Jesus said, despite their superreligious veneer, they did not even have the love of God in them (v. 42). Regarding John the Baptist, He told them, "You were willing for a time to rejoice in his light" (v. 35)—but they never really embraced John's teaching. When it came to Jesus' miracles, Israel's leaders had utterly ignored everything He did, except whatever they thought they could twist against Him. Everything else they doubted (v. 38). As far as the Father was concerned, He said, "You have neither heard His voice at any time, nor seen His form" (v. 37). And with regard to the Scripture, "you do not have His word abiding in you, because whom He sent, Him you do not believe" (v. 38).

The whole discourse is one more example of Jesus' candid straightforwardness. A verse-by-verse analysis of the complete passage is far beyond the scope of this book,[9] but it must be noted that this is a firm and explicit denunciation of Israel's top religious leaders, including several statements that rebuke them as total unbelievers ("How can you believe, who receive honor from one another, and do not seek the honor that comes from the only God?"—v. 44). Jesus closes with a powerful final castigation of their whole system, citing the one source they *claimed* to trust—the books of Moses—as a witness against them: "Do not think that I shall accuse you to the Father; there is one who accuses you—Moses, in whom you trust. For if you believed Moses, you would believe Me; for he wrote about Me. But if you do not believe his writings, how will you believe My words?" (vv. 45–47).

Jesus is not doing any bridge building with the religious establishment here; he is upbraiding them, and none too gently. Rather than tiptoeing around their well-known religious sensibilities and trying to avoid offense, He portrays them as utterly unregenerate, spiritually lifeless men (v. 40). And He drives His point home repeatedly, with some of the sharpest words possible: "You do not have His word abiding in you" (v. 38); "You do not have the love of God in you" (v. 42); "You do not believe" (vv. 38, 47).

On the other hand, Jesus is not trying to provoke them merely for sport. He had a gracious reason for using the kind of harsh speech many today would unthinkingly label ungracious: "I say these things that you may be saved," He told them (v. 34). The religious leaders of Israel were lost and progressively hardening their hearts against Jesus. They *needed* some harsh words. He would not permit them to ignore Him, or to ignore His truth, under the guise of showing them the kind of deference and public honor they craved from Him.

Might Jesus have averted all further conflict with the Sanhedrin simply by toning down His message a little and holding a cordial colloquy with the Jewish council right here? Could He have softened their opposition from the start by muting His criticisms of them? Is it possible that they would have left Him alone if He had simply shown them the kind of respect they craved in public contexts, reserving His disagreements for private, friendly, face-to-face contexts?

Perhaps.

But the cause of truth would not have been served by that, and the price of compromise with Israel's religious elite would have been the loss of redemption for all sinners. So Jesus was in fact showing the utmost righteousness and grace, even though He was deliberately provoking them.

THE AFTERMATH

The end of Jesus' discourse is also the end of John 5. No further comments are recorded from the Jewish authorities. But they were by no means letting the matter drop.

Jesus returned to Galilee (John 6:1), and the Pharisees' Galilean delegation immediately began to scrutinize Him with extra diligence on the Sabbath. If we follow the chronology of gospel events,[10] we discover that almost immediately upon His return to Galilee, Jesus' ministry was marked by a series of conflicts with the Pharisees over His repeated failure to observe the Sabbath on their terms.

The first Galilean conflict over the Sabbath occurred when some Pharisees observed Jesus' disciples picking heads of grain as their path took them through a grain field on the Sabbath. According to Luke 6:1, they were merely "passing through"; they were not out in the fields gleaning. But "His disciples plucked the heads of grain and ate them, rubbing them in their hands."

By the Pharisees' reckoning, the hand-rubbing motion, which separated the wheat from the chaff, technically was a form of winnowing; thus it was work, and prohibited on the Sabbath under their rules. They challenged Jesus; He defended His disciples' actions with a multifaceted argument from the Old Testament.

He pointed out first of all that David had eaten the Tabernacle showbread when he was hungry (Matthew 12:3–4). In that obscure Old Testament incident (1 Samuel 21:3–6), David and his men were desperately hungry, and they sought rest and refuge near the Tabernacle. The showbread on the altar had just been replaced with fresh bread (v. 6). Even after being retired from the altar, the older showbread was deemed holy and normally reserved only for the priests. But David asked for the bread anyway, pointing out that his men were ceremonially clean (v. 5) and the bread was technically now common. So the priest complied and gave him the bread. Neither David, nor his men, nor the priest was ever condemned in Scripture for the act. Jesus cited that as proof that *works of necessity and acts of mercy* override the strict requirements of ceremonial law, and thus such works may be done on the Sabbath. As further evidence,

He pointed out that priests in the Temple *must* work on the Sabbath (Matthew 12:5).

Quoting Hosea 6:6, He then said, "If you had known what this means, 'I desire mercy and not sacrifice,' you would not have condemned the guiltless" (v. 7). He was making a clear distinction between the law's moral significance ("mercy") and its ceremonial features ("sacrifice"), and suggesting that the moral intent of the law always trumps picayune ceremonial technicalities. That, of course, is the same lesson He was pointing to in David's eating of the showbread.

This was the occasion when He made those two definitive statements explaining why He refused to bow to the Pharisees' Sabbath legalism: "The Sabbath was made for man, and not man for the Sabbath. Therefore the Son of Man is also Lord of the Sabbath" (Mark 2:27–28).

FILLED WITH RAGE

Shortly after that ("on another Sabbath"—Luke 6:6), He healed a man with a withered hand in a synagogue where He had gone to teach. Luke says plainly, "The scribes and the Pharisees were watching Him closely to see if He healed on the Sabbath, so that they might find reason to accuse Him. But He knew what they were thinking, and He said to the man with the withered hand, 'Get up and come forward!'" (v. 7 NASB).

Once again Jesus deliberately did something He knew would cause friction. Fully aware that the Pharisees were watching Him closely and that they would be deeply offended if He healed this man on the Sabbath, Jesus brought the man to the front of the synagogue and made the healing as emphatically public as He could. He even preceded the healing by openly challenging the Pharisees' error. "I will ask you one thing," he said. "Is it lawful on the Sabbath to do good or to do evil, to save life or to destroy?" (v. 9). Luke suggests that Jesus then made deliberate eye contact with each of His ecclesiastical adversaries just before He healed the man: "When He had looked around at them all, He said to the man, 'Stretch out your hand'" (v. 10).

It was one of those undeniable, divinely empowered miracles involving the power of creation. The arm that had been "withered" (meaning that it was shriveled and physically deformed) was suddenly made whole! Who could doubt that this was the power of God on display?

But the Pharisees in the audience were unmoved by the miracle. Instead, they were aroused with fury against Jesus. "They were filled with rage" (v. 11).

The conventional wisdom of our age would suggest that the way Jesus handled His differences with these Pharisees was wrong. What did He hope to accomplish by doing something He knew would infuriate the Pharisees? Why would He not rather take them aside and try to correct them privately? Why would He not try to be a bridge builder rather than a wall builder? Why would He purposely provoke strife with them rather than trying to make peace with them? And if it was necessary to set them straight on their views about the Sabbath, would it not be better to keep that conflict between Him and them? Why would He provoke these men in front of a crowd of laypeople in a place of worship? Why pick *this* fight with them over an issue that was so dear to them?

But again, Jesus was not provoking the Pharisees for sport or for pleasure. Moreover, this dispute was not merely about who had the right view of *ceremony.* The bigger, underlying issue was still the principle of justification and how sinners can be made right with God. Justification is not earned by merit, nor is it gained through rituals.

True righteousness cannot be earned by human works, but forgiveness and full justification are freely given to those who believe.

In other words, the difference between Jesus and the Pharisees was not that they had differing customs regarding how to observe the Sabbath; it was that they held contradictory views on the way of salvation. That truth was too important to bury under the blanket of an artificial civility. The gospel must be defended against lies and false teaching, and the fact that gospel truth often offends even the most distinguished religious people is *never* a reason for trying to tame the message or tone it down. Jesus Himself is our model for that.

The scribes and Pharisees in Luke 6 were so deeply offended by Jesus that they gathered afterward "and discussed with one another what they might do to Jesus" (v. 11). Mark 3:6 says they "went out and immediately plotted with the Herodians[11] against Him, how they might destroy Him."

The religious authorities' course was set, and their hearts were steadily hardening. Their determination to see Jesus put to death had suddenly developed into a full-fledged plot. Many more conflicts were yet to come, and neither Jesus nor His religious adversaries showed any signs of backing down.

*W*hy mild? Of all the epithets that could be applied to Christ this seems one of the least appropriate. . . . Jesus Christ might well be called "meek," in the sense of being selfless and humble and utterly devoted to what He considered right, whatever the personal cost; but "mild," never!

—J. B. PHILLIPS[12]

6

Hard Preaching

∾

Does this offend you?

John 6:61

*J*esus' conflict with the Pharisees was not a quiet disagreement carried on in a secret corner. Nor did Jesus Himself seek to tone down the public aspect of His running feud with the religious leaders. He had none of the scruples about propriety and politeness that are so prevalent in public theological discourse nowadays. On the contrary, Jesus' preaching was probably the most important aspect of His relentless polemic against the leaders of the Jewish religious establishment and the institutionalized hypocrisy they embodied. It was clear to everyone that the Pharisees' teaching was one of His primary targets, whether He was giving a discourse for His disciples' benefit or preaching to vast multitudes.

As a matter of fact, the whole theme of the Sermon on the Mount (Luke 6; Matthew 5–7) was a critique of the Pharisees' religion. He condemned their doctrine; their phony approach to practical holiness; their pedantic style of Scripture twisting; and their smug overconfidence. The Bread of Life discourse (John 6) likewise provoked such a conflict with the Pharisees that most of Jesus' own followers became seriously uncomfortable. Many of them stopped following Him altogether after that.

In this chapter, we'll survey both of those pivotal messages. Obviously, there is no practical way to do a verse-by-verse exposition of either passage in a book such as this one,[1] but in order to understand Jesus' preaching style, we need to examine a typical message or two in overview fashion. We especially need to note the main traits that epitomize the prophetic and provocative nature of Jesus' preaching.

THE SERMON ON THE MOUNT

Jesus' best-known and longest recorded sermon comes after the halfway point in a timeline of His public ministry.[2] Just before preaching the sermon, Jesus went to the top of a nearby mountain and spent the entire night in prayer (Luke 6:17). At daybreak, He summoned His apostles and chose twelve of them to accompany Him on a daily basis. He also commissioned them to preach as His representatives. And He gave them authority to cast out demons.

It was clear that something remarkable was happening on the mountain that day, because a great multitude of disciples were awaiting Jesus when He came down from the mountain with the newly appointed group of twelve key disciples.

The Sermon on the Mount derives its name from Matthew's description of what happened next: "Seeing the multitudes, He went up on a mountain" (Matthew 5:1). Some have imagined a contradiction between Matthew's description and Luke's, because Luke says, "He came *down* [from the mountain] with them and stood on a level place with a crowd of His disciples and a great multitude of people from all Judea and Jerusalem" (Luke 6:17, emphasis added). Did He go up, or down; and did he teach from the mountain, or from "a level place"? The answer is all of the above. There is a short, barren mountain peak (about 2,700 feet higher than the Sea of Galilee) six and a half miles north northwest of Capernaum. Descend that mountain taking the most direct route toward the lake, and the path goes directly through the village of Chorazin. Due south of Chorazin and west of Capernaum is a plateau that is part of the mountain's lower base. If Jesus (coming *down* from the mountain) encountered the multitudes arriving from Capernaum near the foot of that plateau, He would have gone back *up* to the plateau (a "level place" on the mountain's large base), where there is a perfect natural amphitheater—an ideal location for teaching a multitude. That is, as a matter of fact, the exact site long held by tradition to be the place where Jesus preached the so-called Sermon on the Mount. Today it is popularly known as "The Mount of the Beatitudes."

THE BEATITUDES

Jesus' sermon begins with the beatitudes—that familiar series of blessings on the poor in spirit, pure in heart, peacemakers, and persecuted. There are eight beatitudes in Matthew's account, and combined, they describe the true nature of saving faith.

> Blessed are the poor in spirit, for theirs is the kingdom of heaven. Blessed are those who mourn, for they shall be comforted. Blessed are the meek, for they shall inherit the earth. Blessed are those who hunger and thirst for righteousness, for they shall be filled. Blessed are the merciful, for they shall obtain mercy. Blessed are the pure in heart, for they shall see God. Blessed are the peacemakers, for they shall be called sons

of God. Blessed are those who are persecuted for righteousness'
sake, for theirs is the kingdom of heaven.

Blessed are you when they revile and persecute you, and say
all kinds of evil against you falsely for My sake. Rejoice and be
exceedingly glad, for great is your reward in heaven, for so they
persecuted the prophets who were before you. (Matthew 5:3–12)

The "poor in spirit" (v. 3) are those who know they have no spiritual
resources of their own. "Those who mourn" (v. 4) are repentant
people, truly sorrowful over their own sin. "The meek" (v. 5) are
those who truly fear God and know their own unworthiness in light
of His holiness. "Those who hunger and thirst for righteousness" (v.
6) are those who, having turned from sin, yearn for what God loves
instead. Those four beatitudes are all *inward qualities* of authentic
faith. They describe the believer's state of heart. More specifically,
they describe how the believer sees himself before God: poor, sorrowful, meek, and hungry.

The final four beatitudes describe the *outward manifestations* of
those qualities. They focus mainly on the believer's moral character,
and they describe what the authentic Christian should look like to an
objective observer. "The merciful" (v. 7) are those who, as beneficiar-
ies of God's grace, extend grace to others. "The pure in heart" (v. 8)
describes people whose thoughts and actions are characterized by
holiness. "The peacemakers" (v. 9) speaks mainly of those who spread
the message of "peace with God through our Lord Jesus Christ"
(Romans 5:1)—which is the only true and lasting peace. And obviously, "those who are persecuted for righteousness' sake" (Matthew
5:10) are citizens of Christ's kingdom who suffer because of their
affiliation with Him and their faithfulness to Him. The world hates
them because it hates Him (John 15:18; 1 John 3:1, 13).

The order is significant. The more faithfully a person lives out the first seven beatitudes, the more he or she will experience the persecution spoken of in the eighth.

All those qualities are radically at odds with the world's values. The world esteems pride more than humility; loves merriment rather than mourning; thinks strong-willed assertiveness is superior to true meekness; and prefers the satiety of carnal pleasure over a thirst for real righteousness. The world looks with utter contempt on holiness and purity of heart, scorns every plea to make peace with God, and constantly persecutes the truly righteous. Jesus could hardly have devised a list of virtues more at odds with His culture.

And that was *especially* true of the style of religion that dominated the culture. Consider this: the Pharisees as a group stood on the wrong side of every one of those lines in the sand. Spiritual self-sufficiency defined their whole system. They refused to acknowledge their sin, much less mourn over it. Far from being meek, they were the very embodiment of stubborn, overbearing self-assertiveness. They didn't hunger and thirst for righteousness; they actually thought they had perfected it. They were not merciful but specialized in "bind[ing] heavy burdens, hard to bear, and lay[ing] them on men's shoulders; but they themselves [would] not move them with one of their fingers" (Matthew 23:4). Their hearts were impure, not pure, and Jesus confronted them about that regularly (Matthew 23:27). They were spiritual troublemakers, not peacemakers. And above all, they were the quintessential persecutors of the righteous. Their dealings with Jesus were already beginning to make that clear.

So the Beatitudes were a rebuke to the Pharisees' whole system. Any Pharisees who might have been in the crowd listening to the sermon would certainly have felt personally attacked and publicly humiliated. And if there were any doubt of His intentions, proof that Jesus *meant* to chide them is seen throughout the rest of the Sermon. In fact, the central message of the Sermon on the Mount is summed up in verse 20: "I say to you, that unless your righteousness exceeds the righteousness of the scribes and Pharisees, you will by no means enter the kingdom of heaven." The sermon is a sustained critique of their whole religious system. The Beatitudes are merely an introduction, contrasting the spirit of authentic faith with the hypocrisy of pharisaical self-righteousness.

YOU HAVE HEARD . . . BUT I SAY

After the Beatitudes, Jesus goes straight into an extended discourse on the true meaning of Old Testament law.[3] The rest of Matthew 5 is a systematic, point-by-point critique of the Pharisees' interpretation of Moses' law. Jesus is correcting some of their representative errors.

Some commentators have suggested that Jesus is altering or expanding the moral requirements of Moses' law for a new dispensation. Jesus Himself emphatically said otherwise: "Do not think that I came to destroy the Law or the Prophets. I did not come to destroy but to fulfill. For assuredly, I say to you, till heaven and earth pass away, one jot or one tittle will by no means pass from the law till all is fulfilled" (vv. 17–18).

Furthermore, every principle Jesus used to refute the Pharisees' interpretation of the law was already either stated or plainly implied in the Old Testament. We'll see that very clearly in our survey of this section.

But what is most important to notice here is that Jesus deliberately sets His description of authentic righteousness *against* the religion of the Pharisees. The brunt of the sermon is aimed squarely at them. The Sermon on the Mount is in essence a jeremiad against their unique brand of hypocrisy. That is the singular theme that ties the whole sermon together.

Furthermore, when He singled out these specific misunderstandings of Moses' law, Jesus was clearly impugning the Pharisees' pet doctrines. He was publicly denouncing what they taught. Everyone in the crowd understood that. It was impossible to ignore. Jesus made no effort to make the dichotomy subtle or to outline His differences with them in a delicate fashion. He went for the jugular against their most closely held beliefs. He even mentioned the Pharisees by name and expressly stated that their righteousness was inadequate—lest there be any ambiguity about *whose* doctrine He was refuting.

Immediately after saying, "Unless your righteousness exceeds the righteousness of the scribes and Pharisees, you will by no means enter the kingdom of heaven" (v. 20), he began dismantling their whole system. He attacked their method of interpreting Scripture, their means of applying the law, their notions of guilt and merit, their infatuation with ceremonial minutiae, and their love for moral and doctrinal casuistry.

The major arguments in this section of the sermon are structured in a way that contrasts the Pharisees' interpretation of the law with the law's real meaning, as expounded by Christ: "You have *heard* that it was said to those of old. . . . But *I* say to you . . ." Six times in the second half of Matthew 5, Jesus used that formula or a variation of it (vv. 21–22, 26–28, 31–32, 33–34, 38–39, 43–44). When He spoke of what "you have heard," He was describing the Pharisees' teaching. And in each case, He refuted it.

Again, He was not changing or expanding the law's moral requirements; He was simply reaffirming what the law always meant. "Your commandment is exceedingly broad," David said, as he meditated on the law (Psalm 119:96). The meaning of the Ten Commandments is not exhausted by the wooden literal sense of the words. Jesus says, for example, that the sixth commandment forbids not only literal acts of murder, but murderous attitudes as well—including undue anger, abusive speech, and an unforgiving spirit (vv. 22–25). The seventh commandment forbids not merely acts of adultery, but even an adulterous heart (v. 28). The command to love your neighbor applies not only to friendly neighbors, but also to those who are our enemies (v. 44).

Superficial readers are sometimes inclined to think Jesus was modifying or raising the bar on the standard of Moses' law. After all, He quoted directly from the sixth and seventh commandments (vv. 21, 27), and He cited the Old Testament principle known as *lex talionis* ("an eye for an eye and a tooth for a tooth"—v. 38; cf. Exodus 21:24, Leviticus 24:20, and Deuteronomy 19:21)—then He followed those quotations with "But I say to you . . ." To a casual listener, it might actually sound as if He were changing the law itself, or making a new law that stood in contrast to what the Old Testament had always taught. But remember: Jesus Himself unequivocally denied that notion in verses 17–18.

Instead, what Jesus is doing in this portion of the sermon is unpacking the true and full meaning of the law as it was originally intended—especially in contrast to the limited, narrow, and woodenly literal approach of the Pharisees. Their hermeneutic (the method by which they interpreted Scripture) was laden with sophistry. They could expound for hours on the law's invisible fine points while inventing technical twists and turns to make exceptions to some of the law's most important moral precepts.

For example, the fifth commandment is clear enough: "Honor your father and your mother" (Exodus 20:12). But the Pharisees had a custom whereby "if a man says to his father or mother, 'Whatever profit you might have received from me is Corban'—(that is, a gift to God), then [the Pharisees] no longer let him do anything for his father or his mother" (Mark 7:11–12). In fact, if someone had thus pledged his inheritance to God and then used any of his resources to care for his parents in their old age, the Pharisees would deem that act of charity a sacrilege, because it was a violation of the *Corban* vow. Jesus told them, "[You have made] the word of God of no effect through your tradition which you have handed down. *And many such things you do*" (v. 13, emphasis added).

That was precisely the kind of hermeneutical tomfoolery Jesus was correcting in the Sermon on the Mount. The Pharisees interpreted the seventh commandment strictly as a narrow prohibition against full-fledged adultery. Of course, by defining adultery only in terms of the outward act, they had left their *hearts* totally unguarded. Like many today who wrongly think fantasies are harmless if not acted upon, they felt free to arouse and indulge in sinful appetites in the privacy of their own imaginations—as if their hearts were somehow exempt from the law's standards. Indeed, that very misconception lay at the root of all the Pharisees' errors. It was how they justified all their hypocrisy.

The Pharisees also had a very liberal standard for divorce, in effect allowing a kind of legalized serial adultery. Jesus corrects that error in verses 31–32.

They likewise applied the sixth commandment as narrowly as possible, believing it forbade only actual crimes of homicide. Meanwhile, they actively encouraged hatred for one's enemies (Matthew 5:43), which in effect nurtured murderous attitudes. Verses 39–47 are an extended refutation of that fallacy.

In fact, it is at this point where Jesus raises the issue of the Old Testament's eye-for-an-eye rule. The context of Exodus 21:24–25, where that standard was given, shows that it was a principle designed to *limit* penalties assessed in civil and criminal court cases. It was never supposed to authorize private retaliation for petty insults and personal infractions. It was a principle that kept the *legal* system in check (cf. Exodus 21:1), not a rule designed to unleash neighbor against neighbor in a back-and-forth war of attacks and counterattacks. But the Pharisees had basically turned it into that. Personal vengeance poisoned the social atmosphere of Israel, and the religious leaders justified it by an appeal to Moses. Jesus said that was a total misuse and abuse of Moses' law.

Further proof that Jesus was not altering the law's legal standard is seen in the fact that every principle He gave in rebuttal to the Pharisees' teaching could already be found in the Old Testament. Psalm 37:8–9, for example, plainly states the same principle Jesus said is implied in the law's ban on murder. It even echoes the language of the Beatitudes regarding meekness: "Cease from anger, and forsake wrath; do not fret—it only causes harm. For evildoers shall be cut off; but those who wait on the LORD, they shall inherit the earth."

Likewise, when Jesus said lust is a violation of the moral principle underlying the seventh commandment, he wasn't adding anything to the law. Lust was *expressly* forbidden by the tenth commandment, and it was identified with the sin of adultery in Proverbs 6:25. Of course, the heart is the most important battlefield in the struggle for moral purity (Proverbs 4:23). And since God sees the heart (1 Samuel 16:7; Psalm 139:2; Proverbs 15:11; Jeremiah 17:10), all the sins that take place in a person's imagination are real sins committed before the very face of God (Psalm 90:8). The Pharisees clearly ought to have known that.

Malachi 2:14–16 condemns divorce in language similar to that of the Sermon on the Mount: "The LORD God of Israel says that He hates divorce, for it covers one's garment with violence"(v. 16). Deuteronomy 23:21–23 forbade casual oaths. Lamentations 3:30 spoke of the virtue of turning the other cheek. The duty of loving one's enemy was very clearly spelled out in Exodus 23:4–5: "If you meet your enemy's ox or his donkey going astray, you shall surely bring it back to him again. If you see the donkey of one who hates you lying under its burden, and you would refrain from helping it, you shall surely help him with it." Proverbs 25:21 likewise taught the same principle: "If your enemy is hungry, give him bread to eat; and if he is thirsty, give him water to drink." Those commandments should have also made it perfectly clear that the eye-for-an-eye principle was not intended to be a recipe for personal retribution. God Himself said, "Vengeance is Mine, and recompense" (Deuteronomy 32:35; cf. Psalm 94:1).

Clearly, Jesus was in no way expressing disagreement with Moses' law or amending its moral content. Every principle in the Sermon on the Mount was either plainly stated or clearly implied in the Old Testament. The Sermon on the Mount therefore must be understood as Jesus' *exposition* of Old Testament law, not a different moral standard altogether. He was simply refuting the Pharisees' misconstrued teaching about the law's moral precepts.

Matthew 5 ends with a brief passage aimed at the Pharisees' self-righteous style of separatism. It is part of the section where Jesus is expounding on the duty to love one's neighbors. The Pharisees, in their passion for ceremonial displays of piety, would even cross the road to avoid contact with their enemies lest they be defiled (cf. Luke 10:31–32). That same way of thinking was also behind their frequent complaints about Jesus' close contacts with sinners (Matthew 9:11; Luke 15:2; 19:7). Jesus pointed out that they had set such a pathetically low standard for the second great commandment ("Love your neighbor as yourself"—Matthew 22:39) that even the rankest sinner would have no trouble obeying: "For if you love those who love you, what reward have you? Do not even the tax collectors do the same? And if you greet your brethren only, what do you do more than others? Do not even the tax collectors do so?" (Matthew 5:46–47). In effect He was teaching that the Pharisees' standard of behavior was no better than the morality of any publican.

Jesus then clearly identified the true standard, and it is infinitely higher than that: "You are to be perfect, as your heavenly Father is perfect" (v. 48 NASB).

Obviously, divine perfection is impossible for fallen sinners. That was a major part of the point Jesus was making. The law itself demands absolute perfection (Leviticus 19:2; 20:26; Deuteronomy 18:13; 27:26; cf. James 2:10). No sinner can possibly live up to that standard, which is why we are dependent on grace for salvation. Our own righteousness can never be good enough (Philippians 3:4–9); we desperately need the perfect righteousness that God imputes to those who believe (Romans 4:1–8).

But the Pharisees epitomized the central fallacy of all human religion. "They being ignorant of God's righteousness, [were] seeking to establish their own righteousness" (Romans 10:3). They believed their best would be good enough for God—especially if they adorned their religion with as many carefully crafted ceremonies and rituals as possible. That's where all their trust and all their hope for heaven lay. They of course formally recognized that they, too, were imperfect, but they minimized their own imperfections and covered them with public exhibitions of piety. They were convinced that would be good enough for God, mainly because it made them *seem* so much better than everyone else.

Naturally, any Pharisee who may have been in the audience for the Sermon on the Mount would have understood Jesus' message plainly enough: Their righteousness, with all its stress on pomp and circumcision, simply did not meet the divine standard. They weren't really any better than the tax collectors. And God would *not* accept their imperfect righteousness. Jesus was as direct as possible about that. He could hardly have spoken any words that would hit them harder. According to Him, their religion was utterly worthless.

DO NOT BE LIKE THE HYPOCRITES

Jesus was far from finished with the point. Practically all of Matthew 6 continues with a hammering, point-by-point critique of the most visible traits of Pharisaism. The sermon was not delivered with chapter divisions, of course, so it's important to keep in mind that the whole catalogue of hypocrisies Jesus attacks in chapter 6 comes hard on the heels of His critique of the Pharisees' misinterpretation of the law in chapter 5. In a way, chapter 5 was merely a warmup for what follows, and chapter 6 is just further development of the key proposition set forth in 5:20: "Unless your righteousness exceeds the righteousness of the scribes and Pharisees, you will by no means enter the kingdom of heaven."

Incidentally, even if Jesus had not specifically named the Pharisees, every person in His audience would have known exactly whom He was talking about, if only from the roster of hypocrisies He outlined in chapter 6. Those were the main badges of the Pharisees' religion. A Pharisee's broad phylacteries and the jumbo-sized tassels on the four corners of his robe (cf. Deuteronomy 22:12) were fitting metaphors for the many ways the Pharisees made their religiosity as ostentatious as possible. They were almost constitutionally incapable of doing any act of charity or piety without making a tawdry public display out of it in the process.

That is precisely what most of Matthew 6 is about. Jesus was contrasting the religious exhibitionism of the Pharisees with the authentic faith he had described in the Beatitudes. Faith has its primary impact on the heart of the believer. The Pharisees' religion, by contrast, was mainly for show, "to be seen" by others (Matthew 6:1).

It is the very same contrast the apostle Paul (himself a converted Pharisee) often highlighted between authentic faith and a religion of mere works. True saving faith inevitably produces good works, because it expresses itself in love (Galatians 5:6); but the superficial displays of "charity" in works-religion are not even truly charitable. Because Pharisee-style religion is motivated mainly by a craving for the praise of men, it is inherently self-aggrandizing, making it the very antithesis of authentic charity.

Jesus was definitive about that. He said the hypocrites in the synagogues and on the streets of Jerusalem sought only praise from men, and since that was the only reward that really mattered to them, that was all the reward they would get (v. 2).

He also portrayed them as sounding a trumpet before them when they did charitable deeds (v. 2). There's no record in any of the literature from that era where anyone *actually* held a parade with trumpets when they did their alms. Jesus was painting a colorful word picture, actually making a humorous parody of the Pharisees' spiritual flamboyance. He was using sanctified mockery to expose the silliness of their system. By the standards of today's overtolerant evangelical subculture, such satire would be deemed a mercilessly cruel way to point out the faults of one's adversaries. But again we see that Jesus was not bound by postmodern scruples.

He went on to rebuke the hypocrisy of loud, long public prayers (another specialty of the Pharisees), again saying that the earthly attention such a practice garners is its only reward (v. 5). It was at this point that He first gave the model prayer that has become known as the Lord's Prayer.[4] That prayer's brevity, simplicity, and Godward focus set it apart from the Pharisees' style of praying.

Next, He turned to the subject of fasting, a practice that was badly abused by the Pharisees. Jesus described how they exploited even this highly personal spiritual discipline as a means of billboarding their own righteousness: "They disfigure their faces that they may appear to men to be fasting" (Matthew 6:16). Specifically, they put on "a sad countenance," ostensibly as a token of solemn devotion and grim self-sacrifice. But it in reality it was all a charade—a thin, worn-out veneer that barely covered their totally selfish motives, which were 180 degrees wrong. Of course, legitimate fasting is supposed to be a means of helping us set aside worldly concerns in order to focus on prayer and spiritual things. The Pharisees instead had turned their fasting into another means of parading their piety in public, proving once more that they could not have cared less about heavenly things. What they really cared for was worldly applause. All their fasting had the exact opposite effect of what a fast should do; it drew attention to them, rather than eliminating things that distract. Jesus exposed the hypocrisy of it.

The rest of Matthew 6 (verses 19–34) is a short lesson on the importance of maintaining a heavenly perspective. It sets forth the same principle the apostle Paul would later summarize in Colossians 3:2: "Set your mind on things above, not on things on the earth." Jesus includes a corresponding warning against being consumed with earthly cares. In this section of the Sermon on the Mount He talks about the proper use of our financial resources (vv. 19–24). He also addresses the sin of worry (vv. 25–34). Those who fret about the future, according to Jesus, manifest a lack of trust in God and a skewed sense of priorities.

All of this, too, is merely a continuation of Jesus' diatribe against the Pharisees' approach to religion. The attitude Jesus was condemning was an inevitable fruit of the Pharisees' infatuation with external things. It colored all their thoughts—making them pathologically superficial; giving them a carnal, earthbound perspective; and keeping them from truly trusting God. That's why they (and their disciples) were obsessed with wealth and asphyxiated with worry. This is clearly seen in the rationale underlying their whole conspiracy against Jesus. All their animosity toward Him was driven by a fear that if He came to power as Messiah, they would lose their status, their means of wealth, and all their earthly advantages (John 11:48).[5] Despite all their pious pretenses, those things meant more to them than righteousness. So when Jesus says, "Seek first the kingdom of God and His righteousness, and all these things shall be added to you," He was teaching yet another truth that directly assaulted the Pharisees' value system (v. 33).

BAD TREES, BAD FRUIT

Matthew 7 continues and concludes the Sermon on the Mount with some of Jesus' most devastating denunciations of Pharisaism so far. The chapter starts with an assault on self-righteous judgmentalism. (The Pharisees were masters at that.) Jesus conjures up the humorous imagery of someone with a large piece of wood imbedded in his eye trying to remove a tiny speck from someone else's eye (vv. 1–5). This was another verbal caricature about the Pharisees, who would do things like criticizing the disciples for rubbing a handful of grain on the Sabbath (Matthew 12:2), but whose own hearts and minds were private dens of iniquity, given over to all kinds of evil thinking (v. 34).

It is crucial to understand verse 1 properly. "Judge not, that you be not judged" is not a blanket condemnation of all kinds of judgment—just the hypocritical, superficial, and misguided kinds of judgments the Pharisees made. The context makes clear that this is a call for charity and generosity in the judgments we make, "For with what judgment you judge, you will be judged; and with the measure you use, it will be measured back to you" (v. 2). It is often necessary to make judgments, and when we do, we must "not judge according to appearance, but judge with righteous judgment" (John 7:24).

Jesus' own words make it clear that He expects us to make discerning judgments, because He goes on to say, "Do not give what is holy to the dogs; nor cast your pearls before swine" (v. 6). "Swine" and "dogs" in that verse refer to people who are chronically antagonistic to the gospel—those whose predictable response to sacred things is that they will "trample them under their feet, and turn and tear [the messenger] in pieces" (v. 6). Obviously, in order to obey that command, we have to know who the swine and dogs are. So an underlying assumption is that we *must* judge carefully and biblically.

But what is most intriguing here is that Jesus was clearly alluding to the Pharisees and others like them, not to the Gentiles and moral pariahs who were normally labeled "swine" and "dogs" by Israel's religious elite. Pigs and dogs were unclean animals under Old Testament law, of course. So swine were never raised by Jewish people as domesticated livestock. Dogs were not kept as house pets. Both species were generally thought of only as wild, bad-tempered scavengers. Naturally, those labels carried a very strong connotation of uncleanness and inhumanity. They were normally applied only to society's lowest outcasts and untouchables.

Remember, however, that Jesus had a vibrant ministry among the very people who were usually on the receiving end of such epithets. That is why the Pharisees derisively called Him "a glutton and a winebibber, a friend of tax collectors and sinners" (Luke 7:34). Given the context of the Sermon on the Mount and Jesus' relentless assault on the Pharisees' hypocrisy and religious exhibitionism, it is clear whom He had in mind when He forbade casting pearls before swine. It was not the repentant publicans and sinners to whom He regularly showed mercy.

Jesus Himself modeled the kind of discretion He is calling for here. He regularly "[hid] things from the wise and prudent and revealed them to babes" (Luke 10:21). In other words, to humble and repentant people, He always gave more and taught more. But He deliberately concealed truth from arrogant and self-righteous people, "so that 'seeing they may see and not perceive, and hearing they may hear and not understand'" (Mark 4:12). His parables served this very purpose: they obscured the truth from people whose hearts had grown dull and whose spiritual ears were hard of hearing (Matthew 13:15). He did not give sacred things to dogs or cast His pearls before swine.

In short, swine and dogs represent the spiritual antitheses of "those who hunger and thirst for righteousness" (Matthew 5:6). The former are puffed up with self and predisposed to reject *any* truth that does not fit their agenda. They will then turn against the messenger and rend him or her in pieces. That is precisely what the Pharisees and their co-conspirators were already poised to do to Jesus.

But the spiritually famished—those who know they are sick and need a physician (Luke 5:31)—will turn from everything else for the life-giving, thirst-quenching, soul-satisfying truth they seek. Jesus always reached out tenderly to all such people.

This sermon is no exception. Although the sermon is full of criticisms aimed at Pharisee-style religiosity, remember that it started with words of grace for the poor in spirit, parched souls, and the pure in heart. As Jesus begins the concluding section of His message, He returns to that same theme:

> "Ask, and it will be given to you; seek, and you will find; knock, and it will be opened to you. For everyone who asks receives, and he who seeks finds, and to him who knocks it will be opened. Or what man is there among you who, if his son asks for bread, will give him a stone? Or if he asks for a fish, will he give him a serpent? If you then, being evil, know how to give good gifts to your children, how much more will your Father who is in heaven give good things to those who ask Him!" (Matthew 7:7–11)

The remainder of Jesus' sermon includes a summary and final appeal. The summary is a single verse, the so-called Golden Rule: "Therefore, whatever you want men to do to you, do also to them, for this is the Law and the Prophets" (v. 12). (Notice, by the way, that a right understanding of the Law's moral demands is the polar opposite of the Pharisees' misinterpretation of the Law's *lex talionis*. They twisted a statement meant to limit penalties into a principle that justified personal revenge—doing to others whatever they have done to offend you. Jesus said the true governing moral principle of the law, rightly understood, is *love*—meaning preemptively doing to others what you want them to do to you.)

By saying, "this is the Law and the Prophets" Jesus did not mean, of course, that the law was thereby reduced to the horizontal demands of the Golden Rule alone. He was saying the principle of love that defines the Golden Rule is the underlying principle of all the law. Elsewhere (Matthew 22:36–40) Jesus made it clear that the law demands love for God as well as love for one's neighbors. A true love for God is also implicit in the Golden Rule, given the full context of the larger sermon—especially Matthew 5:45, which states that loving one's neighbors is the way to be like our heavenly Father.

THE BROAD WAY TO DESTRUCTION

The final plea of the Sermon on the Mount is a general invitation to "enter by the narrow gate; for wide is the gate and broad is the way that leads to destruction, and there are many who go in by it. Because narrow is the gate and difficult is the way which leads to life, and there are few who find it" (Matthew 7:13–14). The narrow gate and difficult road are references to the gospel's demand for total self-denial and humility—and all the other qualities highlighted in the beatitudes.

Proud and unbroken sinners always choose the wrong road. That's why it is full of travelers. It's broad enough for everyone from out-and-out libertines to the strictest Pharisees. All of them like it, because no one has to bow low or leave any baggage behind in order get on this highway. Furthermore, all the road signs promise heaven.

There's just one problem, and it's a significant one: the road does not actually go to heaven. It leads instead to utter destruction.

Furthermore, Jesus says, the world is full of false prophets who steer people onto the broad road. Beware of them. They "come to you in sheep's clothing, but inwardly they are ravenous wolves" (v. 15). He might well be painting a verbal portrait of the Pharisees. This is, in fact, a generic description of *all* false prophets in all ages, but the religious elite of Israel epitomized everything He was talking about. That fact was surely not lost on them, or on the general audience.

"You will know them by their fruits," Jesus said (v. 16). The imagery of bad trees with bad fruit had special significance for the Pharisees. Some Pharisees and Sadducees had come to John the Baptist not many months before this. Apparently they saw how popular John was, and they wanted the admiration of his followers. John called them the offspring of vipers and told them to "bear fruits worthy of repentance" (Matthew 3:7–8). Then he added, "Even now the ax is laid to the root of the trees. Therefore every tree which does not bear good fruit is cut down and thrown into the fire" (v. 10)—and began to prophesy about Jesus. Now, in wrapping up His Sermon on the Mount, Jesus employed the very same imagery, and even quoted John the Baptist's exact words: "Every good tree bears good fruit, but a bad tree bears bad fruit. A good tree cannot bear bad fruit, nor can a bad tree bear good fruit. *Every tree that does not bear good fruit is cut down and thrown into the fire.* Therefore by their fruits you will know them" (7:17–20, emphasis added). Those were strong words of condemnation, and though Jesus' admonition was not limited to religious leaders only, no one could possibly miss the fact that Jesus was treading directly on the toes of the Pharisees and Sadducees.

A MESSAGE FOR THE MASSES

Nevertheless, it would be wrong to conclude that the Sermon on the Mount was only—or even *mainly*—preached for the benefit of Israel's hypocritical religious leaders. While the Pharisees and Sadducees epitomized the hypocrisy and self-righteousness Jesus targeted, they were by no means the only ones with whom He was pleading. He was speaking to everyone on the broad road. His description of the judgment that awaits at the end of that road is chilling:

> "Not everyone who says to Me, 'Lord, Lord,' shall enter the kingdom of heaven, but he who does the will of My Father in heaven. Many will say to Me in that day, 'Lord, Lord, have we not prophesied in Your name, cast out demons in Your name, and done many wonders in Your name?' And then I will declare to them, 'I never knew you; depart from Me, you who practice lawlessness!' Therefore whoever hears these sayings of Mine, and does them, I will liken him to a wise man who built his house on the rock: and the rain descended, the floods came, and the winds blew and beat on that house; and it did not fall, for it was founded on the rock. But everyone who hears these sayings of Mine, and does not do them, will be like a foolish man who built his house on the sand: and the rain descended, the floods came, and the winds blew and beat on that house; and it fell. And great was its fall." (Matthew 7:21–27)

The word *many* echoes through the passage. *Many* go in by the wide gate onto the broad road (v. 13). *Many* will say "Have we not . . .

done *many* wonders?" (v. 22). But notice: It's not merely Pharisees and Sadducees who will try to argue at the judgment seat that their works ought to be sufficient to get them into heaven. Jesus is describing people who profess to be Christians. They call Jesus "Lord, Lord." They claim to have done mighty works *in His name.* But He sends them away with these soul-shattering words: "I never knew you; depart from Me."

So it turns out the Sermon on the Mount is not a message just for the Pharisees, even though Jesus attacked their beliefs from the start of the sermon through its conclusion. The underlying message is chiefly for disciples, and it is a warning to them, lest they fall into the very same errors that turned the Pharisees' religion into a monstrosity that was odious to God and made them hostile to the truth.

MORE HARD WORDS FOR DISCIPLES

Those final words from the Sermon on the Mount left people breathless. They "were astonished at His teaching, for He taught them as one having authority, and not as the scribes" (vv. 28–29).

The Pharisees could not teach without citing this or that rabbi and resting on the pedigree of centuries-long traditions. Their religion was academic in practically every sense of that word. And to many of them, teaching was just another opportunity to seek praise from men—by showing off their erudition. They took great pride in citing as many sources as possible, carefully footnoting their sermons. They were more concerned with what others said about the law than they were with what the law itself actually taught. They had thus learned the law without ever really listening to it (cf. Galatians 4:21).

Jesus, by contrast, quoted no authority other than the Word of God itself. He gave its interpretation without buttressing His point of view with endless quotations from earlier writers. If he cited religious scholars at all, it was to refute them. He spoke as one who *has* authority, because He does. He is God, and His style of delivery reflected that. His words were full of love and tenderness toward repentant sinners—but equally full of hard sayings and harsh-sounding words for the self-righteous and self-satisfied. As we have seen from the start, He wasn't inviting an exchange of opinions, giving an academic lecture, or looking for common cause with the religious leaders of the land; He was declaring the Word of God *against* them.

That was every bit as shocking in Jesus' culture as it would be in ours. Don't miss the real import of verses 28–29. People weren't exactly delighted by Jesus' approach. They were "astonished" at first. Soon they would grow angry.

For His part, the more Jesus preached to the same crowds again and again, the more His messages were filled with rebukes and urgent pleas for their repentance. He was not impressed with the size or enthusiasm of large crowds. He was not interested in accumulating the kind of disciples whose main concern was for what they might get out of the relationship. He never upholstered his message to make it more cushy for popular opinion, and he never turned down the rhetorical heat in order to keep the congregation as comfortable as possible. If anything, His approach was the exact opposite. He seemed to do everything He could to disquiet the merely curious who were unconverted. They absolutely loved it when He did miracles. He rebuked them for that, and He made sure they could not ignore His *message*.

As we noted earlier, the site where Jesus preached the Sermon on the Mount was situated somewhere between the villages of Capernaum and Chorazin. Not many days after He gave that sermon, Jesus preached another sermon at or very near the same spot. Matthew 11:20–24 describes what happened:

Then He began to rebuke the cities in which most of His mighty works had been done, because they did not repent: "Woe to you, Chorazin! Woe to you, Bethsaida! For if the mighty works which were done in you had been done in Tyre and Sidon, they would have repented long ago in sackcloth and ashes. But I say to you, it will be more tolerable for Tyre and Sidon in the day of judgment than for you. And you, Capernaum, who are exalted to heaven, will be brought down to Hades; for if the mighty works which were done in you had been done in Sodom, it would have remained until this day. But I say to you that it shall be more tolerable for the land of Sodom in the day of judgment than for you."

Harsh words, indeed. That reproof signaled another major change in Jesus' public ministry. From that time forth, He moved around Galilee more and focused more on private instruction for a steadily decreasing circle of the most devoted disciples. His subsequent public discourses tended to be more urgent and more severe.

THE BREAD OF LIFE DISCOURSE

John 6 contains one of the best-known examples of Jesus' hard preaching. The chapter also chronicles the rejection of Jesus by a large number of people who had once followed Him closely enough to be numbered among His disciples. When His message began to sound harsh and offensive, they turned away in droves.

The beginning of John 6 features the feeding of the five thousand. (That is the only one of Jesus' miracles besides His resurrection to be recorded in all four gospels, so it is clearly an important event.) As the chapter begins, Jesus is ministering near the shore of Galilee (v. 1) to that "great multitude" (vv. 2, 5) of *at least* five thousand people (v. 10).

The gospel writers all agree on that number. It was a sizable crowd (especially given the fact that Jesus spoke to them outdoors without any amplification or acoustical aids). It is an especially astonishing number considering that the total population of Capernaum could not have been more than 1,700.[6] But some of the people following Jesus had come from fair distances. Mark 3:7–8 says, "A great multitude from Galilee followed; and also from Judea, and from Jerusalem, and from Idumea, and beyond the Jordan, and the vicinity of Tyre and Sidon, a great number of people heard of all that He was doing and came to Him." They must have filled every available place of lodging in Capernaum, Chorazin, Bethsaida, and all the surrounding villages. Those who could not find lodging would find places to camp in the region. All of Galilee was abuzz with activity and talk about Jesus.

That is the picture we see at the start of John 6: enthusiastic multitudes coming to see Jesus from faraway regions, all of them excited about His miracles and devoted enough to come and learn from Him in person. The natural human response would be to take this as a wholly positive sign that Jesus was making a major impact on His culture. He was accumulating followers who would be able to take His message back to their own communities. It looked for all the world like it might be the start of a grassroots movement that had the potential of influencing the whole world.

Indeed, it was that. But the big picture was not nearly as positive as it appeared at first glance. Jesus' strategy was not to accumulate crowds of thousands whose main interest was seeing miracles. His energies were focused on training eleven disciples who were the backbone of His entire plan. *They* were the key to the church's eventual worldwide expansion. As for the crowds, there were no doubt many true believers among them, as well as many halfhearted hangers-on. Jesus fearlessly and unapologetically gave them all the message they

153

needed to hear—in unvarnished terms. He was impossible to ignore, and the truth He taught was impossible to miss.

John 6 is a record of how all the public goodwill generated by Jesus' miracles gave way to anger and outrage because of the message He proclaimed. The massive crowds dwindled to virtually nothing in the course of a few verses.

Jesus' deity is a major theme in John 6. We have already surveyed the Sabbath controversy in Jerusalem recorded in John 5. You will recall that Jesus' deity became the focus of that conflict, too, when He responded to the charge of Sabbath breaking by claiming the prerogatives of God (John 5:17)—and even claiming that He is worthy of equal honor from all who truly worship God: "so that all will honor the Son even as they honor the Father. He who does not honor the Son does not honor the Father who sent Him" (5:23). As we noted, the rest of John 5 is a catalog of witnesses who affirmed Jesus' deity.

John 6 continues with more proofs of Jesus' deity as He feeds the five thousand, walks on water, and declares that He is the bread of life.

But the majority of the chapter is devoted to a sermon known as the "Bread of Life discourse."

The setting is important. Jesus had fed the multitudes somewhere on the eastern shore of Galilee, then (walking on water in stormy weather) had gone back to Capernaum (on the North shore) to get away from the passionate crowd. When word reached Tiberias (on the western shore) about the feeding of the five thousand, many more people came looking for Jesus, hoping for a repeat performance.

The multitudes, now numbering more than five thousand, found Jesus in Capernaum (John 6:24–25; cf. v. 59). His message began with a rebuke of their motives: "Most assuredly, I say to you, you seek Me, not because you saw the signs, but because you ate of the loaves and were filled. Do not labor for the food which perishes, but for the food which endures to everlasting life, which the Son of Man will give you, because God the Father has set His seal on Him" (vv. 26–27).

He wanted to talk to them about spiritual things; they were interested mainly in lunch. They began to bargain for a repeat performance of the previous day's miracle. They said they would hear what He had to say *if* He would give them food. As if to put a spiritual spin on the demand, they pointed out that, after all, the manna of Moses' day was literal food that could be eaten: "Our fathers ate the manna in the desert; as it is written, 'He gave them bread from heaven to eat'" (v. 31).

Jesus continued to speak of a different kind of food from heaven—"*true* bread." But, He said, the bread that gives life is a Person, not an edible substance that could be kept in a jar like manna: "For the bread of God is He who comes down from heaven and gives life to the world" (v. 33).

They were still looking for lunch—still seeking a way to feed their physical appetites—when they said, "Lord, give us this bread always" (v. 34).

The back-and-forth dialogue makes a frustrating study in misunderstanding and spiritual blindness. The voices from the crowd were demanding literal food; Jesus was speaking of something infinitely more important. But they would not see it. There was clearly a tone of testiness and arrogance in their repeated demands (v. 30). It was also obvious that they would not be satisfied with a single encore of the previous day's miracle. "Give us this bread *always*" implies that they wanted Jesus to produce food from heaven every day from then on—like a genie who would magically grant them any wish that struck their fancy. After all, they suggested, that's very much like what Moses did for the Israelites in the wilderness. The manna came every day.

These people were basically offering to make a deal with Jesus: they would believe in Him if He would agree to make food for them from now on, whenever they demanded it.

Jesus certainly *could* have given them food (or anything else they wanted) whenever they wanted. It would have been a very seeker-sensitive way to guarantee that the ranks of His followers would never diminish. Who would not be willing to forsake everything and become His disciple if He could guarantee a life of ease and perpetual food from heaven?

But Jesus was not there to discuss the lunch menu with them, much less barter for their faith by doing miracles on demand. He was going to talk to them about spiritual things. So He said plainly: "I am the bread of life" (v. 35).

That statement instantly brought murmuring protests from the religious leaders in the crowd. They saw clearly that He was claiming to be more than a mere man. They "complained about Him, because He said, 'I am the bread which came down from heaven.' And they said, 'Is not this Jesus, the son of Joseph, whose father and mother we know? How is it then that He says, 'I have come down from heaven'?" (vv. 41–42).

Jesus met their disapproval head-on: "Do not murmur among yourselves. . . . I am the bread of life" (vv. 43, 48). It ought to have been perfectly clear that He was speaking of *spiritual* nourishment and *spiritual* life, because He also said, "He who believes in Me has everlasting life" (v. 47). The doctrine of justification by faith was clearly implied in that statement. He was giving them the very heart of gospel truth, if they had spiritual ears to hear.

He even explained why the true bread of life is superior to Moses' manna: "Your fathers ate the manna in the wilderness, and are dead. This is the bread which comes down from heaven, that one may eat of it and not die" (vv. 49–50). So this bread could give them spiritual life instead of mere physical nourishment, and the bread was Christ Himself. He was clearly explaining a profound spiritual reality, not describing literal food to be ingested by mouth.[7]

John the Baptist had publicly testified that Jesus was the Lamb of God to take away the sin of the world. Jesus' words echoed that prophecy: "The bread that I shall give is My flesh, which I shall give for the life of the world" (v. 51). The words are full of paschal imagery, revealing Christ as the fulfillment of everything the sacrificial system signified. Just as the symbolic Passover lamb was a feast designed to be eaten, Christ (the *true* paschal Lamb) was a spiritual banquet to be received by faith. He was the fulfillment of everything the manna and the Passover feast symbolized, and more.

If the multitudes had shown the least bit of interest in hearing the truth, they would have sought clarification of what they did not understand. Jesus was clearly speaking to them about spiritual realities. From the beginning of this increasingly contentious conversation, they had resisted that and clamored for a free lunch instead. Now they were incapable of thinking in other than literal terms.

"The Jews therefore quarreled among themselves, saying, 'How can this Man give us His flesh to eat?'" (v. 52). Remember that John regularly uses the expression "the Jews" to signify the hostile religious leaders. They were apparently at the head of this crowd.

Notice that Jesus did not stop them at that point and say, "No, you misunderstand. Let me explain what I mean." They had shown no interest in understanding Him, so He persisted with His difficult analogy. In fact, He pressed the metaphor even harder this time: "Most assuredly, I say to you, unless you eat the flesh of the Son of Man and drink His blood, you have no life in you. Whoever eats My flesh and drinks My blood has eternal life, and I will raise him up at the last day. For My flesh is food indeed, and My blood is drink indeed. He who eats My flesh and drinks My blood abides in Me, and I in him" (vv. 53–56). Four times in quick succession He spoke of not only eating His flesh, but also drinking His blood.

The symbolic meaning of eating His flesh might have been somewhat transparent to anyone who remembered that the Messiah was the sacrificial lamb who would take away the sin of the world. But when He spoke of drinking His blood, He was using language guaranteed to offend His Jewish audience. The consumption of blood of any kind was deemed grossly unclean under Old Testament law. "You shall not eat the blood of any flesh, for the life of all flesh is its blood. Whoever eats it shall be cut off" (Leviticus 17:14). Kosher food preparation to this day involves carefully removing every trace of blood from meat. In that culture, the idea of consuming blood was considered repulsive in the extreme.

The voices in the crowd had been stubbornly insistent on talking about literal food. The clearer Jesus made it that He was speaking figuratively about spiritual life and spiritual nourishment, the angrier the contrarians became, and the more offensive His words sounded—especially to the Jewish leaders who considered themselves guardians of public piety and ceremonial purity. But finally, even some of Jesus' own disciples began to whisper among themselves, "This is a hard saying; who can understand it?" (v. 60).

Jesus, knowing full well what they were thinking, simply said, "Does this offend you? What then if you should see the Son of Man ascend where He was before? It is the Spirit who gives life; the flesh profits nothing. The words that I speak to you are spirit, and they are life. But there are some of you who do not believe" (vv. 61–64). Thus He declared plainly that He was using spiritual words to speak of spiritual things. He offered no exegesis of His symbolism and no clarification for the benefit of those who had already become angry with Him. Their failure to grasp His meaning was a fruit of their own belief, He said. And John reminds us, "Jesus knew from the beginning who they were who did not believe, and who would betray Him" (v. 64). That, of course, is another echo of John 2:24 ("Jesus did not commit Himself to them, because He knew all men").

It was the end of the discourse. Jesus punctuated it with these words: "Therefore I have said to you that no one can come to Me unless it has been granted to him by My Father" (v. 65). He was referring to an earlier statement, recorded in verse 44: "No one can come to Me unless the Father who sent Me draws him." The implication was that wickedness and rebellion are so deeply ingrained in the character of fallen sinners that apart from divine grace, no one would ever believe. Those were no doubt the final words many of them ever heard from Jesus. After all the miracles and gracious works they had seen Him do, this ought to have moved them to plead for grace, mercy, and new hearts. Instead, John says, "From that time many of His disciples went back and walked with Him no more" (v. 66). The verb tense means they ceased following Him permanently. What a tragedy! They had heard Jesus preach in person. They had seen Him do miracles. They had even followed Him around like disciples. But they turned away without ever really knowing what it was to have a true disciple's heart; without coming to authentic faith in Him; without understanding even the basics of His message.

Jesus did not run after them with an explanation of what He really meant. He let the multitudes leave, then turned to the Twelve and said, "Do you also want to go away?" Peter, speaking as usual for the group, assured Him of their intention to stay on as disciples, and Jesus simply replied, "Did I not choose you, the twelve, and one of you is a devil?" (v. 70).

Jesus was not being pugnacious, though He probably would be accused of that by some of today's sensitive evangelicals who think conflict of any kind is always unspiritual. He was being *truthful*—in a bold, clear way calculated to force them to declare whether or not they likewise loved the truth. He was asking true disciples to declare themselves; he was exposing the enmity of His antagonists; and He was forcing the halfhearted multitudes who were halting between two decisions to choose either one side or the other.

There were clearly aspects of the Pharisees' doctrine Jesus *could* have singled out to declare that He had some "common ground" with them. There was much positive energy in the initial eagerness of the crowds who followed Jesus. He might have harnessed that and doubled or tripled the size of His congregation.

He did not do that. He did the exact opposite—deliberately. Again, He was not interested in increasing the ranks of halfhearted disciples. His preaching had one aim: to declare truth, not to win accolades from the audience. For those who were not interested in hearing the truth, He did not try to make it easier to receive. What He did instead was make it impossible to ignore.

NOT A TAME PREACHER

Before we wrap up this chapter, it's worth pausing to consider how Jesus' preaching might come across if He spoke that way in a stadium filled with typical twenty-first-century evangelicals. Because let's be candid: Jesus' style of preaching was nothing at all like most of the popular preaching we hear today—and His style of preaching isn't likely to generate the kind of enthusiastic arm waving and feel-good atmosphere today's Christians typically like to see at their mass meetings and outdoor music festivals.

Survey the current plethora of websites devoted to supplying preachers with prefabricated sermon material, and you'll get a very clear picture of what constitutes "great preaching" in the minds of most twenty-first-century evangelicals: trendiness; funny anecdotes; slick packaging; clever audio-visual aids; and short, stylish, topical homilies on themes borrowed from pop culture. Favorite subjects include marriage and sex, human relationships, self-improvement, personal success, the pursuit of happiness, and anything else that pleases audiences—especially if the topic or sermon title can easily be tied into the latest hit movie, must-watch TV series, or popular song. In the trendiest churches, you are more likely to hear the preacher quote lyrics from Bono and U2 than from David and the Psalms. One megachurch sponsored a four-part sermon series in which their pastor did a word-by-word exegesis of passages taken from Dr. Seuss books, starting with *Horton Hatches the Egg.* The pastor of one of America's five largest churches put a king-sized bed on the platform as a prop while he preached a five-week series on sex. A year or so later, the same church made national headlines by promoting yet another series with a "sex challenge" so blatantly inappropriate that even some in the secular media expressed shock and outrage.

Such shenanigans come under the rubric of *relevance* in the catalog of contemporary church-growth strategies. Sermons featuring straight biblical exposition, precise doctrine, difficult truths, or negative-sounding topics are strongly discouraged by virtually all the leading gurus of cultural relevance. And the people filling evangelical pews "love to have it so" (Jeremiah 5:31). "Speak to us smooth things" (Isaiah 30:10) is their constant demand. Teaching, reproof, correction, and training in righteousness (cf. 2 Timothy 3:16) are out. Catering to itchy ears is in (cf. 4:3). No truly clued-in preacher nowadays would think to fill his message with reproof, rebuke, or exhortation (cf. 4:2). Instead, he does his best to suit the felt needs, preoccupations, and passions of the audience. Many contemporary pastors study pop culture as diligently as the Puritans used to study Scripture. They let congregational opinion polls determine what they should preach, and they are prepared to shift directions quickly if the latest survey tells them their approval ratings are beginning to drop.

That, of course, is precisely what Paul told Timothy *not* to do. "Preach the word! . . . in season and out of season" (v. 2).

The contemporary craving for shallow sermons that please and entertain is at least partly rooted in the popular myth that Jesus Himself was always likable, agreeable, winsome, and at the cutting edge of His culture's fashions. The domesticated, meek-and-mild Savior of today's Sunday-school literature would never knowingly or deliberately offend someone in a sermon—would He?

As we have seen, even a cursory look at Jesus' preaching ministry reveals a totally different picture. Jesus' sermons *usually* featured hard truths, harsh words, and high-octane controversy. His own disciples complained that His preaching was too hard to hear!

That's why Jesus' preaching heads the list of things that make Him impossible to ignore. No preacher has ever been more bold, prophetic, or provocative. No style of public ministry could possibly be more irksome to those who prefer a comfortable religion. Jesus made it impossible for any hearer to walk away indifferent. Some left angry; some were deeply troubled by what He had to say; many had their eyes opened; and many more hardened their hearts against His message. Some became His disciples, and others became His adversaries. But no one who listened to Him preach for very long could possibly remain unchanged or apathetic.

I believe it to be a grave mistake to present Christianity as something charming and popular with no offence in it. Seeing that Christ went about the world giving the most violent offense to all kinds of people, it would seem absurd to expect that the doctrine of his person can be so presented as to offend nobody. We cannot blink at the fact that gentle Jesus, meek and mild, was so stiff in His opinions and so inflammatory in His language that He was thrown out of church, stoned, hunted from place to place, and finally gibbeted as a firebrand and a public danger. Whatever His peace was, it was not the peace of an amiable indifference.

—DOROTHY SAYERS[8]

7

Unpardonable Sin

❧

Brood of vipers! How can you, being evil, speak good things?
For out of the abundance of the heart the mouth speaks.

Matthew 12:34

𝒪ne other major turning point in Jesus' public dealings with the Jewish leaders must be mentioned. Some of the Pharisees who had been stalking Jesus suddenly went from accusing Him of blasphemy to committing an unpardonable blasphemy of their own. These religious experts, who were so outraged when Jesus declared a publican's sins instantly forgiven, were about to hear Him pronounce their sin *un*forgivable.

According to the best, simplest harmonies of the Gospels, this chapter of Jesus' conflict with the Pharisees began with a spectacular healing that occurred sometime after the Sermon on the Mount but before the events of John 6. During this period of His ministry, Jesus was doing some itinerant preaching in the villages of Galilee (Luke 8:1). He was traveling with the Twelve, plus a small group of women who no doubt cared for the domestic needs of Jesus and His disciples—and who, according to Luke, "provided for Him from their substance" (Luke 8:3). One of the women was the wife of Herod's personal steward, so they obviously had means by which to help meet whatever financial needs were associated with travel and ministry.

However, the daily demands on Jesus' time were so overwhelming in those days that the little group "could not so much as eat bread" (Mark 3:20).

During that phase of His ministry, Jesus had a significant run-in with a group of Pharisees whose antagonism to Him literally knew no bounds. They were so set on discrediting Him that they committed an act of gross blasphemy against the Spirit of God and thereby sealed their doom with absolute finality. Jesus' condemnation of their blasphemy stands out as one of the most chilling warnings in all of Scripture.

Matthew recounts the incident and its aftermath immediately after describing the healing of the man with a withered hand. The two events no doubt happened in quick succession—separated, perhaps, by a few days at most. So the Pharisees were still fuming over Jesus' supposed violation of their Sabbath rules. They continued to look for ways to discredit Him, but frankly, they had run out of arguments. It was absolutely clear to the multitudes that Jesus spoke for God, because there was no miracle He could not accomplish, no ailment He could not heal, and no argument from the Jewish leaders He could not answer.

Israel's religious elite were desperate. The apostle John describes a major council meeting in Jerusalem that took place either during this same phase of Jesus' ministry or shortly afterward. It gives us a window into how the Sanhedrin were thinking and what they were planning: "Then the chief priests and the Pharisees gathered a council and said, 'What shall we do? For this Man works many signs. If we let Him alone like this, everyone will believe in Him, and the Romans will come and take away both our place and nation'" (John 11:47–48).

Notice: they did not dispute the legitimacy of His claim that He was the Messiah or the reality of His miracles. They had no real argument against His doctrine, either—other than the fact that He represented a serious threat to their power.

In short, they feared the Romans more than they feared God. They wanted to hang on to the clout they had, rather than yield their honor and obedience to Israel's rightful Messiah. They loved their own artificial piety more than they craved authentic righteousness. They were satisfied with their own merits and contemptuous of anyone who questioned their godliness—as Jesus had done publicly and repeatedly. From the time He first entered public ministry, he had stood resolutely against their whole system of religion, and they hated Him for it.

That is why Jesus' miracles made no impact on them whatsoever. They would not have thought differently about Him even if He had called down fire from heaven in their presence. They would not have liked him any more if He had literally banished every last vestige of illness and suffering from the entire nation. They would have hated Him no matter what He did, as long as He refused to affirm and honor *them*. And He steadfastly refused to do that under any circumstances.

No wonder. Their own words reveal the evil in their hearts. They had all the evidence they needed in order to believe He was who He claimed to be. In fact, they were now convinced that if they simply "let Him alone like this, everyone [would soon] believe in Him" (John 11:48). They were determined to keep that from happening at all costs. As we have seen, they were already aggressively conspiring to kill Him. But that would take time. (For a helpful gauge of how much planning and premeditation went into the murder of Jesus, simply note that the crucifixion was still at least a year away at this point.) In the meantime, the Pharisees would resort to whatever means they could to discredit or embarrass Him. They stepped up their efforts to shadow Him wherever He went. From here on, whenever Jesus taught in public, the Sanhedrin had their representatives there, ready to criticize His every word and action from the sidelines.

THE HEALING AND DELIVERANCE

As we have seen already, the withered-hand healing of Matthew 12 was one of the most remarkable of all Jesus' miracles, because the man's desiccated arm was instantly made whole and healthy before everyone's eyes. That healing, which we examined from Luke's account, filled the Pharisees with rage (Luke 6:11). It thus became the incident that sparked their determination to put Him to death. In Matthew's words, "The Pharisees went out and plotted against Him, how they might destroy Him" (Matthew 12:14).

The very next account in Matthew's narrative describes another healing. Once more it is the kind of healing that involves an indisputable miracle: "Then one was brought to Him who was demon-possessed, blind and mute; and He healed him, so that the blind and mute man both spoke and saw" (v. 22). The miracle was instantaneous, comprehensive, and triumphant on multiple levels. The man's physical disabilities were instantly healed, and he was freed from demonic bondage all at once.

Matthew says "multitudes" witnessed the miracle. Some of those people surely knew the man and his history, because the response to the healing was unusually strong. Matthew uses an especially intense Greek word (*exist'mi,* "amazed") which speaks of more than mere surprise; it suggests they were practically out of their minds with awe. Of all the miracles they had seen, this one had a particular shock value—no doubt because the man's case was so severe. His blindness and inability to speak cut him off completely from all possible means of communication. That, combined with whatever grotesque manifestations his demonic possession might have caused, put him far beyond all earthly hope in the minds of everyone who knew him. But Jesus instantly made him completely well.

No one, including the Pharisees, could dispute the *fact* of the miracle. Immediately, a ripple of excitement went through the multitudes. They "were amazed and said, 'Could this be the Son of David?'" (v. 23). It was not an expression of doubt, nor was it a profession of faith. It was an exclamation of wonder and amazement. The miracle, on top of everything else they had seen and heard from Jesus, has them seriously pondering the possibility that He might indeed be the promised Messiah. He did not fit their expectations in most ways, because they were looking for the Messiah to explode on the scene as a conquering hero and glorious king, not as a simple carpenter's son from a family who lived in their midst. But they could not see so many dramatic miracles without beginning to wonder whether Jesus was indeed the One.

THE BLASPHEMY

Hearing such talk surge through the multitudes, the Pharisees reacted quickly, with the strongest denunciation of Jesus they could possibly put into words: "This fellow does not cast out demons except by Beelzebub, the ruler of the demons" (v. 24).

Beelzebub (or *Beelzebul,* as the best manuscripts have it) was a name borrowed and slightly altered from Baal-zebub (literally, "lord of the flies"), a deity of the Philistines (2 Kings 1:2–3, 6, 16). The alteration may have been deliberate, because *Beel-zebul* in Syriac means "god of dung." The name was used of Satan in Jesus' time. In other words, while the Pharisees could not deny that a bona fide miracle had occurred before their very eyes, they immediately began to insist that the power to perform the miracle came straight from Satan.

As usual, they muttered that charge in the midst of the multitude, out of earshot from Jesus. They were probably doing their best to discredit Him without catching His notice. They surely did not want another public confrontation. Every public clash they ever provoked with Him ended in embarrassment for them. They weren't bold enough to confront Jesus directly and make their charge to His face. But Matthew says:

> Jesus knew their thoughts, and said to them: 'Every kingdom divided against itself is brought to desolation, and every city or house divided against itself will not stand. If Satan casts out Satan, he is divided against himself. How then will his kingdom stand? And if I cast out demons by Beelzebub, by whom do your sons cast them out? Therefore they shall be your judges. But if I cast out demons by the Spirit of God, surely the kingdom of God has come upon you'" (vv. 25–28).

Surely by now you have noticed that Jesus' omniscience, particularly His ability to know what is going on in people's hearts, has been a consistent theme in His disputes with the Pharisees. John mentions it repeatedly (John 2:24–25; 6:64). Matthew mentions it here and in Matthew 9:4. Luke notes the same fact in an account that closely parallels this incident (Luke 11:17). If the stridency of Jesus' dealings with the Jewish leaders shocks you, bear in mind that He had the advantage of knowing their hearts even more perfectly than they themselves did. The fallen human heart is "deceitful above all things, and desperately wicked; who can know it?" (Jeremiah 17:9). The potential for self-deception is so profound that we are not to trust our own hearts (Proverbs 28:26). Only God knows how to judge a human heart perfectly (Jeremiah 11:20; 17:10; 20:12). Jesus *is* God, and therefore we can rest assured that His unrelenting harshness with the Pharisees was fully justified (Luke 16:15), even when He seemed to respond to them without much visible provocation.

Obviously you and I cannot assess other people's hearts perfectly—much less trust our own hearts (1 Samuel 16:7; John 7:24). Therefore we are also cautioned repeatedly to deal with others as patiently and as gently as possible (Galatians 6:1; Ephesians 4:2; Philippians 4:5; 2 Timothy 2:24–26). So let's be absolutely clear about this once more: Jesus' harshness with the Pharisees does not give us an unrestricted license to deal roughly with others every time we happen to disagree. *Gentleness* should characterize our relationships with people, including those who persecute us (Luke 6:27–36). *Love* "suffers long and is kind . . . bears all things, believes all things, hopes all things, endures all things" (1 Corinthians 13:4, 7). Those are general rules that should be paramount in all our interaction with others.

Nevertheless, Jesus' constant friction with the Pharisees does show that conflict is sometimes necessary. Harsh words are not always inappropriate. Unpleasant and unwelcome truths sometimes need to be voiced. False religion always needs to be answered. Love may cover a multitude of sins (1 Peter 4:8), but the gross hypocrisy of false teachers desperately needs to be *un*covered—lest our silence facilitate and perpetuate a damning delusion. The truth is not always "nice."

In this case, Jesus took the Pharisees' murmured accusation, set it front and center before the whole multitude, and then deconstructed the logic of the charge. He pointed out first of all that a divided kingdom cannot stand. (Israel knew that fact all too well from her own history.) He noted that there were supposed exorcists among the Pharisees' disciples, and He raised the question of whose power *they* employed to cast out demons. The remark is tinged with sarcasm, because while there were exorcists in the Pharisees' system, they were notoriously unsuccessful—like the sons of Sceva ("a Jewish chief priest") mentioned in Acts 19:13–16, who tried using Jesus' name as an abracadabra to exorcise a demon-possessed man in Ephesus. Scripture says "the man in whom the evil spirit was leaped on them, overpowered them, and prevailed against them, so that they fled out of that house naked and wounded." The prevalence of so many extreme cases of demon possession in Galilee during Jesus' ministry bears testimony to what a large convocation of the forces of hell were arrayed against Him, as well as how ineffectual the exorcisms of the Pharisees had been. When Jesus challenged the Pharisees—"If I cast out demons by Beelzebub, by whom do your sons cast them out?" (v. 27)—it is not difficult to envision a wave of laughter moving through the watching crowd.

Given Jesus' one-hundred-percent success rate in casting out demons, the only reasonable and rational conclusion was that He was doing it by God's power—because only God is greater than the entire kingdom of Satan. "How can one enter a strong man's house and plunder his goods, unless he first binds the strong man? And then he will plunder his house" (Matthew 12:29).

Jesus' short reply to the Pharisees contained a couple of significant, ominous statements. He told them, for example, "If I cast out demons by the Spirit of God, surely the kingdom of God has come upon you" (v. 28). In other words, if they were wrong about Jesus (and they clearly were; even they knew so in their hearts), then He was indeed Israel's Messiah, and they were setting themselves against the power and authority of the kingdom of God in the very presence of the eternal King!

Furthermore, Jesus drew a stark line in the sand: "He who is not with Me is against Me" (v. 30). That statement, it appears, was mainly for the benefit of those in the multitude who were not fully committed disciples yet. They could not remain halfhearted and aloof while pretending to be His followers. By trying to sit on the fence between Jesus and the Pharisees, they were actually hardening their hearts against Christ. The proof that they were "against Him" would eventually be manifest in their own apostasy. Judas was the classic example of this. He had never once been overtly hostile to Jesus, until the day he betrayed Him for money. But that made it clear that Judas was never really "with" Jesus to begin with (cf. 1 John 4:19). I'm convinced there are more people like that in evangelical churches than the typical Christian imagines, even today. They may identify with Jesus superficially and blend in well with true disciples, but they are not truly committed to Him and therefore they are *against* Him. Jesus' line in the sand was a challenge for such people to examine themselves honestly and commit themselves to Him in earnest.

For the Pharisees who uttered the blasphemy, however, Jesus had even more solemn words.

BROOD OF VIPERS!

If it seems Jesus was pronouncing a final judgment of damnation against these Pharisees right then and there, I believe that is precisely what He was doing. Having demonstrated the utter irrationality and irresponsibility of their accusation, he added this: "Therefore I say to you, every sin and blasphemy will be forgiven men, but the blasphemy against the Spirit will not be forgiven men. Anyone who speaks a word against the Son of Man, it will be forgiven him; but whoever speaks against the Holy Spirit, it will not be forgiven him, either in this age or in the age to come" (vv. 31–32). Mark records the same statement in slightly different words: "Assuredly, I say to you, all sins will be forgiven the sons of men, and whatever blasphemies they may utter; but he who blasphemes against the Holy Spirit never has forgiveness, but is subject to eternal condemnation" (Mark 3:28–29). Mark adds this editorial comment, however: "because they said, 'He has an unclean spirit.'" (v. 30). Thus Mark makes it inescapably clear that Jesus' words about unpardonable sin were His response to the Pharisees' blasphemy. What is the unpardonable sin? What does Jesus mean when He speaks of "the blasphemy against the Holy Spirit?" The context, as usual, gives a clear answer. It is the very blasphemy those men had just uttered.

The divine wrath that provoked those words of judgment is evident in the way He spoke to them: "Brood of vipers! How can you, being evil, speak good things? For out of the abundance of the heart the mouth speaks" (Matthew 12:34). The fruit of their own words demonstrated their true character (v. 33). Their condemnation was just.

FORGIVENESS AND UNFORGIVABILITY

People are often troubled by the notion that there is such a thing as unforgivable sin. Some worry about whether they might have inadvertently committed it. Some, noticing that Jesus did not elaborate a lot about the nature of the sin, try all kinds of hermeneutical gymnastics to define it as precisely as possible. Some have difficulty reconciling the notion of unpardonable sin with the doctrine of justification by faith and end up with a twisted idea of how salvation works. If it is possible to commit a blasphemy that can never be forgiven, they reason, then it must be possible for Christians to commit the sin and lose their salvation.

All those concerns and misunderstandings are easily answered, if we keep the context of this passage in view. These Pharisees were guilty of unpardonable sin because they knowingly—not in ignorance or by accident, but *deliberately*—wrote Jesus' work off as the work of the devil. Moreover, their rejection of Christ was a full, final, settled renunciation of Christ and everything He stood for. Contrast their sin with that of Peter, who later denied knowing Christ and punctuated his denials with swearing and curses. But Peter found forgiveness for his sin. If we think carefully about what was happening here and what Jesus actually said, the notion of unpardonable sin is not really so mysterious.

Notice, first of all, that this passage and its cross-references (Mark 3:28–29; Luke 12:10) are the only places where Scripture mentions unpardonable sin.[1] Hebrews 6:4–6 and 10:26 describe a kind of willful apostasy for which there is no remedy, and 1 John 5:16 mentions "a sin unto death" (KJV). But the "sin unto death" is best understood as a sin that results in *physical* death. The New King James Version renders it accordingly: "sin leading to death." It is not one specific sin, but any sin whose direct consequence is death, including sins that God judges with death (of 1 Corinthians 11:30). The passages in Hebrews 6 and 10 describe a deliberate turning away from the truth. It is very similar to the blasphemy these Pharisees committed, and there may indeed be a legitimate correlation between those passages and the unpardonable sin. but the stress in Hebrews is on the impossibility of *repentance* (6:6), not the unobtainability of *forgiveness*.

Second, don't miss the fact that Jesus' words about this one unpardonable sin begin with a sweeping promise of forgiveness for "every sin and blasphemy" (Matthew 12:31). Our God is a forgiving God; that is His nature. "Who is a God like You, pardoning iniquity and passing over the transgression of the remnant of His heritage? He does not retain His anger forever, because He delights in mercy" (Micah 7:18). "For You, Lord, are good, and ready to forgive, and abundant in mercy to all those who call upon You" (Psalm 86:5). Scripture is full of texts like those.

Jesus emphatically states that the *severity* of sin never hinders God's forgiveness. "All manner of sin and blasphemy" is forgivable (Matthew 12:31 KJV). After all, the grossest sin ever committed was the crucifixion of Jesus (Acts 2:23), and yet one of Jesus' last sayings before He died was a prayer for forgiveness for His executioners and the crowd who mocked Him (Luke 23:34). The *number* of sins a person commits does not make his case unpardonable. The redemption purchased by Christ will "cover a multitude of sins" (James 5:20). The *species* of sin isn't the factor that makes it unpardonable. "If we confess our sins, He is faithful and just to forgive us our sins and to cleanse us from *all* unrighteousness" (1 John 1:9). Over the course of His ministry, Jesus forgave every conceivable kind and category of wickedness. Even as He hung on the cross, He granted full and immediate pardon to a thief who had lived a full life of sin—because the man was truly repentant.

Here, then, was the issue with the Pharisees. Their hatred for Jesus was fixed and utterly immovable. They would never repent, and their blasphemy simply demonstrated beyond doubt how inexorably hardened their hearts had become. In the face of a miracle that completely shocked and amazed all who saw it, they were concerned only with how to discredit Christ.

Not only were their hearts permanently hardened against Christ; they were fully resolved to do everything possible to turn as many others as possible against Him. Their hatred for Him was driven by murderous intentions, and now it was compounded with the ultimate blasphemy.

The language Jesus used ("sin and blasphemy") clearly sets blasphemy apart from all other sins, signifying that *any* blasphemy is worse than other sins. That's because it is a sin directly against God, with no motive other than dishonoring Him. Most sins are at least partly motivated by desires for pleasure, money, self-indulgence, or other complex motives. But blasphemy fulfills no craving, offers no reward, and gratifies no human need. Of all sins, this one is purely and simply an act of defiance against God. That's why in any biblical taxonomy of evil deeds, blasphemy ranks worse than even murder and adultery. Nevertheless, Jesus expressly states that even acts of blasphemy are forgivable when the blasphemer repents.

Notice that He refers to the unpardonable sin as *"the* blasphemy against the Spirit" (Matthew 12:31, emphasis added). The definite article is significant. Jesus clearly was speaking about one particular act of blasphemy—the ultimate, conclusive, in-your-face expression of blasphemy that rises above all other forms of blasphemy. He was not suggesting that a slip of the tongue invoking the Holy Spirit's name in a blasphemous oath is automatically unpardonable. Some people labor under the delusion that if they even question any of the various phenomena that people claim are manifestations of the Holy Spirit's power today, they risk committing an unpardonable sin. And thus their fear squelches discernment. That is not at all what Jesus was saying here. He was not naming a broad category of offenses and declaring them all unpardonable. He was dealing with one very specific exhibition of gross blasphemy, and *that* is what He said was unforgivable. It was the sin of those Pharisees: closing one's heart permanently against Christ even after the Holy Spirit has brought full conviction of the truth. In effect, Jesus closed the door of heaven against these Pharisees who had so utterly and deliberately shut their hearts against Him.

Why did He characterize their sin as blasphemy against the Holy Spirit? Because Jesus' miracles were done in the power of the Holy Spirit. (Even the Pharisees knew that in their hearts.) And yet they claimed He was operating in Satan's power. In effect, they were calling the Holy Spirit the devil, and giving the devil credit for what the Spirit of God had done.

But what made this particular sin unpardonable was the finality of it. It was deliberate. It was an expression of coldhearted, determined unbelief. These Pharisees had seen, up close, more evidence than they could possibly ever need that Jesus was God incarnate. And yet they continued to press for more dramatic signs. In fact, right after Jesus admonished them about the danger of unpardonable sin, they demanded another sign—suggesting that they wanted to see a sign of cosmic proportions (v. 38)—"a sign from heaven," in the words of Luke 11:16.

The fact is, their hearts were already settled. They would never believe, no matter what Jesus ever did or said. Therefore their sin was unforgivable. The Holy Spirit had already opened their eyes to see the truth and convicted their hearts of their own guilt, and yet they persisted in coldhearted unbelief. That is what made this particular blasphemy against the Holy Spirit more wicked and more personally dishonoring to God than any casual blasphemy they might ever have uttered against Jesus Himself (v. 32).

Immediately after that day, Jesus began to teach in parables (13:3). From that day forward, when He taught in public settings, "Jesus spoke to the multitude in parables; and without a parable He did not speak to them" (v. 34). That was at least in part an expression of judgment against the hardheartedness of the Pharisees. Quoting from Isaiah 6:9–10 and 44:18, Jesus explained to His disciples the reason for the parables: "To you it has been given to know the mystery of the kingdom of God; but to those who are outside, all things come in parables, so that 'seeing they may see and not perceive, and hearing they may hear and not understand; lest they should turn, and their sins be forgiven them'" (Mark 4:11–12). If Israel's religious elite were so determined to reject the truth, He would conceal the truth from them with parables, while using those same parables to illustrate the truth for His disciples. And "when they were alone, He explained all things to His disciples" (v. 34).

But the parables also served a *merciful* purpose in Jesus' dealings with the Pharisees. With their hearts now permanently hardened against the truth, the more truth they heard, the greater their final judgment would be. Because their determination to oppose the truth was now permanent and final, the less truth they heard from Jesus, the better it would be for them.

Not many weeks after this conflict with the Pharisees came the Bread of Life discourse and the large-scale defection of followers, which we examined in the previous chapter. After that, Jesus ended the Galilean phase of His ministry and began to travel into further regions. His ministry took Him from Tyre and Sidon on the northern Mediterranean coast (Matthew 15:21), to Caesarea Philippi in the north near the Syrian border (Matthew 16:13), to Decapolis (Mark 7:31) and Perea, east of the Jordan (John 10:40). He also moved back and forth between Galilee and Judea during these months. Of course, the Pharisees followed Him everywhere He went and continued more aggressively than ever to oppose Jesus at every opportunity, but He now turned His attention mainly to the training of His own disciples.

If time and space permitted us to survey each one of the various challenges and confrontations the Pharisees brought to Jesus, you would see that their pattern of antagonism toward Him continued unabated and in fact dramatically increased as the end of Jesus' public ministry drew near. Luke 20:20 says, "They watched Him, and sent spies who pretended to be righteous, that they might seize on His words, in order to deliver Him to the power and the authority of the governor." They continually put Him to the test (Luke 11:54; Matthew 15:39; 22:15), and they repeatedly embarrassed themselves in the process. Every subsequent encounter He had with them was more of the same.[2]

Jesus always withstood them, and He invariably put them to silence. He often warned His disciples about the tendencies of the Pharisees' system, referring to their hypocrisy as "leaven" (Matthew 16:6; Luke 12:1). But he had little else to say *to* them other than the same truths they had already heard from Him.

In the end, during that final week before the crucifixion, He would sum up His views about Israel's religious leaders and their hypocrisy in a scalding diatribe in their front yard—the Temple grounds in Jerusalem. That sermon would leave them fuming and outraged, and it would seal their determination to kill Him as soon as they possibly could.

We have all heard people say a hundred times over, for they seem never to tire of saying it, that the Jesus of the New Testament is indeed a most merciful and humane lover of humanity, but that the Church has hidden this human character in repellent dogmas and stiffened it with ecclesiastical terrors till it has taken on an inhuman character. This is, I venture to repeat, very nearly the reverse of the truth. The truth is that it is the image of Christ in the churches that is almost entirely mild and merciful.

—G. K. CHESTERTON[3]

8

Woe

Woe to you, scribes and Pharisees, hypocrites! For you are like whitewashed tombs which indeed appear beautiful outwardly, but inside are full of dead men's bones and all uncleanness. . . . See! Your house is left to you desolate.

Matthew 23:27, 38

*A*ll of Matthew 23 is the record of one sermon. It is the last public sermon Jesus ever preached. Its subject matter is not the gospel or the kingdom of God *per se;* it is a powerful onslaught of rebuke against the religious sins of Israel, and her leaders in particular. How ironic (and how supremely significant) it is that the One of whom it was said, "God did not send His Son into the world to condemn the world, but that the world through Him might be saved" (John 3:17) made His last public sermon an extended message of condemnation.

It was the middle of Passion Week. The events of that tumultuous week began with Jesus entering Jerusalem on the back of a donkey with shouts of "Hosanna!" reverberating through the city.[1] It looked for all the world as if He would be swept on a massive wave of public support into prominence and power in some political capacity—and then He would finally inaugurate His promised kingdom. But the public's enthusiasm for Christ was an illusion. Their expectation was for a Messiah who would quickly liberate Israel from the dominion of Rome and establish a political kingdom that would ultimately rule over even Caesar. Jerusalem was happy to have a worker of miracles and the hope of a conquering King like that. But they did not want Jesus' hard preaching. They were shocked that He seemed more interested in challenging their religious institutions than He was in conquering Rome and liberating them from political oppression. They were stunned by His treatment of Israel's religious elite—as if they were pagans. He spent more time calling *Israel* to repentance than He did criticizing her oppressors. On top of that, they did not appreciate His refusal to be Messiah on *their* terms (John 6:15). Before the week was over, the same crowd who praised Him with Hosannas would be screaming for His blood.

NOT IN MY FATHER'S HOUSE

On Tuesday morning of that fateful week, Jesus repeated the cleansing of the temple. Almost exactly three years had elapsed since He first came on the scene as a prophet with a whip of cords, chasing the unscrupulous animal merchants and money changers from the temple. That, you will recall, was His first public act in Jerusalem. Back then, it seemed as if He stormed into the Temple compound out of nowhere, and He took the religious authorities completely by surprise. It was clear they did not know what to do with Him.

Now, three years later, the profiteering money changers were back on the job, as were the unscrupulous animal sellers. Not much had changed, except that the Jewish leaders' hearts had grown harder and colder—and now they knew exactly what they wanted to do with Jesus.

All three Synoptic Gospels describe the second temple cleansing, but Mark gives the fullest account:

Jesus went into the temple and began to drive out those who bought and sold in the temple, and overturned the tables of the money changers and the seats of those who sold doves. And He would not allow anyone to carry wares through the temple. Then He taught, saying to them, "Is it not written, 'My house shall be called a house of prayer for all nations'? But you have made it a 'den of thieves.'" And the scribes and chief priests heard it and sought how they might destroy Him; for they feared Him, because all the people were astonished at His teaching. (Mark 11:15–18)

It makes perfect sense that Jesus would conclude His ministry by making the very same point He made at the outset. The idea that He cleansed the temple twice does not strain common sense or credulity in the least.[2] What is truly remarkable is that Jesus did not do this every time He visited Jerusalem over the course of His ministry. He did it just once at the beginning and then again at the end, bracketing his public ministry.

These dramatic public displays of Jesus' divine authority highlight His opposition to the religious institutions of apostate Judaism. They stress the prophetic nature of His message and explain to a large degree why His interactions with the Jewish leaders were always heavily flavored with gall.

By now, the rank and file members of the Sanhedrin, the Pharisees, the chief priests, the leading Sadducees, and the temple guard all hated Him more than ever. But they also still feared Him (Mark 11:18)—mainly because He seemed so popular with the people. So instead of arresting Him then and there on the temple grounds, their plan was to lie in wait for an opportunity to arrest Him in secret. That's why this time Jesus was able to drive the money changers from the temple and walk away from the scene totally unchallenged. (Remember that the first time Jesus drove out the money changers, the temple guard responded by demanding that He give a sign that would prove His prophetic authority. This time, their response was just mute amazement.) But while they remained largely in the background, the Sanhedrin quietly renewed their resolve to get rid of Him—that very week, if possible.

For His part, immediately after driving out the money changers, Jesus more or less moved into the temple grounds for the week. The temple courts became both classroom and headquarters for His public teaching ministry, right under the Sanhedrins' nose. Most of Matthew 21–25; Mark 11–13; Luke 19–21, and John 12 record what He taught and things that happened there during that week. The religious leaders repeatedly challenged Him, trying to trap Him or confound Him some way—and they always failed. Luke says, "He was teaching daily in the temple. But the chief priests, the scribes, and the leaders of the people sought to destroy Him, and were unable to do anything; for all the people were very attentive to hear Him" (Luke 19:47–48).

John adds this ominous note about the crowds who listened to Jesus' teaching that week: "But although He had done so many signs before them, they did not believe in Him" (John 12:37).

MAKING AN IMPACT

Someone might wonder why Jesus continued teaching in the temple courts when He knew the hearts of so many of His hearers were dull and cold. He also certainly knew that His very presence provoked the Jewish leaders and inflamed their determination to destroy Him. He was fully aware of where all this was headed. A pragmatist might suggest that He ought to have kept a lower profile—perhaps even gone underground, and ministered in less public ways just to the people who were receptive, rather than continually antagonize people whom He knew would never believe anyway. After all, stirring up strife like this could not possibly do anyone any good, could it?

But as we have seen consistently from the very start, the truth mattered more to Jesus than how people felt about it. He wasn't looking for ways just to make people "like" Him; he was calling people who were willing to bow to Him unconditionally as their Lord. He wasn't interested in reinforcing the "common-ground" beliefs where His message overlapped with the Pharisees' worldview. On the contrary, He stressed (almost exclusively) the points on which He *disagreed* with them. He never acted as if the best way to turn people away from the damnable heresies of Pharisee-religion was to make His message sound as much as possible like the popular beliefs of the day. Instead, He stressed (and reiterated again and again) the points of doctrine that were most at odds with the conventional wisdom of Pharisaism.

His strategy frankly would not have been any more welcome in the typical twenty-first-century evangelical gathering than it was right there in the Sanhedrin's backyard.

And yet, in modest but significant ways, Jesus was making an impact. John 12:42–43, describing Jesus' ministry that week in the temple courtyard, says this: "Nevertheless even among the rulers many believed in Him, but because of the Pharisees they did not confess Him, lest they should be put out of the synagogue; for they loved the praise of men more than the praise of God." Evidently, Nicodemus and Joseph of Arimathea were representative of a small, quiet, almost invisible group of council members and influential rabbis who listened to Jesus and were persuaded of the truth of His message. Because love for the praise of men was so deeply ingrained in their worldview, they kept silent. Were they genuine believers—regenerate men—or was their "faith" of the spurious, temporary, nonredemptive kind?

Notice that John does not speak very highly of them. Whatever the nature of their "belief," they still were concerned more about their membership in the synagogues than they were about Christ. It seems certain that the vast majority of them were convinced but uncommitted and therefore not authentic believers—not yet, at least. Some of them may have come to true faith at some later time—perhaps after the resurrection. Joseph of Arimathea and Nicodemus were Pharisees—council members—who came slowly and haltingly to Christ but who ultimately showed their true commitment to Him at a pivotal moment (Luke 23:51; John 19:38–39). There may well have been others like them.

But apparently, some of them continued to be double-minded. The first major doctrinal crisis that arose in the early church stemmed from some heretics who taught that Gentiles coming to Christ could not be saved without being circumcised. They therefore made the believer's own works—rather than Christ's perfect righteousness alone—the ground of a right standing with God, and thus they corrupted the simplicity of the gospel. In Acts 15, a council was convened to address that error. Luke records that the culprits who had introduced this doctrine were "some of the sect of the Pharisees who believed" (Acts 15:5).

In other words, some of the earliest heretics in the primitive church were former Jewish leaders who had been persuaded of the truth about Christ, but rather than repenting of their own self-righteousness, they had dragged their pharisaical perspective into the church, corrupting the message of Christianity in the process. So thoroughly embedded in all their thoughts was a love for the praise of men that even after being persuaded of the truth, some Pharisees were unable to lose the works-based orientation of their religion.

That's why the apostle Paul was so emphatic about His own break from Pharisaism. He described his former religion as "dung" in Philippians 3:8 (KJV).

If the apostle John seems somewhat less than exuberant in John 12:42–43 about council members who "believed" but kept quiet about it—now you know why. Any Pharisee who never fully repented of his own "good works" would perish in his sins, even if he did believe that Jesus was the true Messiah. And it was clear by the time John wrote his gospel that the spurious "faith" of such men was already a huge and widespread problem in the early church—the first truly significant threat to the purity of the gospel message.

Among the common people, spurious faith and halfhearted Messianic hope in Jesus was likewise a significant problem. It always had been. Remember that John drew attention to the problem at the very start, in John 2:23–24: "Many believed in His name when they saw the signs . . . but Jesus did not commit Himself to them, because He knew all men." John 6 described in detail how such halfhearted faith so quickly gave way to hostility. It was about to happen again. Regarding those appreciative crowds who listened to Jesus eagerly during that final week in Jerusalem, "hanging on to every word He said" (Luke 19:48 NASB)—there must have been countless people who would be chanting "Crucify him!" (Mark 15:13) before the week was over.

And yet there was a remnant in both groups—the Jewish leaders and the common people—who either were or would become true disciples. Jesus kept preaching for their benefit, even though He knew full well that the more visible He made His ministry in the public eye, the more the Sanhedrin's resolve to crucify Him intensified.

THE FINAL SERMON

The content of Jesus' message demonstrates, however, that He was teaching not only for the benefit of the believing remnant, but also as a final warning and instruction to the Jewish leaders themselves.

Our Lord's last public sermon took place on Wednesday of that final week. Matthew 23:1 says He delivered His message "to the crowds and to his disciples." But it is clear from the message itself that members of the council were among the bystanders, because Jesus called them out and addressed major portions of the sermon directly to them. They were not only standing on the perimeter as usual, but actually mixing in with the crowds incognito, and pretending to be sympathetic hearers. They were listening carefully for anything they might use "to trap Him in his words" (22:15) or to twist into an accusation against Him. Here is where Luke says, "The teachers of the law and the chief priests were afraid of the people. Keeping a close watch on him, they sent spies, who pretended to be sincere. They hoped to catch Jesus in something he said, so that they might hand Him over to the power and authority of the governor" (Luke 20:19–20).

Of course, Jesus *still* knew their thoughts, and He confronted them more directly than ever before. He used some of the sharpest language He ever employed. He called them names. He let loose with waves of condemnation against their hypocrisy, their scripture-twisting, and their self-righteousness. He pronounced woe after woe against them. And the expression "woe" was no mild imprecation; it was the strongest conceivable prophetic curse. And you can be certain its meaning was not lost on them.

HOW TO LOSE FRIENDS AND INFLAME ENEMIES

From His opening words to His final sentence, Jesus was stern, candid, passionate, and intense—even fierce. Someone steeped in modern and postmodern styles of "contextualization" might allege that His message and his style of delivery were insensitive and hurtful to His intended audience. That would be a gross misjudgment. *Sensitivity* entails being perceptive of others' feelings. There is no way Jesus, who could see directly into the Pharisees' hearts, could possibly have failed to perceive what they were feeling. Furthermore, as personally aggravating as it might be to find oneself on the receiving end of a tirade like this, what would have been truly *hurtful* would have been for Jesus to pretend the spiritual danger posed by the Pharisees' doctrine and behavior was not really so grave after all. So as always, He told them what they most needed to hear, declaring the truth to them in unvarnished language. Under the circumstances, this was the greatest kindness he could possibly have shown to them. The tenor of His words reminds us that spiritual warfare is just that: a battle. It is a fierce conflict against spiritual lies, damnably erroneous doctrine, and destructive false religion.

It is significant that Jesus, who as omniscient God incarnate, was the most sensitive Person ever to walk the earth, and yet in circumstances like these, He refused to tone down the message, adopt a delicate tone, or handle His spiritual adversaries as fragile souls. Too much was at stake.

He began the message in a comparatively low-key fashion, mocking the Pharisees' proud self-righteousness and calling His followers to be as humble as the Pharisees were arrogant:

> "The scribes and the Pharisees sit in Moses' seat. Therefore whatever they tell you to observe, that observe and do, but do not do according to their works; for they say, and do not do. For they bind heavy burdens, hard to bear, and lay them on men's shoulders; but they themselves will not move them with one of their fingers. But all their works they do to be seen by men. They make their phylacteries broad and enlarge the borders of their garments. They love the best places at feasts, the best seats in the synagogues, greetings in the marketplaces, and to be called by

men, 'Rabbi, Rabbi.' But you, do not be called 'Rabbi'; for One is your Teacher, the Christ, and you are all brethren. Do not call anyone on earth your father; for One is your Father, He who is in heaven. And do not be called teachers; for One is your Teacher, the Christ. But he who is greatest among you shall be your servant. And whoever exalts himself will be humbled, and he who humbles himself will be exalted." (Matthew 23:2–12)

His description fit the Pharisees and their followers to a T.

Notice that Jesus said, "Whatever they tell you to observe, that observe and do, but do not do according to their works" (v. 3). The Pharisees' practice was certainly a more conspicuous problem than their doctrine. Nevertheless, Jesus was not making a wholesale endorsement of their teaching and criticizing only their practice. Far from it. The root problem was their belief system, not just their behavior. Their whole interpretation of the law was faulty, as Jesus had demonstrated in His Sermon on the Mount. They "trusted in themselves that they were righteous, and despised others" (Luke 18:9). And thus the entire foundation of their soteriology (their view of the doctrine of salvation) was askew. So Jesus was certainly not indicating that the Pharisees were doctrinally orthodox and only wrong in their practice. He would go on to expose some of the more egregious errors in their teaching before this sermon ended.

On the other hand, they were not wrong in *everything* they taught. It would be a total misapplication of Jesus' teaching to take His condemnation of Pharisee religion and conclude that He endorsed whatever seemed to be the opposite of what they advocated. In their emphasis on the authority and gravity of the law, especially as it governed public morality, they were generally right. When it came to those issues, what Jesus abhorred about them was not what they said people should or shouldn't do; it was their failure to live in accord with their own teaching. That was the great danger posed by their obsession with externals. They paid careful attention to what they wore, but not so much to what they thought about. They were deeply concerned with how they were perceived by other people but not so concerned with what God thought of them. They were passionate about making sure *they* received earthly honor, but they hardly cared about God's honor. *Don't be like them* was the starting point of the whole sermon.

Then Jesus turned His attention directly to the scribes and Pharisees who were there: "But woe to you, scribes and Pharisees, hypocrites!" (v. 13). And thus he launched into a diatribe against them that consumes the rest of the chapter. From that point to the end of the message, Jesus speaks directly to the Jewish leaders in the second person—his most blistering attack on them to date.

The sermon is much too long to analyze word for word,[3] but it is worth reading the entire portion that was addressed directly to Israel's religious elite, and then we'll note some of the sermon's major features.

"But woe to you, scribes and Pharisees, hypocrites! For you shut up the kingdom of heaven against men; for you neither go in yourselves, nor do you allow those who are entering to go in. Woe to you, scribes and Pharisees, hypocrites! For you devour widows' houses, and for a pretense make long prayers. Therefore you will receive greater condemnation.

"Woe to you, scribes and Pharisees, hypocrites! For you travel land and sea to win one proselyte, and when he is won, you make him twice as much a son of hell as yourselves.

"Woe to you, blind guides, who say, 'Whoever swears by the temple, it is nothing; but whoever swears by the gold of the temple, he is obliged to perform it.' Fools and blind! For which is greater, the gold or the temple that sanctifies the gold? And, 'Whoever swears by the altar, it is nothing; but whoever swears by the gift that is on it, he is obliged to perform it.' Fools and blind! For which is greater, the gift or the altar that sanctifies the gift? Therefore he who swears by the altar, swears by it and by all things on it. He who swears by the temple, swears by it and by Him who dwells in it. And he who swears by heaven, swears by the throne of God and by Him who sits on it.

"Woe to you, scribes and Pharisees, hypocrites! For you pay tithe of mint and anise and cummin, and have neglected the weightier matters of the law: justice and mercy and faith. These you ought to have done, without leaving the others undone. Blind guides, who strain out a gnat and swallow a camel!

"Woe to you, scribes and Pharisees, hypocrites! For you cleanse the outside of the cup and dish, but inside they are full of extortion and self-indulgence. Blind Pharisee, first cleanse the inside of the cup and dish, that the outside of them may be clean also.

"Woe to you, scribes and Pharisees, hypocrites! For you are like whitewashed tombs which indeed appear beautiful outwardly, but inside are full of dead men's bones and all uncleanness. Even so you also outwardly appear righteous to men, but inside you are full of hypocrisy and lawlessness.

"Woe to you, scribes and Pharisees, hypocrites! Because you build the tombs of the prophets and adorn the monuments of the righteous, and say, 'If we had lived in the days of our fathers, we would not have been partakers with them in the blood of the prophets.'

"Therefore you are witnesses against yourselves that you are sons of those who murdered the prophets. Fill up, then, the measure of your fathers' guilt. Serpents, brood of vipers! How can you escape the condemnation of hell? Therefore, indeed, I send you prophets, wise men, and scribes: some of them you will kill and crucify, and some of them you will scourge in your synagogues and persecute from city to city, that on you may come all the righteous blood shed on the earth, from the blood of righteous Abel to the blood of Zechariah, son of Berechiah, whom you murdered between the temple and the altar. Assuredly, I say to you, all these things will come upon this generation.

"O Jerusalem, Jerusalem, the one who kills the prophets and stones those who are sent to her! How often I wanted to gather your children together, as a hen gathers her chicks under her wings, but you were not willing! See! Your house is left to you desolate; for I say to you, you shall see Me no more till you say, 'Blessed is He who comes in the Name of the LORD!'" (vv. 13–39).

Jesus had said many of those same things before. Once a private lunch meeting in a Pharisee's home had dissolved into a conflict[4] when it became obvious that He had been invited mainly so that they could observe and criticize things like His failure to observe their ceremonial washings. On that occasion, in the presence of several Pharisees, Jesus delivered a scathing tongue-lashing in which He said many of these same things (Luke 11:37–54). But this was the first time where it is recorded that Jesus had made such a sustained attack on official Judaism publicly—in Jerusalem, at the temple, no less.

Eight times He pronounces *woe* against them. Remember that the Sermon on the Mount began with eight beatitudes. These pronouncements of woe are the polar opposite of those, and they stand in stark contrast. These are curses rather than blessings.

And yet even in the curses, there is a poignancy that reflects Jesus' sorrow. He is not expressing a *preference* for their condemnation, because, after all, He came to save, not to condemn (John 3:17). The word *woe* in Greek as well as in English is an *onomatopoeia*—a word whose meaning is derived from its sound rather than from a semantic root. It sounds like a wail of grief or sorrow. It is a one-word verbal parallel of Jesus' lament for the entire city (Luke 19:41–44), reflecting the same kind of sorrow. That sorrow, I believe, is a reflection of God's own heart, not merely a manifestation of Jesus' human nature. God takes no pleasure in the destruction of the wicked (Ezekiel 18:32; 33:11).

On the other hand, Jesus' profound sorrow over the hardhearted rebellion of the Pharisees did not move Him to soften His words or soft-sell the reality of the spiritual calamity they had brought upon themselves. If anything, that was why He delivered this final message to them with such passion and urgency.

The other word that dominates this sermon besides *woe* is *hypocrites*—which likewise appears eight times. In the course of pronouncing those eight woes, Jesus was addressing many of the doctrinal and practical errors that illustrated what deplorable hypocrites they were. These included their pretentious praying (v. 14); their misguided motives for "ministry" to others (v. 15); their tendency to swear casually by things that are holy, plus the corresponding habit of playing fast and loose with their vows (vv. 18–22); their upside-down approach to priorities, by which they had elevated obscure ceremonial precepts over the moral law (vv. 23–24); and above all, their blithe toleration of many gross, often ludicrous, manifestations of hypocrisy (vv. 27–31).

One other characteristic that makes this sermon stand out is Jesus' liberal use of derogatory epithets. Those who think name-calling is inherently un-Christlike and always inappropriate will have a very hard time with this sermon. In addition to the eight times Jesus emphatically calls them "hypocrites!" He calls them "blind guides" (vv. 16, 24); "fools and blind!" (v. 17, 19); "blind Pharisee[s]" (v. 26); and "serpents, brood of vipers!" (v. 33).

This was not an attempt to win esteem in their eyes. It was not an attempt to persuade them with smooth words or a friendly overture. It was not the kind of soft word that turns away wrath.

But it was the truth, and it was what the Pharisees, as well as those potentially influenced by them, desperately needed to hear.

NOT SO MEEK AND MILD

Sadly, this sermon was also a pronouncement of final judgment against the religious leaders and their followers who had rejected Christ and who by now had so hardened their hearts against Him that they would never believe. It underscored in a verbally graphic way the finality of the judgment Jesus had rendered when He pronounced the Pharisees' blasphemy unpardonable. It also effectively expanded that judgment to include not only other hardened unbelievers, but also the institutions that had become monuments to that corrupt religious system—the Sanhedrin, the corrupt priesthood, the Pharisees and Sadducees—the whole religious hierarchy that had in effect taken over the temple.

At the end of the message, when Jesus said, "See! Your house is left to you desolate" (v. 38), He was pronouncing *Ichabod* ("the glory has departed") on the temple. Instead of "My Father's house" (John 2:16), it was now "your house." The Glory of Israel departed the temple for good, not to return again until all Israel says, "Blessed is He who comes in the Name of the Lord!"

Before that generation passed from the scene, Roman armies laid waste to Herod's temple. From then until now, Israel has had no temple, no sacrifices, no means of fulfilling the most important aspects of their ceremonial law, no other means of atonement apart from the Lamb of God who took away the sin of the world. Thus His dramatic departure from the temple was a major turning point for all Israel.

No wonder He spoke with such passion and intensity.

We can learn a lot from observing how Jesus dealt with false religion and its purveyors. The boldness with which He assaulted error is very much in short supply today, and the church is suffering because of it.

We don't need a return to the brand of fundamentalism whose leaders fought all the time, and fought over practically everything—often attacking one another over obscure and insignificant differences. Much less do we need to persist in the misguided course of so-called neoevangelicalism, where the overriding concern has always been academic respectability and where conflict and strong convictions are automatically regarded as uncouth and uncivil.

In fact, the very *last* thing we can afford to do in these postmodern times, while the enemies of truth are devoted to making everything fuzzy, would be to pledge a moratorium on candor or agree to a cease-fire with people who delight in testing the limits of orthodoxy. Being friendly and affable is sometimes simply the *wrong* thing to do (cf. Nehemiah 6:2–4). We *must* remember that.

Someone who makes a loud profession of faith but constantly fails to live up to it needs to be exposed for his own soul's sake. More than that, those who set themselves up as teachers representing the Lord and influencing others while corrupting the truth need to be denounced and refuted. For their sake, for the sake of others who are victimized by their errors, and especially for the glory of Christ, who *is* Truth incarnate.

Jesus Himself reminded us of those things, in the last biblical passage where He spoke to His church.

*H*ow different is that honey-mouthed, tear-stained, soup-kitchen Jesus Christ of our poor shovel-hatted modern Christians from that stern-visaged Christ of the gospels, proclaiming aloud in the marketplace (with such a total contempt of the social respectabilities): "Woe unto you, Scribes and Pharisees, hypocrites"! Descend from your Gigs, ye wretched scoundrels, for the hour is come! . . .

Jesus of Nazareth was of all men the least of a "Penny Lady," or comprehensive universal Soup-Kitchen character; he pitied sorrow and sin and pain, with an infinite, outbursting, helpful pity, wheresoever he met with it; but so likewise did he smite with an infinite, withering indignation whatsoever deserved that; and on the whole went about with a quite other object than consciously seeking either of these. "To do the will of My Father,"—were it even that of being scourged out of existence, as a failure and a nonentity, and disgrace to the world.

—THOMAS CARLYLE[5]

Epilogue

❦

I have a few things against you, because you allow that woman Jezebel, who calls herself a prophetess, to teach and seduce My servants.

Revelation 2:20

*J*esus' final public diatribe in Matthew 23 against the lawyers, Scribes, and Pharisees was by no means the end of His long conflict with them. Just days after He delivered that message, Jewish authorities turned Him over to the Romans to be crucified.[1] It was the most drawn-out and demeaning form of execution they could possibly subject Him to. Thus the conspiracy first hatched in John 11:43 finally came to fruition. And the true evil of Israel's religious establishment was manifest in the most wicked act of cruelty and injustice ever committed. The "sons of those who murdered the prophets" (Matthew 23:31) finally murdered their Messiah—the only truly innocent, fully righteous human being ever.

Anyone watching Jesus die must have thought they were observing the final triumph of the Sanhedrin over their most outspoken

Adversary. It seemed as if Jesus would be permanently silenced. From the religious leaders' perspective, that should have been the end of the matter. They must have expected that His teaching would eventually fade from memory and His Name would remain only as a warning to anyone else inclined to oppose the doctrine and the authority of the mighty Sanhedrin.

Of course that was not at all what really happened. Days later, Christ rose triumphantly from the grave, emboldening His followers and unleashing an army of disciples to carry on His work. "Go into all the world and preach the gospel to every creature," He told them (Mark 16:15). "[Teach] them to observe *all things* that I have commanded you" (Matthew 28:20). Implicit in that commission was a command to contend for the truth in the same way He had done.

WALKING AS HE WALKED

Some readers might question whether Christ is really the example we should follow in confronting error. After all, He was God incarnate, with all the wisdom of divine omniscience available to Him. He could see into other people's hearts and read their thoughts. He knew truth perfectly without any of the limitations we suffer from as fallen creatures. We're naturally prone to error; He was immune from error of any kind.

And didn't Jesus Himself say we should *not* try to separate wheat from tares? "Lest while you gather up the tares you also uproot the wheat with them. [But] let both grow together until the harvest" (Matthew 13:29-30). He also said, "Judge not, and you shall not be judged. Condemn not, and you shall not be condemned" (Luke 6:37). After all, "The Father . . . has committed all judgment to the

Son" (John 5:22). Who are we to step into that role and usurp authority that is explicitly given to Christ?

That is exactly right when it comes to judging the secrets of men's hearts—their motives, their private thoughts, or their hidden intentions. We cannot see those things, so we cannot judge them adequately. We're not even supposed to try. "He who judges me is the Lord. Therefore judge nothing before the time, until the Lord comes, who will both bring to light the hidden things of darkness and reveal the counsels of the hearts" (1 Corinthians 4:4-5). "Who are you to judge another's servant? To his own master he stands or falls" (Romans 14:4). "God will judge the secrets of men by Jesus Christ" (Romans 2:16).

That is the whole point of the parable of the tares: the tares *look* like wheat in every superficial way. Until they bear fruit and it ripens it is virtually impossible to tell wheat from tares. The tares therefore represent people who look and act like Christians—false professors. They blend into the fellowship of the church, give a fine-sounding testimony about their faith in Christ, and otherwise *seem* exactly like authentic believers. But they are not authentic. Their faith is a sham. They are unregenerate hangers-on. We know there are tares in almost every fellowship of believers, because Jesus gave that parable as an illustration of what His kingdom would be like in the church age, and because from time to time one of the tares will abandon the faith completely, embrace some damnable heresy, or sell out to some sin which he or she is unwilling to abandon or repent from. In such cases, we *are* supposed to confront the individual, call them to repentance, and put them out of the church if they steadfastly refuse to repent (Matthew 18:15-18).

Phony Christians and worldly pretenders are permitted by God to fall away for the very purpose of reminding us that not everyone who claims to be a Christian really is. "They went out from us, but they were not of us; for if they had been of us, they would have continued with us; but they went out that they might be made manifest, that none of them were of us" (1 John 2:19).

But notice: people who actively *teach* serious error—especially doctrines that corrupt vital gospel truth—are to be confronted and opposed. Their false ideas are to be refuted. They are to be called to repentance. And if they refuse the admonition and continue their assault against truth, we have a duty to denounce their error and do everything we can to thwart their efforts to spread it. Such false teachers are not "tares" to be tolerated in the church; they are accursed antichrists (1 John 2:18) to be exposed, contradicted, denounced, and disavowed. Paul was clear about this: "Even if we, or an angel from heaven, preach any other gospel to you than what we have preached to you, let him be accursed. As we have said before, so now I say again, if anyone preaches any other gospel to you than what you have received, let him be accursed" (Galatians 1:8-9). The apostle John was likewise adamant:

> Many deceivers have gone out into the world who do not confess Jesus Christ as coming in the flesh. This is a deceiver and an antichrist. Look to yourselves, that we do not lose those things we worked for, but that we may receive a full reward. Whoever transgresses and does not abide in the doctrine of Christ does not have God. He who abides in the doctrine of Christ has both the Father and the Son. If anyone comes to you and does not bring this doctrine, do not receive him into your house nor greet him; for he who greets him shares in his evil deeds. (2 John 7-11)

As we have noted from the beginning, we do indeed need to exercise due caution in making judgments about the gravity of someone else's error. We must never judge superficially. We need to remember that we are indeed prone to misjudgments and errors of our own. "We all stumble in many things" (James 3:2).

It is quite true that those things should keep us humble. As a matter of fact, almost every time Scripture holds up Christ as our example to follow, the stress is on His humility—especially His willingness to bear personal insult without lashing back or being belligerent:

> When you do good and suffer, if you take it patiently, this is commendable before God. For to this you were called, because Christ also suffered for us, leaving us an example, that you should follow His steps: "who committed no sin, nor was deceit found in His mouth"; who, when He was reviled, did not revile in return; when He suffered, He did not threaten, but committed Himself to Him who judges righteously. (1 Peter 2:20-23)

It was immediately after He washed the disciples' feet that Jesus said, "I have given you an example, that you should do as I have done to you" (John 13:15). And when the apostle John writes, "He who says he abides in Him ought himself also to walk just as He walked" (1 John 2:6)—the context is all about love.

In other words, following Christ's steps starts with being willing to give of oneself—being willing to suffer as He suffered, loving as He loved, and being humble as He was humble. "The fruit of the Spirit is love, joy, peace, longsuffering, kindness, goodness, faithfulness, gentleness, [and] self-control" (Galatians 5:22-23). We are forbidden to be pugnacious and urged to "pursue righteousness, faith, love, peace with those who call on the Lord out of a pure heart" (2 Timothy 2:22). Scripture commends meekness, commands us to be peacemakers, instructs us to be gentle, and forbids us to judge what we cannot appraise righteously.

JUDGE WITH RIGHTEOUS JUDGMENT

But none of that gives us any reason to suspend judgment altogether. In fact, it would be sinful to do so. Discernment is every Christian's duty: "Test all things; hold fast what is good. Abstain from every form of evil" (1 Thessalonians 5:21-22). "Judge with righteous judgment" (John 7:24). We are also called to be soldiers for the cause of truth. The spiritual conflict between the forces of darkness and the truth of God is, after all, *war.*

That means, among other things, that we have some fighting to do. As we have seen throughout this book, the popular notion that conflict is always to be avoided is simply wrong. There are times when we *must* be confrontive rather than collegial. "For there are many insubordinate, both idle talkers and deceivers, especially those of the circumcision, whose mouths must be stopped" (Titus 1:10-11).

If you wince at that or think there's no way such an aggressive attitude could possibly be a sanctified response to doctrinal error in a postmodern culture, you need to review and rethink what the entire New Testament says about false teachers and how Christians should respond to them—especially from Jesus' point of view.

A FINAL WORD FROM CHRIST

I mentioned at the very start of this epilogue that Jesus' crucifixion did not put an end to his conflict with false religion. Neither did His ascension into heaven.

In His final recorded messages to the church, given to the apostle John in a vision several decades after Christ's ascension into heaven, we see that the silencing of false teachers was still one of our Lord's primary concerns, even from His throne in heaven. He addressed seven churches—Ephesus, Smyrna, Pergamos, Thyatira,

Sardis, Philadelphia, and Laodicea. Only two of the churches, Smyrna and Philadelphia, were commended for their faithfulness without any qualification or hint of rebuke. Both of them had remained true to Christ despite the influence of "those who say they are Jews and are not, but are a synagogue of Satan" (Revelation 2:9; 3:9). All five other churches received various measures of rebuke, based on how corrupt, unfaithful, or spiritually lethargic they were.

A prominent theme in practically all Jesus' messages to those seven churches is the issue of how they responded to false teachers and rank heretics in their midst. Ephesus, of course, was the church Jesus rebuked with these words: "I have this against you, that you have left your first love" (2:4). But Ephesus was nonetheless strongly commended *twice* because they refused to tolerate false teachers. Before He admonished them about leaving their first love, Jesus praised them for their steadfast resistance to false apostles: "I know your works, your labor, your patience, and that you cannot bear those who are evil. And you have tested those who say they are apostles and are not, and have found them liars" (v. 2). Afterward, He told them, "But this you have, that you hate the deeds of the Nicolaitans, which I also hate" (v. 6).

The epistle to Pergamos was basically the flip side of that message to Ephesus. Christ commended the saints at Pergamos for holding fast to His name and not denying the faith, even though they dwelt where Satan's throne was. In other words, they had successfully persevered in the faith despite *external* threats of persecution. Unlike Ephesus, they had not left their first love. Nevertheless, Christ had a list of rebukes for them, and these were all related to their tolerance of false doctrine in their own midst. It was as if they were utterly insensible to *internal* dangers that came with a tolerant attitude toward deviant doctrines. He wrote, "I have a few things against you, because you have there those who hold the doctrine of

Balaam. . . . You also have those who hold the doctrine of the Nicolaitans, which thing I hate" (vv. 14-15).

Likewise to Thyatira, He wrote: "I have a few things against you, because you allow that woman Jezebel, who calls herself a prophetess, to teach and seduce My servants" (v. 20).

The church at Sardis was spiritually dead, and the church at Laodicea was lukewarm and smug. Those churches had clearly already lost their will to oppose false doctrine and purge sin from their midst. Their lack of zeal, lack of energy, and (in the case of Sardis) lack of any life was a direct result of their failure to keep themselves and their fellowship pure. They had not been sufficiently wary of false teaching, and therefore they had not remained devoted to Christ alone. The warnings Christ gave them are chilling reminders that churches do go bad. When that happens, it is almost never because they succumb to dangers from the outside. Rather, it is almost always because they let down their guard and allow false doctrines to be disseminated freely inside the church. Apathy sets in, followed inevitably by spiritual disaster.

It is clear from those letters to the churches in Revelation that battling heresy is a duty Christ expects every Christian to be devoted to. Whether we like it or not, our very existence in this world involves spiritual warfare—it is not a party or a picnic. If Christ Himself devoted so much of His time and energy during His earthly ministry to the task of confronting and refuting false teachers, surely that must be high on our agenda as well. His style of ministry ought to be the model for ours, and His zeal against false religion ought to fill our hearts and minds as well.

"He who has an ear, let him hear what the Spirit says to the churches" (Revelation 2:7, 11, 17, 29; 3:6, 13, 22).

Appendix

❧

JOSEPHUS ON THE MAJOR JEWISH SECTS

The following excerpt is from William Whiston's 1737 translation of Josephus's Antiquities of the Jews, *book 18, chapter 1, paragraphs 2–6:*

2. The Jews had for a great while had three sects of philosophy peculiar to themselves; the sect of the Essens, and the sect of the Sadducees, and the third sort of opinions was that of those called Pharisees; of which sects, although I have already spoken in the second book of the Jewish War, yet will I a little touch upon them now.

3. Now, for the Pharisees, they live meanly, and despise delicacies in diet; and they follow the conduct of reason; and what that prescribes to them as good for them they do; and they think they ought earnestly to strive to observe reason's dictates for practice. They also pay a respect to such as are in years; nor are they so bold as to contradict them in any thing which they have introduced; and when they determine that all things are done by fate, they do not take away the freedom from men of acting as they think fit; since their notion is, that it hath pleased God to make a temperament, whereby what he wills is done, but so that the will of man can act virtuously or

viciously. They also believe that souls have an immortal rigor in them, and that under the earth there will be rewards or punishments, according as they have lived virtuously or viciously in this life; and the latter are to be detained in an everlasting prison, but that the former shall have power to revive and live again; on account of which doctrines they are able greatly to persuade the body of the people; and whatsoever they do about Divine worship, prayers, and sacrifices, they perform them according to their direction; insomuch that the cities give great attestations to them on account of their entire virtuous conduct, both in the actions of their lives and their discourses also.

4. But the doctrine of the Sadducees is this: That souls die with the bodies; nor do they regard the observation of any thing besides what the law enjoins them; for they think it an instance of virtue to dispute with those teachers of philosophy whom they frequent: but this doctrine is received but by a few, yet by those still of the greatest dignity. But they are able to do almost nothing of themselves; for when they become magistrates, as they are unwillingly and by force sometimes obliged to be, they addict themselves to the notions of the Pharisees, because the multitude would not otherwise bear them.

5. The doctrine of the Essens is this: That all things are best ascribed to God. They teach the immortality of souls, and esteem that the rewards of righteousness are to be earnestly striven for; and when they send what they have dedicated to God into the temple, they do not offer sacrifices (3) because they have more pure lustrations of their own; on which account they are excluded from the common court of the temple, but offer their sacrifices themselves; yet is their course of life better than that of other men; and they entirely addict

themselves to husbandry. It also deserves our admiration, how much they exceed all other men that addict themselves to virtue, and this in righteousness; and indeed to such a degree, that as it hath never appeared among any other men, neither Greeks nor barbarians, no, not for a little time, so hath it endured a long while among them. This is demonstrated by that institution of theirs, which will not suffer any thing to hinder them from having all things in common; so that a rich man enjoys no more of his own wealth than he who hath nothing at all. There are about four thousand men that live in this way, and neither marry wives, nor are desirous to keep servants; as thinking the latter tempts men to be unjust, and the former gives the handle to domestic quarrels; but as they live by themselves, they minister one to another. They also appoint certain stewards to receive the incomes of their revenues, and of the fruits of the ground; such as are good men and priests, who are to get their corn and their food ready for them. They none of them differ from others of the Essens in their way of living, but do the most resemble those Dacae who are called Polistae (4) [dwellers in cities].

6. But of the fourth sect of Jewish philosophy, Judas the Galilean was the author. These men agree in all other things with the Pharisaic notions; but they have an inviolable attachment to liberty, and say that God is to be their only Ruler and Lord. They also do not value dying any kinds of death, nor indeed do they heed the deaths of their relations and friends, nor can any such fear make them call any man lord. And since this immovable resolution of theirs is well known to a great many, I shall speak no further about that matter; nor am I afraid that any thing I have said of them should be disbelieved, but rather fear, that what I have said is beneath the resolution

they show when they undergo pain. And it was in Gessius Florus's time that the nation began to grow mad with this distemper, who was our procurator, and who occasioned the Jews to go wild with it by the abuse of his authority, and to make them revolt from the Romans. And these are the sects of Jewish philosophy.

Notes

PROLOGUE

1. Doug Pagitt, *Reimagining Spiritual Formation* (Grand Rapids: Zondervan, 2003), 92.
2. I covered this issue in detail in *Reckless Faith* (Wheaton: Crossway, 1994), 91–117.

INTRODUCTION

1. Some readers might think I'm employing hyperbole or overstating the decline of evangelical conviction, but I don't believe I am. Practically every biblical doctrine you could name (from historic trinitarianism to justification by faith) is currently being questioned or attacked by one or another influential figure on the contemporary evangelical landscape. These are no longer anomalies that belong only to the movement's fringe. One of Christian publishing's top-selling authors for the past decade is non trinitarian; a sitting president of the Evangelical Theological Society recently converted to Roman Catholicism; and it has become commonplace for evangelical leaders to voice skepticism about the authority of Scripture, justification by faith alone, substitutionary atonement, and practically every other distinctive of historic evangelical doctrine. This flood of cynicism has arisen not because some new fact has come to light that raises serious questions about something evangelical Protestants formerly believed, but simply because certainty itself is no longer in vogue. I've documented many of these things—and more—in *The Truth War* (Nashville: Thomas Nelson, 2007), so I won't belabor the point further here.
2. Evangelical publications reflect an obsession with the church's relationship to "the culture." In practical terms, this has come to mean familiarity with secular fads and a craving to fit comfortably into pop culture. That ambition is evident in the undue importance so many churches place on being "contemporary." A recent survey of church websites revealed hundreds that featured the slogan "We're just like you"—or some near variant on the front page.
3. "An Evangelical Manifesto: A Declaration of Evangelical Identity and Public Commitment" (Washington DC, May 7, 2008), 9. The Manifesto describes fundamentalism as "an overlay on the Christian faith and . . . an essentially modern reaction to the modern world."
4. All those things are good in proper proportions and appropriate circumstances, of course. But inherently subjective ideals like those have in effect been made into absolute and inviolable standards. (Ironically, this postmodernized taxonomy of virtues is championed mainly by people who say they don't like either absolutes or standards.) Synthetic rules like those now govern the evangelical conversation, while authentically *biblical* values—such as boldness, steadfastness, stoutheartedness, and assurance—have been reclassified as arrogant and pushed to the back of the bus.
5. "CNN Presents: God's Christian Warriors" (aired August 23, 2007). I was a guest on an episode of *Larry King Live* three days before that segment aired ("God's Warriors': Fighters for Faith," aired August 20, 2007). Ms. Amanpour showed preview clips from the extended series, and Larry King interviewed a diverse panel of religious leaders (including a Jewish rabbi and an Islamic theologian). I pointed out that authentic Christianity is defined by Scripture, and the Bible says the kingdom of Christ is not advanced by political clout or military might. So the Christian concept of spiritual warfare has nothing whatsoever in common with Islamic jihad. The one other professing Christian on the panel was a politi-

cal and theological liberal. (Although this man used the title "Reverend," Larry King introduced him by saying he believed the man was an agnostic.) The man could hardly contain his disagreement with me until it was his turn to speak. He suggested that Christians who take the Bible literally are as dangerous as Muslim suicide bombers, because their worldview "divides and makes it very difficult to have the kind of dialogue that we might use to find common ground, common values and move forward."

6. http://russandrebecca.wordpress.com/2007/08/27/gods-warriors-wrap-up/
7. http://christianresearchnetwork.info/2007/11/01/jesus-didnt-fight-a-truth-war/

CHAPTER ONE: WHEN IT'S WRONG TO BE "NICE"

1. Josephus, *Jewish Wars,* (Preface, 1).
2. Josephus, *The Life,* 2.
3. Josephus, *Antiquities,* 18:3–4 (see Appendix).
4. "An Evangelical Manifesto: A Declaration of Evangelical Identity and Public Commitment" (Washington, DC, May 7, 2008), 8.
5. Ibid., 9.
6. Ibid., 4.
7. Ibid., 5.
8. Ibid., 3
9. Tony Campolo with Shane Claiborne,, "On Evangelicals and Interfaith Cooperation," *Cross Currents,* Vol. 55, no. 1. Spring 2005, (online at http://www.crosscurrents.org/CompoloSpring2005.htm). Campolo is not advocating dialogue merely for the sake of political peace or cultural harmony. He is expressly calling for *religious* dialogue between evangelicals and Muslims with a goal of "interreligious cooperation." Underlying the whole interview seems to be the suggestion that Christians should regard Islam as an equal (and potentially a partner) in spiritual matters (starting with the pursuit of "goodness"). Claiborne introduces the interview by saying it was done at the request of "a devout Muslim brother." Although Campolo claims this newfound spirit of brotherhood with other religions does not necessarily mean we have to "give up trying to convert each other," he immediately adds that it *does* mean we should stop saying that Muslims who reject Christ are in peril of eternal judgment. He even strongly implies that this is one way Muslims are morally superior to Christians: "The Muslim community is very evangelistic, however what Muslims will not do is condemn Jews and Christians to hell if in fact they do not accept Islam. . . Islam is much more gracious towards evangelical Christians who are faithful to the New Testament, than Christians are towards Islamic people who are faithful to the Koran." Being "gracious" by Campolo's definition, seems to entail refusing to say plainly that someone else's beliefs are wrong—even when they are damnably wrong. Campolo adds this: "I think there are Muslim brothers and sisters who are willing to say, 'You live up to the truth as you understand it. I will live up to the truth as I understand it, and we will leave it up to God on judgment day.'" Then he adds, "There is much in Christianity that would suggest exactly the same thing." In reality, there is *nothing* in Scripture that justifies embracing people from other religions as "brothers and sisters" or holding this kind of interfaith dialogue. In fact, Scripture emphatically forbids us to seek spiritual common ground or cooperation with false religions (2 Corinthians 6:14–17).
10. Brian McLaren, *The Secret Message of Jesus: Uncovering the Truth That Could Change Everything* (Nashville: Thomas Nelson, 2006), 4.
11. See note 1 in the Introduction.
12. R. C. H. Lenski, The Interpretation of John (Minneapolis: Augsburg Publishing House, 1943), 205–07.

CHAPTER TWO: TWO PASSOVERS

1. *The Interpretation of St. John's Gospel* (Columbus, OH: Wartburg, 1943), 207.
2. Throughout his gospel, John uses the expression "the Jews" as a reference to the Sanhedrin and their representatives. It is not a reference to the Jewish race in general. (Some have suggested that John's gospel has an anti-Semitic overtone because when he mentions "the Jews" it is usually in a disparaging way. But remember that John himself was Jewish. He was certainly not making a slur against his own ethnic heritage.) A careful comparison of all the places where John speaks of "the Jews" confirms that he never uses that expression in a negative sense to speak of

Jewish people in general. In fact, John makes a clear distinction between "the Jews" (speaking of ruling elders) and "the people" (speaking about the common people of Israel) in John 7:11–13. On rare occasions he employs the expression "the Jews" in contrast to Samaritans or Romans. But in every case where he is making that kind of ethnic distinction, his point is either positive (John 4:22) or neutral (John 18:33). Whenever John speaks of "the Jews" in a negative sense, it is always a shorthand reference to the Jewish rulers or their deputies. It is John's abbreviated version of the expression found in Luke 7:3: "elders of the Jews."

3. George Swinnock, "Do You Worship God," a sermon from the Puritan era on 1 Timothy 4:7, reprinted in *Free Grace Broadcaster*, Issue 177, (Summer 2001), 21–22.

CHAPTER THREE: A MIDNIGHT INTERVIEW
1. The Shining of the Face of Moses, 1890

CHAPTER FOUR: THIS MAN SPEAKS BLASPHEMIES
1. Robert L. Thomas and Stanley N. Gundry, *A Harmony of the Gospels* (Chicago: Moody, 1978), 348.
2. Nazareth is situated in a bowl-shaped depression between hills. A mile and a half due south of the town is a prominent hill known as Mount Precipice, with a sheer drop on its southern face. That is the traditional spot where the crowd tried to throw Jesus to His death. If Jesus was marched that far by this angry crowd, their determination to kill Jesus was perhaps more fierce and less impulsive than it might seem at first glance. There is also a more modest stone ledge with a sheer forty-foot drop-off on the edge of a hill just a short distance *above* where the synagogue is thought to have been located. That, too, fits Luke's description of the "brow of the hill."
3. "Sweet Savour," 1866.

CHAPTER FIVE: BREAKING THE SABBATH
1. For more on Matthew's conversion, see John MacArthur, *The Gospel According to Jesus* (Grand Rapids: Zondervan, 2008), 73–79.
2. Luke may seem to suggest that the Pharisees countered with a question about why the disciples of John the Baptist and their own disciples fast, while Jesus' disciples did not. But a comparison of the gospels shows that Luke's use of "they" is generic; Matthew expressly says it was some disciples of John the Baptist, not the Pharisees, who subsequently raised a question about fasting.
3. "Now when He was in Jerusalem at the Passover, during the feast . . . " John (2:23); "Now the Passover, a feast of the Jews, was near" (6:4); "Now the Jews' Feast of Tabernacles was at hand" (7:2); "Now it was the Feast of Dedication in Jerusalem, and it was winter" (10:22); "And the Passover of the Jews was near, and many went from the country up to Jerusalem" (11:55).
4. The following year's Passover is mentioned in John 6:4, and that year's Feast of Tabernacles follows in 7:2. If the feast mentioned in 5:1 is also the Feast of Tabernacles, then chapters 5–6 would mark the passing of a full year in John's gospel, and that seems to fit best with everything we can legitimately deduce from Scripture about the chronology of Jesus' life.

   Also, it would be uncharacteristic for the apostle John to speak of Passover merely as "the feast." He consistently refers to it as "the Passover" (2:13, 23; 6:4; 11:55; 12:1; 18:28, 39; 19:14), or "the Feast of the Passover" (John 13:1). In John 7:2, however, John describes events from the following year's Feast of Tabernacles, and then he repeatedly refers to it simply as "the feast" (vv. 8, 10, 11, 14, 37). In all likelihood, then, John 5:1 is a reference to the Feast of Tabernacles, which fell at the end of the summer, in the second year of Jesus' public ministry.
5. I've omitted a portion of this passage because it does not appear in the oldest and best manuscripts of John's gospel. It has the earmarks of a marginal note inserted by a scribe that found its way into later copies of the actual text. The omitted section attempts to explain the stirring of the water mentioned in verse 7 by suggesting this was the work of an angel and that it resulted in miraculous healing for the first person in the pool after the water began moving. But nothing else in the text mentions an angel or suggests that the water's healing power was supernatural. More likely, the pool was fed by an intermittent spring of mineral water with medicinal qualities, and the stirring of the waters would occur when the

spring flowed, signifying a fresh infusion of soothing warmth and minerals. The man's comment in verse 7 may indicate a popular or superstitious belief that when the water began to flow, the first person in the pool would benefit the most.

Incidentally, this is also the only mention of Bethesda in Scripture. The existence of the pool—described here as a large cistern surrounded by five covered colonnades—was questioned by skeptics until archaeologists discovered it in the nineteenth century, complete with the ruins of the five porticoes.

6. D. A. Carson, *The Gospel According to John,* in *The Pillar New Testament Commentary* (Grand Rapids: Eerdmans, 1991), 243.

7. The statement that "the Father . . . has granted the Son to have life in Himself" cannot possibly mean that the Son's *existence* is derived from the Father, because that would flatly contradict the assertion that He has life in Himself. The expression simply acknowledges the personal distinction that exists between Father and Son, while still affirming the absolute equality of essence they share. This, of course, is one of the great mysteries of the Trinity. It is identical to the difficulties posed by the expression "only-begotten" in John 1:14, 18; 3:16, 18; 1 John 4:19. How can Christ be "begotten" and yet eternal and self-existent? The answer, of course, is that the word *begotten* with respect to God the Father and Christ the Son describes the *eternal relationship* between the first and second members of the Trinity, not the Son's *ontological origin,* for He had no beginning in either time or eternity but has always been (Revelation 1:8, 11).

Here in John 5, Jesus is not giving a lecture on the fine points of the Trinity; He is simply declaring His own absolute equality with God. The entire context makes that point clearly, and the religious leaders of Israel certainly got it, even though latter-day Arians and others who deny the deity of Christ sometimes try to twist verse 26 to make it seem like a denial of the very thing it asserts.

8. Likewise, in John 14:28, when Jesus says to the disciples, "If you loved Me, you would rejoice because I said, 'I am going to the Father,' for *My Father is greater than I,"* that statement (italics added) has to be interpreted in its larger context. Only moments before, Jesus had told Philip, "He who has seen Me has seen the Father" (v. 9), plainly affirming once more His absolute equality and oneness-of-essence with God. Verse 28, however, is clearly speaking about the divine glory. Christ had stepped down from that glory during His incarnation, and in that sense *and that sense only,* the Father was "greater than" the Son. Jesus was about to return to heaven and step back into the fullness of the divine glory, so He tells the disciples, "If you loved me, you would rejoice." In context, then, John 14:28 poses no conflict at all with the many clear affirmations of Jesus' deity in John's gospel; rather that verse simply affirms that once Christ was risen and glorified, He would return to the full glory of the Godhead. Read correctly, it is yet another affirmation of Jesus' deity.

9. For a full exposition of the entire chapter, see John MacArthur, *The MacArthur New Testament Commentary: John 1–11* (Chicago: Moody, 2006), 169–216.

10. Assuming John 5 describes events that occurred during the Feast of Tabernacles (see note 4 of this chapter), that would have been about the third week of October on our calendars. That would also be the time for gleaning grain. So the events of John 5 and the controversy in the grain fields (described in Matthew 21:1–8; Mark 2:23–28; and Luke 6:1–5) could quite possibly have occurred on successive Sabbaths.

11. The Herodians were a political party, not a religious sect. As their name suggests, they supported the Herodian dynasty—which set them at odds with the Pharisees on most spiritual matters. But they believed Herod was the true king of the Jews; therefore, all Jesus' talk about the kingdom of God must have been deeply unsettling to them. That the Pharisees would conspire with them against Jesus reveals just how desperate the religious elite in Israel were to get rid of Him. Near the end of Jesus' earthly ministry, the Herodians will appear once more working in concert with the Pharisees against Jesus (Matthew 22:15–16).

12. *Your God Is Too Small* (New York: Macmillan, 1953), 27.

CHAPTER 6: HARD PREACHING

1. For a verse-by-verse exposition of the Sermon on the Mount, see *The MacArthur New Testament Commentary: Matthew 1–7* (Chicago: Moody, 1985), 130–489. For the Bread

of Life discourse (John 6), see *The MacArthur New Testament Commentary: John 1–11* (Chicago: Moody, 2006), 217–74.

2. Matthew's gospel is not a strictly chronological account. He sometimes arranges incidents in a topical fashion. His ordered telling of the Sabbath controversies, for example, including the grain field incident and the man with the withered hand, are found in Matthew 12. Although the Sermon on the Mount comes *after* the earliest Sabbath controversy in any chronological survey of Jesus' ministry, the sermon was of such importance in the way it summarized Jesus' teaching that Matthew put it as close as possible to the beginning of his gospel; thus prior to his account of the Sabbath conflicts. Matthew also records the details of the Sermon in much greater detail than Luke (the only other evangelist to include an account of that message). Once past the Sermon (Matthew 8:2), Matthew begins dealing with events from Jesus' life in a much more chronological fashion. Even so, he occasionally groups incidents from different periods of Jesus' Galilean ministry in topical order rather than strict chronological sequence. He does that deliberately, but his approach must be borne in mind by readers, or the chronology can become confusing.

   Luke's stated intention, by way of contrast, is to "set in order [the] narrative." Even that expression doesn't necessarily preclude a logical and topical order as opposed to a strict timeline, but Luke does seem to follow the actual chronology more closely than any other gospel. (Luke and Mark both order their narratives essentially the same.)

3. Remember that space does not permit us to examine every verse in the sermon; we are limited here to a bird's eye survey of its major themes. Those who know me will understand that my preferred mode of teaching is verse by verse, but in this case, the big picture is what's most important.

   Without going into any great detail about verses 13–16, however, it is worth adding as a footnote that those verses are a perfect transition from the Beatitudes into the section where Jesus systematically explains the fuller sense of the law. The Beatitudes themselves are a fine summary of the moral principles of Moses' law. Moreover, those qualities that are enumerated in the Beatitudes *are* the salty flavor of which Jesus speaks in verse 13 and the radiance He mentions in verse 14. He is telling His disciples that even though the world devalues virtue and persecutes the righteous, if true believers will live out their faith boldly and openly, their holy character and behavior will have an effect like salt to preserve and flavor, and light to brighten and show the way, in an otherwise dark and unsavory world. Some try to interpret this passage as a mandate for political or cultural activism. It is not that; it is simply a call to bold, holy living, even in the face of persecution.

4. Luke records a slightly different, even shorter, version of the prayer in a different context at a later point in Jesus' ministry (Luke 11:1–3).

5. In the chapter that follows, we'll look more closely at the motives that made the Sanhedrin so determined to reject and destroy Jesus. ·

6. Jonathan L. Reed, *Archaeology and the Galilean Jesus* (Harrisburg, PA: Trinity, 2000), 83.

7. John 6 is not about transubstantiation (the Roman Catholic belief that the communion elements literally become flesh and blood). It is not even a reference to the communion ordinance, which was yet to be established. The symbolic language Jesus used employs the very same figure as Christian communion, which pictures our partaking by faith in Jesus' atoning work (which of course involved the giving of His body and blood). But when Jesus spoke of "eating . . . flesh" and "drinking . . . blood," He was describing what the ordinance signifies, not the ordinance itself. Otherwise, the communion elements would be the instruments of our justification, and Scripture is clear in teaching that faith alone is the instrument of justification (Romans 4:4–5).

8. *Letters to a Diminished Church* (Nashville: Thomas Nelson, 2004).

CHAPTER SEVEN: UNPARDONABLE SIN

1. Luke 12:10 comes at a different time in Jesus' ministry but under circumstances almost identical to what occurs in Matthew 12. The sin Jesus calls unpardonable in Luke 12:10 must therefore also be understood in light of this passage. Both passages are clearly warning against a specific sin, not setting up a broad category of sins that are deemed unpardonable. And it is the very same sin in each of the two incidents.

NOTES

2. As a matter of fact, Luke 11:14–36 is so similar to Matthew 12:22–45 that some commentators believe they describe the same incident. Jesus heals a man and some Pharisees accuse Him of using satanic power to do it. But the setting and some of the details are different. Luke, who follows chronological order more closely, describes an event that took place almost a year later, in Judea. So it seems a different group of Pharisees, in an almost identical situation, likewise spoke the same unpardonable blasphemy against the Spirit of God.
3. *The Everlasting Man* (New York: Dodd, Mead, 1925), 187.

CHAPTER EIGHT: WOE
1. Christians have traditionally celebrated the Christ's triumphal entry on Palm Sunday. The New Testament is not specific as to the day, however, and the chronology of Passion Week seems to work best if we take Monday as the day of the Triumphal Entry. See Harold Hoehner, *Chronological Aspects of the Life of Christ* (Grand Rapids: Zondervan, 1977), 91.
2. Bible scholars sometimes debate whether there were really two temple cleansings. Those who believe Jesus cleansed the temple only once usually suggest that John simply gave his account out of order. There are several reasons to reject that view. First, if we take John's account at face value, there is nothing that would indicate he was jumping around chronologically in that part of his narrative. If he was describing the same event as Mark 11:15–18, John didn't merely get it out of order; he moved a major event from the very end of Jesus' public ministry to the very beginning. Second, the details of the two accounts are significantly different. In the early incident, for example, Jesus made a whip and used it to drive the animals out. In this later incident, He overturned seats and tables and expelled the evil merchants, but there is no mention of either a whip or an animal stampede.

     Jesus' words are also different. All three Synoptics say He quoted from Isaiah 56:7 and Jeremiah 7:11; but in the event John describes, He speaks words of His own, without quoting Scripture. Furthermore, *only* John records that He said, "Destroy this temple, and in three days I will raise it up" (John 2:19). Matthew and Mark both say the Pharisees cited that statement against Him in His trials (Matthew 26:61; Mark 14:58), and that the hostile crowd threw that statement in His face while He hung on the cross (Matthew 27:40; Mark 15:29). But the only gospel that records when and where Jesus actually said those words is John.
3. A full commentary on the passage is available in *The MacArthur New Testament Commentary: Matthew 16–23* (Chicago: Moody, 1988), 353–404.
4. Here was a perfect opportunity for Jesus to have a friendly conversation with His adversaries, if He had thought that an effective way to minister to them. It was not a formal setting. It was not in a synagogue or any public setting where Jesus might be concerned about the impression such a friendly overture might leave on innocent bystanders. This was a casual lunch in a Pharisee's private home. And yet Jesus' demeanor and His dialogue were no different—no more gentle and no more amicable—from any other time when He had an opportunity to challenge pharisaical hypocrisy.
5. Cited in Mark Cumming, *The Carlyle Encyclopedia* (Madison, NJ: Fairleigh Dickenson University, 2004), 251.

EPILOGUE
1. See John MacArthur, *The Murder of Jesus* (Nashville: Word, 2000) for a thorough exposition of the biblical narrative dealing with Jesus' arrest and crucifixion.

About the Author

❧

Widely known for his thorough, candid approach to teaching God's Word, John MacArthur is a popular author and conference speaker and has served as pastor-teacher of Grace Community Church in Sun Valley, California since 1969. John and his wife, Patricia, have four grown children and fifteen grandchildren.

John's pulpit ministry has been extended around the globe through his media ministry, Grace to You, and its satellite offices in seven countries. In addition to producing daily radio programs for nearly two thousand English and Spanish radio outlets worldwide, Grace to You distributes books, software, audiotapes, and CDs by John MacArthur.

John is president of The Master's College and Seminary and has written hundreds of books and study guides, each one biblical and practical. Best-selling titles include *The Gospel According to Jesus*, *Truth War*, *The Murder of Jesus*, *Twelve Ordinary Men*, *Twelve Extraordinary Women*, and *The MacArthur Study Bible*, a 1998 ECPA Gold Medallion recipient.

An Excerpt from *Slave*

❧

"*I* am a Christian."

The young man said nothing else as he stood before the Roman governor, his life hanging in the balance. His accusers pressed him again, hoping to trip him up or force him to recant. But once more he answered with the same short phrase. "I am a Christian."

It was the middle of the second century, during the reign of emperor Marcus Aurelius.[1] Christianity was illegal, and believers throughout the Roman Empire faced the threat of imprisonment, torture, or death. Persecution was especially intense in southern Europe, where Sanctus, a deacon from Vienna, had been arrested and brought to trial. The young man was repeatedly told to renounce the faith he professed. But his resolve was undeterred. "I am a Christian."

No matter what question he was asked, he always gave the same unchanging answer. According to the ancient church historian Eusebius, Sanctus "girded himself against [his accusers] with such firmness that he would not even tell his name, or the nation or city to which he belonged, or whether he was bond or free, but answered in the Roman tongue to all their questions, 'I am a Christian.'"[2] When at last it became obvious that he would say nothing else, he was condemned to severe torture and a public death in the amphitheater. On the day of his execution, he was forced to run the gauntlet, subjected to wild beasts, and fastened to a chair of burning iron. Throughout all

221

of it, his accusers kept trying to break him, convinced that his resistance would crack under the pain of torment. But as Eusebius recounted, "Even thus they did not hear a word from Sanctus except the confession which he had uttered from the beginning."[3] His dying words told of an undying commitment. His rallying cry remained constant throughout his entire trial. "I am a Christian."

For Sanctus, his whole identity—including his name, citizenship, and social status—was found in Jesus Christ. Hence, no better answer could have been given to the questions he was asked. He was a Christian, and that designation defined everything about him.

This same perspective was shared by countless others in the early church. It fueled their witness, strengthened their resolve, and confounded their opponents. When arrested, these courageous believers would confidently respond as Sanctus had, with a succinct assertion of their loyalty to Christ. As one historian explained about the early martyrs:

> They [would reply] to all questionings about them [with] the short but comprehensive answer, 'I am a Christian.' Again and again they caused no little perplexity to their judges by the pertinacity with which they adhered to this brief profession of faith. The question was repeated, 'Who are you?' and they replied, 'I have already said that I am a Christian; and he who says that has thereby named his country, his family, his profession, and all things else besides.'[4]

Following Jesus Christ was the sum of their entire existence.[5] Thus, at the moment when life itself was on the line, nothing else mattered besides identifying themselves with Him.

For these faithful believers, the name "Christian" was much more than just a general religious designation. It defined everything about them, including how they viewed both themselves and the

AN EXCERPT FROM *SLAVE*

world around them. The label underscored their love for a crucified Messiah, along with their willingness to follow Him no matter the cost. It told of the wholesale transformation God had produced in their hearts and witnessed to the fact that they had been made completely new in Him. They had died to their old way of life, having been born again into the family of God. "Christian" was not simply a title, but an entirely new way of thinking—one which had serious implications for how they lived and, ultimately, how they died.

WHAT DOES IT MEAN TO BE A CHRISTIAN?

The early martyrs were crystal clear on what it meant to be a Christian. But ask what it means today and you're likely to get a wide variety of answers, even from those who identify themselves with the label.

For some, being "Christian" is primarily cultural and traditional, a nominal title inherited from a previous generation, the net effect of which involves avoiding certain behaviors and occasionally attending church. For others, being a Christian is largely political, a quest to defend moral values in the public square or perhaps to preserve those values by withdrawing from the public square altogether. Still more define their Christian experience in terms of a past religious experience, a general belief in Jesus, or a desire to be a good person. Yet all of these fall woefully short of what it truly means to be a Christian from a biblical perspective.

Interestingly, the followers of Jesus Christ were not called "Christians" until ten to fifteen years after the church began. Before that time, they were kn own simply as disciples, brothers, believers, saints, and followers of the Way (a title derived from Christ's reference to Himself, in John 14:6, as "the way, the truth, and the life"). According to Acts 11:26, it was in Antioch of Syria that "the disciples were first called Christians," and since that time the label has stuck.

The name was initially coined by unbelievers as an attempt to deride those who followed a crucified Christ.[6] But what began as a ridicule soon became a badge of honor. To be called "Christians" (in Greek, *Christianoi*) was to be identified as Jesus' disciples and to be associated with Him as loyal followers. In a similar fashion, those in Caesar's household would refer to themselves as *Kaisarianoi* ("those of Caesar") in order to show their deep allegiance to the Roman Emperor. Unlike the *Kaisarianoi*, however, the Christians did not give their ultimate allegiance to Rome or any other earthly power; their full dedication and worship were reserved for Jesus Christ alone.

Thus, to be a *Christian*, in the true sense of the term, is to be a wholehearted follower of Jesus Christ. As the Lord Himself said in John 10:27, "My sheep hear My voice, and I know them, and *they follow Me*" (emphasis added). The name suggests much more than a superficial association with Christ. Rather, it demands a deep affection for Him, allegiance to Him, and submission to His Word. "You are My friends if you do what I command you," Jesus told His disciples in the Upper Room (John 15:14). Earlier He had told the crowds who flocked to hear Him, "If you continue in My word, then you are truly disciples of Mine" (John 8:31); and elsewhere: "If anyone wishes to come after Me, he must deny himself, and take up his cross daily and follow Me" (Luke 9:23; cf. John 12:26).

When we call ourselves *Christians,* we proclaim to the world that everything about us, including our very self-identity, is found in Jesus Christ because we have denied our*selves* in order to follow and obey *Him.* He is both our Savior and our Sovereign, and our lives center on pleasing Him. To claim the title is to say with the apostle Paul, "To live is Christ, and to die is gain" (Phil. 1:21).

A WORD THAT CHANGES EVERYTHING

Since its first appearance in Antioch, the term *Christian* has become the predominant label for those who follow Jesus. It is an appropriate designation because it rightly focuses on the centerpiece of our faith: Jesus Christ. Yet ironically, the word itself appears only three times in the New Testament—twice in the book of Acts and once in 1 Peter 4:16.

In addition to the name *Christian,* the Bible uses a host of other terms to identify the followers of Jesus. Scripture describes us as children of God, citizens of heaven, and lights to the world. We are heirs of God and joint heirs with Christ, members of His body, sheep in His flock, ambassadors in His service, and friends around His table. We are called to compete like athletes, to fight like soldiers, to abide like branches in a vine, and even to desire His Word as newborn babies long for milk. All of these descriptions—each in its own unique way—help us understand what it means to be a Christian.

The Bible uses one metaphor more frequently than any of these. It is a word picture you might not expect, but it is absolutely critical for understanding what it means to follow Jesus.

It is the image of a *slave.*

Time and time again throughout the pages of Scripture, believers are referred to as *slaves of God* and *slaves of Christ.*[7] In fact, whereas the outside world called them "Christians," the earliest believers repeatedly referred to themselves in the New Testament as the Lord's slaves.[8] For them, the two ideas were synonymous. To be a Christian was to be a slave of Christ.[9]

The story of the martyrs confirms that this is precisely what they meant when they declared to their persecutors, "I am a Christian." A young man named Apphianus, for example, was imprisoned and tortured by the Roman authorities. Throughout his trial, he would only reply that he was the slave of Christ.[10] Though he was finally sentenced to death and drowned in the sea, his allegiance to the Lord never wavered.

Other early martyrs responded similarly: "If they consented to amplify their reply, the perplexity of the magistrates was only the more increased, for they seemed to speak insoluble enigmas. 'I am a slave of Caesar,' they said, 'but a Christian who has received his liberty from Christ Himself;' or, contrariwise, 'I am a free man, the slave of Christ;' so that it sometimes happened that it became necessary to send for the proper official (the *curator civitatis*) to ascertain the truth as to their civil condition.[11]

But what proved to be confusing to the Roman authorities made perfect sense to the martyrs of the early church.[12] Their self-identity had been radically redefined by the gospel. Whether slave or free in this life, they had all been set free from sin, yet having been bought with a price, they had all become slaves of Christ. That is what it meant to be a *Christian*.[13]

The New Testament reflects this perspective, commanding believers to submit to Christ completely, and not just as hired servants or spiritual employees but as those who belong wholly to Him. We are told to obey Him without question and follow Him without complaint. Jesus Christ is our Master—a fact we acknowledge every time we call Him "Lord." We are His slaves, called to humbly and wholeheartedly obey and honor Him.

We don't hear that concept much in churches today. In contemporary Christianity the language is anything but slave language.[14] It is about success, health, wealth, prosperity, and the pursuit of happiness. We often hear that God loves people unconditionally and wants them to be all *they* want to be. He wants to fulfill every desire, hope, and dream. *Personal* ambition, *personal* fulfillment, *personal* gratification—these have all become part of the language of evangelical Christianity—and part of what it means to have a "*personal* relationship with Jesus Christ." Instead of teaching the New Testament gospel—where sinners are called to submit to Christ, the contemporary message is exactly the opposite: Jesus is here to fulfill all *your* wishes. Likening Him to a personal assistant or a personal trainer, many churchgoers speak of a *personal* Savior who is eager to do their bidding and help them in their quest for self-satisfaction or individual accomplishment.

The New Testament understanding of the believer's relationship to Christ could not be more opposite. He is the Master and Owner; we are His possession. He is the King, the Lord, and the Son of God. We are His subjects and His subordinates.

In a word, we are His *slaves*.

LOST IN TRANSLATION

Scripture's prevailing description of the Christian's relationship to Jesus Christ is the slave-master relationship.[15] But do a casual read through your English New Testament and you won't see it. The reason for this is as simple as it is shocking: the Greek word for *slave* has been covered up by being mistranslated in almost every English version—going back to both the King James Version and the Geneva Bible that predated it.[16] Though the word *slave* (*doulos* in Greek) appears 124 times in the original text,[17] it is correctly translated only once in the King James. Most of our modern translations do only slightly better.[18] It almost seems like a conspiracy.

Instead of translating *doulos* as "slave," these translations consistently substitute the word *servant* in its place. Ironically, the Greek language has at least half a dozen words that can mean *servant*. The word *doulos* is not one of them.[19] Whenever it is used, both in the New Testament and in secular Greek literature, it always and only means *slave*. According to the *Theological Dictionary of the New Testament*, a foremost authority on the meaning of Greek terms in Scripture, the word *doulos* is used exclusively "either to describe the status of a slave or an attitude corresponding to that of a slave."[20] The dictionary continues by noting that "the meaning is so unequivocal and self-contained that it is superfluous to give examples of the individual terms or to trace the history of the group. . . . [The] emphasis here is always on 'serving as a slave.' Hence we have a service which is not a matter of choice for the one who renders it, which he has to perform whether he likes it or not, because he is subject as a slave to an alien will, to the will of his owner. [The term stresses] the slave's dependence on his lord."

While it is true that the duties of *slave* and *servant* may overlap to some degree, there is a key distinction between the two: servants are *hired*; slaves are *owned*.[21] Servants have an element of freedom in whom they choose to work for and in what they are willing to do. The idea of servanthood maintains some level of autonomy and personal rights. Slaves, on the other hand, have no freedom, autonomy, or rights. In the Greco-Roman world, slaves were considered property, to the point that, in the eyes of the law they were regarded as *things* rather than *persons*.[22] Thus, to be someone's slave was to be his possession, bound to obey his will without hesitation or argument.[23]

Why have modern English translations consistently mistranslated *doulos* when its meaning is unmistakable in Greek? There are at least two answers to this question. First, given the stigmas attached to slavery in Western society, translators have understandably wanted to avoid any association between biblical teaching and the slave trade of the British Empire and American Colonial era.[24] For the average reader today, the word *slave* does not conjure up images of Greco-Roman society, but rather an unjust system of oppression that was finally ended by parliamentary rule in England and by civil war in the States. In order to avoid both potential confusion and negative imagery, modern translators have replaced slave language with servant language.

Second, from a historical perspective, in late-medieval times it was common to translate *doulos* with the Latin word *servus*. Some of the earliest English translations, influenced by the Latin version of the Bible, translated *doulos* as "servant" because it was a more natural rendering of *servus*.[25] Added to this, the term *slave* in sixteenth-century England generally depicted someone in physical chains or in prison. Since this is quite different from the Greco-Roman idea of slavery, the translators of early English versions (like the Geneva Bible and the King James) opted for a word they felt better represented Greco-Roman slavery in their culture. That word was *servant*. These early translations continue to have a significant impact on modern English versions.[26]

But whatever the rationale behind the change, something significant is lost in translation when *doulos* is rendered "servant" rather than "slave." The gospel is not simply an invitation to become Christ's associate; it is a mandate to become His slave.

REDISCOVERING THIS ONE HIDDEN WORD

The Bible's emphasis on slavery to God is missing from the pages of most English translations. But that which is hidden in our modern versions was a central truth for the apostles and the generations of believers who came after them.

Early Christian leaders, like Ignatius (who died around AD 110) and his coworkers, saw themselves as "fellow slaves" of Christ.[27] Polycarp (c. 69–155) instructed the Philippians, "Bind up your loose robes and serve as God's slaves in reverential fear and truth."[28] The *Shepherd of Hermas* (written in the second century) warns its readers that "there are many [wicked deeds] from which the slave of God must refrain."[29] The fourth-century writer known as Ambrosiaster explained that "the one who is liberated from [the Mosaic Law] 'dies' and lives to God, becoming his slave, purchased by Christ."[30] Augustine (354–430) simply asked his congregation this rhetorical question, "Does your Lord not deserve to have you as his trustworthy slave?"[31] Elsewhere, he rebuked those who would exhibit foolish pride: "You are a creature, acknowledge the Creator; you are a slave, do not disdain the Master."[32] Ancient Bible expositor John Chrysostom (347–407) comforted those who were in physical bondage with these words: "In things that relate to Christ, both [slaves and masters] are equal; and just as you are the slave of Christ, so also is your master."[33]

Even in more recent history, in spite of the confusion caused by English translations, leading scholars and pastors have recognized the reality of this vital concept.[34] Listen to the words of Charles Spurgeon—the great British preacher of the nineteenth century:

Where our Authorized [King James] Version softly puts it "servant" it really is "bond-slave." The early saints delighted to count themselves Christ's absolute property, bought by him, owned by him, and wholly at his disposal. Paul even went so far as to rejoice that he had the marks of his Master's brand on him, and he cries, "Let no man trouble me: for I bear in my body the marks of the Lord Jesus." There was the end of all debate: he was the Lord's, and the marks of the scourges, the rods, and the stones were the broad-arrow of the King which marked Paul's body as the property of Jesus the Lord. Now if the saints of old time gloried in obeying Christ, I pray that you and I . . . may feel that our first object in life is to obey our Lord.[35]

Scottish pastor Alexander MacLaren, a contemporary of Spurgeon, echoed these same truths:

> The true position, then, for a man is to be God's slave. . . . Absolute submission, unconditional obedience, on the slave's part; and on the part of the Master complete ownership, the right of life and death, the right of disposing of all goods and chattels . . . the right of issuing commandments without a reason, the right to expect that those commandments shall be swiftly, unhesitatingly, punctiliously, and completely performed—these things inhere in our relation to God. Blessed [is] the man who has learned that they do, and has accepted them as his highest glory and the security of his most blessed life! For, brethren, such submission, absolute and unconditional, the blending and the absorption of my own will in His will, is the secret of all that makes manhood glorious and great and happy. . . . [I]n the New Testament these names of slave and owner are transferred to Christians and Jesus Christ.[36]

As these voices from church history make so abundantly clear, our slavery to Christ has radical implications for how we think and live. We have been *bought with a price*. We *belong to Christ*. We are part of a people for *His own possession*. And understanding all of that changes everything about us, starting with our perspective and our priorities.

True Christianity is not about adding Jesus to *my* life. Instead, it is about devoting myself completely to *Him*—submitting wholly to His will and seeking to please Him above all else. It demands dying to self and following the Master, no matter the cost. In other words, to be a Christian is to be Christ's *slave*.

In the pages that follow, we will examine the profound depths of that one hidden word, and in the process we'll discover the life-changing difference it makes.

Notes

1. Marcus Aurelius reigned from AD 161 to 180. The intense persecution described here likely took place around 177.
2. Eusebius, *Church History*, 5.1.20, quoted in Philip Schaff, *Nicene and Post-Nicene Fathers*, 2nd ser. (Grand Rapids: Eerdmans, 1971), I:214. (Hereafter, *Nicene and Post-Nicene Fathers* will be referred to as *NPNF*.)
3. Ibid.
4. J. Spencer Northcote, *Epitaphs of the Catacombs or Christian Inscriptions in Rome During the First Four Centuries* (London: Longman, Green & Co., 1878; repr., Whitefish, MT: Kessinger Publishing, 2007), 139.
5. Such was the attitude of Ignatius, a pastor from Antioch and a disciple of the apostle John. Upon being condemned to death in Rome (around AD 110), Ignatius wrote, "It is not that I want merely to be called a Christian, but actually to be one. Yes, if I prove to be one [by being faithful to the end], then I can have the name. . . . Come fire, cross, battling with wild beasts, wrenching of bones, mangling of limbs, crushing of my whole body, cruel tortures of the devil—only let me get to Jesus Christ!" (Ignatius, *Epistle to the Romans*, 3, 5, 6, quoted in Cyril C. Richardson, *Early Church Fathers* [Louisville: Westminster John Knox Press, 1953], 104–5.)
6. As the apostle Paul explained in 1 Corinthians 1:23, the idea of a crucified Christ was "to the Jews a stumbling block and to the Gentiles foolishness." Those who followed Jesus Christ (having been labeled as *Christians*) were denounced as heretics by unbelieving Jews and derided as fools by unbelieving Gentiles.
7. The Hebrew word for slave, *'ebed,* can speak of literal slavery to a human master. But it is also used metaphorically to describe believers (more than 250 times), denoting their duty and privilege to obey the heavenly Lord. The New Testament's use of the Greek word, *doulos,* is similar. It too can refer to physical slavery. Yet it is also applied to believers—denoting their relationship to the divine Master—at least 40 times (cf. Murray J. Harris, *Slave of Christ* [Downers Grove, Ill.: InterVarsity Press, 1999], 20–24). An additional 30-plus NT passages use the language of *doulos* to teach truths about the Christian life.
8. See, for example, Romans 1:1; 1 Corinthians 7:22; Galatians 1:10; Ephesians 6:6; Philippians 1:1; Colossians 4:12; Titus 1:1; James 1:1; 1 Peter 2:16; 2 Peter 1:1; Jude 1; and Revelation 1:1.
9. According to the *International Standard Bible Encyclopedia*, some commentators have proposed that the term Christian literally means "slave of Christ." For example, "Deissmann (*Licht vom Osten*, 286) suggests that *Christian* means *slave of Christ,* as *Caesarian* means *slave of Caesar*" (John Dickie, "Christian," in James Orr, ed., ISBE, [Chicago: Howard-Severance Company, 1915], I:621–22).
10. Stringfellow Barr, *The Mask of Jove* (Philadelphia: Lippincott, 1966), 483.
11. Northcote, *Epitaphs of the Catacombs*, 140.
12. Karl Heinrich Rengstorf, under "doulos" in the *Theological Dictionary of the New Testament* (hereinafter referred to as *TDNT*) notes that "in the early Church the formula [slave of God or slave of Christ] took on a new lease of life, being used increasingly by Christians in self-designation (cf. 2 Clem. 20, 1; Herm. m. 5, 2, 1; 6, 2, 4; 8, 10 etc.)." (Gerhard Kittel and Gerhard Friedrich, eds., Geoffrey Bromiley, trans., *TDNT*, 10 vols. [Grand Rapids: Eerdmans, 1964], 2:274.)

13. In a second-century letter from the churches of Lyons and Vienne to the churches of Asia and Phrygia, the anonymous authors began by designating themselves the "slaves of Christ" (Eusebius, *Ecclesiastical History*, 5.1–4). They continued by describing the widespread persecution they had endured, including the martyrdoms that many in their midst had experienced.

14. As Janet Martin Soskice points out, "talk of the Christian as 'slave of Christ' or 'slave of God' which enjoyed some popularity in the Pauline Epistles and early Church is now scarcely used, despite its biblical warrant, by contemporary Christians, who have little understanding for or sympathy with the institution of slavery and the figures of speech it generates" (*The Kindness of God: Metaphor, Gender, and Religious Language* [New York: Oxford University Press, 2007], 68).

15. For example, Rengstorf, under "Doulos," in *TDNT*, notes the prominence "in the NT [of] the idea that Christians belong to Jesus as His δοῦλοι [slaves], and that their lives are thus offered to Him as the risen and exalted Lord" (2:274).

16. Even earlier, John Wycliffe and William Tyndale rendered the Greek *doulos* with the English word "servant."

17. According to Harris, "this word [*doulos*] occurs 124 times in the New Testament and its compound form *syndoulos* ('fellow-slave') ten times" (*Slave of Christ*, 183). The verb form also occurs an additional eight times.

18. Two exceptions to this are E. J. Goodspeed's *The New Testament: An American Translation* (1923) and the Holman Christian Standard Version (2004), both of which consistently render *doulos* as "slave."

19. Cf. Harris, *Slave of Christ*, 183.

20. Rengstorf, "Doulos," *TDNT*, 2:261.

21. As Walter S. Wurzburger explains, "To be a slave of God . . . involves more than merely being His servant. Servants retain their independent status. They have only specific duties and limited responsibilities. Slaves, on the other hand, have no rights vis á vis their owners, because they are deemed the property of the latter" (*God Is Proof Enough* [New York: Devora Publishing, 2000], 37).

22. Speaking of Roman slavery in particular, Yvon Thébert noted that the slave "was equated with his function and was for his master what the ox was for the poor man: an animated object that he owned. The same idea is a constant in Roman law, where the slave is frequently associated with other parts of a patrimony, sold by the same rules that governed a transfer of a parcel of land or included with tools or animals in a bequest. Above all he was an object, a *res mobilis*. Unlike the waged worker, no distinction was made between his person and his labor" ("The Slave," 138–174 in Andrea Giardina, ed., *The Romans* [Chicago: University of Chicago, 1993], 139).

23. John J. Pilch, under "Slave, Slavery, Bond, Bondage, Oppression," in Donald E. Gowan, ed., *The Westminster Theological Wordbook of the Bible* (Louisville, KY: Westminster John Knox Press, 2003), 472, notes that "the Greek noun *doulos* is a sub-domain of the semantic field 'control, rule' and describes someone who is completely controlled by something or someone."

24. Ibid., 474. The author points out that "slavery in the ancient world had practically nothing in common with slavery familiar from New World practice and experience of eighteenth and nineteenth centuries. It would distort the interpretation of the Bible to impose such an understanding on its books."

25. Cf. Harris, *Slave of Christ*, 184.

26. For an intriguing look at the early English Bible translators' reticence to translate *doulos* as "slave," see Edwin Yamauchi, "Slaves of God," *Journal of the Evangelical Theological Society* 9/1 (Winter 1966): 31–49. Yamauchi shows that by the late thirteenth century, "slavery disappeared from northwestern Europe. . . . Slavery therefore was known to the 17th century Englishmen—at least at the beginning of that century—not as an intimate, accepted institution but rather as a remote phenomenon" (p. 37). Their concept of a "servant" was shaped by their knowledge of serfdom—a kind of servitude in which the laborer was bound to the land he worked. Although he was duty-bound to the landowner, his services could only be sold when the land itself was sold. By contrast, "slavery" in their minds evoked "the extreme case of a captive in fetters" (p. 37), an image of cruelty that they understandably wished to avoid. But in so doing they unwittingly diminished the force of the actual biblical expression.

In Yamauchi's words, "If we keep in mind what 'slavery' meant to the ancients, and not what it means to us or the 17th-century theorists, we shall gain a heightened understanding of many passages in the New Testament" (p. 37). See also Harris, *Slave of Christ*, 184.

27. Cf. *Epistle to the Philadelphians*, 3; *Epistle to the Magnesians*, 2; *Epistle to Smyrna*, 12.

28. Polycarp, *Letter to the Philippians*, 1–2, in Bart D. Ehrman, trans., *The Apostolic Fathers* (Harvard, 2003), I:335.

29. *Shepherd of Hermas*, Exposition on the Eighth Commandment, 38.3–6, in ibid., II:270. This is just one of several instances in which *Hermas* used the phrase "slave of God."

30. *Corpus Scriptorum Ecclesiasticorum Latinorum*, 81.3: 28.21–23, quoted in Eric Plumer's critical notes on *Augustine's Commentary on Galatians* (New York: Oxford University Press, 2003), 30, n. 153.

31. Augustine, "Sermon 159," in John E. Rottelle, trans., *Sermons* (Hyde Park, NY: New City Press, 1992), 124.

32. Augustine, *Homilies on the Gospel of John 1–40*. Homily 29. Translated by Edmund Hill (Hyde Park, NY: New City Press, 2009), 495. Capitalization of divine names added.

33. John Chrysostom, *Homilies on First Corinthians*. Homily 19.5–6 (on 1 Cor. 7:22–23), quoted in Schaff, *NPNF*, 12:108–9.

34. See the appendix for additional quotations from recent church history.

35. Charles Spurgeon, "Eyes Right," sermon no. 2058, in *The Metropolitan Tabernacle Pulpit* (Pasadena, TX: Pilgrim Publications, 1974), 34:689.

36. Alexander MacLaren, *Expositions of Holy Scripture: Acts*, commenting on Acts 4:26, 27, 29 (n.p.: BiblioLife, 2007), 148–49.